Interpretations of Hope

in

Chinese Religions and Christianity

Interpretations of Hope
in
Chinese Religions and Christianity

Daniel L. OVERMYER and Chi-tim LAI

Editors

CSCCRC

Christian Study Centre on Chinese Religion and Culture

Interpretations of Hope in Chinese Religions and Christianity
Editors: Daniel L. OVERMYER, Chi-tim LAI
Assistant Editor: Wai-yin CHOW

ISBN 962-7706-04-3

Christian Study Centre on Chinese Religion and Culture
G/F., Theology Building, Chung Chi College, Shatin, N.T., Hong Kong.
Tel   : (852) 2770 3310
Fax   : (852) 2603 5224
E-mail : csccrc@yahoo.com.hk

Printed in Hong Kong

Contents

Notes on Contributors

Judith A. BERLING, Professor of Chinese and Comparative Religions at Graduate Theological Union, Berkeley, California, the USA

Xiaogan LIU, Professor in the Department of Philosophy at the Chinese University of Hong Kong, Hong Kong

Mu-chou POO, Research Fellow of the Institute of History and Philology at Academia Sinica,Taipei,Taiwan

Chi-tim LAI, Associate Professor in the Department of Religion at the Chinese University of Hong Kong, Hong Kong

John LAGERWEY, Professor at the Ecole Pratique des Hautes Études, Paris, Fance

Daniel L. OVERMYER, Professor Emeritus in the Department of Asian Studies at the University of British Columbia, Vancouver, Canada

Frank E. REYNOLDS, Professor of Buddhist Studies and History of Religions at the University of Chicago Divinity School, Chicago, the USA

Yün-hua JAN, Professor Emeritus in the Department of Religious Studies at McMaster University, Hamilton, Canada

Wai-lun TAM, Associate Professor in the Department of Religion at the Chinese University of Hong Kong, Hong Kong

David TRACY, Distinguished Service Professor of Catholic Studies and Professor of Theology and of the Philosophy of Religion at the University of Chicago Divinity School, Chicago, the USA

Choan-Seng SONG, Professor of Theology and Asian Cultures at Pacific School of Religion and the Graduate Theological Union, Berkeley, California, the USA

Pan-chiu LAI, Associate Professor in the Department of Religion at the Chinese University of Hong Kong, Hong Kong

Archie C. C. LEE, Professor in the Department of Religion at the Chinese University of Hong Kong, Hong Kong

Chee-pang CHOONG, Academic Consultant of the Lutheran World Federation;Visiting Professor at Peking Univerity and Fmdan University, China

Introduction

Religion and Human Hope — Interpretations of Hope in Chinese Religions and Christianity

HOPE represents a universal quest of the human race. It is essentially a concern for and a speculation of one's own future. Ever since the emergence of any form of religions, they have been closely associated with the human quest for hope. Historically, Eastern and Western religions have constructed different models to answer this quest in response to suffering, anxiety, or calamities, concern for world crises and the consummation of history, taking into account their own respective cultural characteristics.

An international conference under the theme of "Interpretations of Hope in Chinese Religions and Christianity", co-sponsored by the Department of Religion of the Chinese University and the Graduate Theological Union in Berkeley, U.S.A., was held at the Chinese University of Hong Kong in 1996. The conference provided a forum for a total of fifty scholars from Hong Kong, Mainland China, Taiwan, Korea, Singapore, France, the United States and Canada. They specialize in Western Christianity, philosophy of religion, Taoism, Chinese popular religion, Chinese Buddhism, and the Zen school. Focused on the subject of human hope, the presentations centered around the following questions: how the symbol of "hope" is expressed in the religious traditions and beliefs of China and Christianity. The participants' presentation in that conference, after revision, were collected in this book.

The operative definition of "hope" in this book is "to wish for something in expectation of its fulfillment." All the essays focus on how such hope is expressed in some of the religious traditions and beliefs of China and Christianity. Some of these essays are historical and descriptive; others more normative and theological. They are deliberately presented here according to their different religious traditions they study. Here the reader will find essays on hope in early Chinese traditions both popular and philosophical, on Taoism, Buddhism and in late popular religious texts. On the side of Christianity there are essays on hope in the Hebrew scriptures and the Christian New Testament, on the Christian theology, ethics and on Christianity as a whole. Hence, the coverage of this book is considerably comprehensive.

Nevertheless, the similarities and differences between Chinese religions (Confucianism, Buddhism and Taoism and folk religions) and Christianity dealing with the universal notion of hope are investigated here. This book pays full respect to the difference between religions and cultures, and yet scholars in different disciplines were encouraged to compare the hope notion in different traditions in all open-mindedness. Some of the essays indicate that Chinese and Western religions shared the same concern and commitment towards human suffering and anxiety. On the other hand, differences in language and history and culture inevitably gave rise to different interpretations. As a matter of fact, a self-correcting process can be seen in the same religious tradition which demonstrates different interpretations under different contexts in different times.

Judith A. Berling's essay looks at the hope notion in Chinese religions from the Confucian and Taoist perspectives. Contrary to the Western tradition, the Chinese did not express hope through a certain idea or eschatological event. They sought to build a harmonious society through the practice of morality. Confucians stressed political and cultural morality. The Confucian ideal was the rule of a saintly king. Both Confucians and Taoists emphasized the return to Nature and its values. This hope, however, was not intended for realization in another world, nor was it anticipating the end of the present world. Rather, a Confucian or Taoist follower was asked to pursue a transcendent dimension and imagination that was not bound by the present, physical existence. Judith Berling believes that these seemingly contradictory perspectives represent the two extremes of the horizon of Chinese religion and culture. Both were looking for hope in the existing, inherent values of the human person.

Frank E.Reynolds's essay indicates that religious traditions had been exercising a positive influence by imparting hope and inspiring social and historical changes towards the cause of justice. However, for a religious perspective on hope to be truly constructive, it should remain open-ended and placed in a pluralistic dimension, which made human integrity possible. In other words, the religious hope should be "for this world," so that it calls for a positive attitude towards life. Yet, it should also be transcendent over the present world and the self, so that it would also be able to address the personal needs of the individual.

Yün-hua Jan's essay points out that the Chinese understanding of hope was not necessarily related to God. He explains this by quoting from the popular Buddhist wish incantations in medieval China. If a Chinese had hope for the future, it would be expressed in the reform of political/ social relationships and personal pursuit of happiness. The wishes of Chinese Buddhists were related to well-being of individual families (ancestors and descendants), peace of the royal reign and the absence of pain and suffering.

David Tracy's essay points out that modern Western theology had over-emphasized the participation of the holy in human progress. In fact, Tracy had always deliberately substituted the reference to "God" with the word "Holy." By doing that, modern theology had become a spokesperson for none but the admirers of the Western civilization. One of Tracy's famous theological propositions was "Let God be God," which suggested that the Christian culture of the West should liberate God from their preconceptions. Tracy also believed that if God were to intervene with human history anew, this intervention should first and foremost be associated with the suffering and fear of the oppressed and the marginalized. True hope should mean, nonetheless than Christian confrontation with the human pain that suffering brought and Christian struggle with the sinful forces of this world.

Choan-seng Song's essay focuses on the inseparability of religious Hope from the life of the masses. Theologically, he believed that the discussion of hope should be done in the light of the pursuit of justice. Hope should never be reduced to theological speculations. Rather, genuine hope should find expression in the future as well as present life of the community, such as hope for the hungry, and freedom and justice for the oppressed.

Archie C.C.Lee's essay points out that religious communities in history had sometimes been confused by different or conflicting hopes. He quoted as an example the Book of Isaiah in the Old Testament of the Bible, which told the story of how the exiled Jews returned from their Babylonian captivity to find themselves in conflict with their compatriots at home. The Jews of different parties had to discover the hope they once had and reconciled different concepts of hope.

Daniel L. Overmyer also uncovered the rich expressions of hope contained in the *Precious Volumes (Baojuan)*, particularly passages that express hope for a coming savior deity in the near future to save pious believers from destruction at the end of age.

Turning mto the transforming religious imagination and actions arising from human suffering. Feng-mou Li explained how Taoist priests guided the mass to pass through the realities of wars and calamities through expiation from the scriptures of *Lingpao* of the Six-Dynasties period. On the one hand, the Ling-pao Taoists coined suffering as eschatological sign. On the other hand, the scriptures contain many promises of salvation, namely the restoration of the natural order, to those who cultivate the Way through the means of reciting and distributing scriptures, writing charms, refining one's inner elixir of immortality, and having faith in the Tao.

Chi-tim Lai analyzed the confession rites in the Taoist sect of Celestial Masters recorded in the *Taiping jing* from the perspective of psychology of religion. He explained how Taoism, through the means of confession rites, had cultivated the personal sense of morality of its followers and relived the fear of Chinese people for disease and death and the unknown world of afterlife.

This book emphasizes that the study of religion has definitely been established as an important discipline that has made unique contributions to the broader cultural studies. Moreover, the fact that the concept of hope in religions has been interpreted from the perspectives of different disciplines, including Chinese philosophy, religious studies, Western theology, history, studies of ancient Egypt, Buddhism and classical Chinese literature, etc. is a strong evidence for the manifold significance of religion as a unique phenomenon of human culture. Precisely because of this, no study in religion would be complete unless it is engaged in cross-discipline dialogue, so that religious traditions can be offered, in an enlivened manner, as an invaluable cultural heritage and source of imagination to the modern man and woman who seek to reshape their present context of existence and hope for the future.

Nevertheless, some important areas of investigation are not included here, such as the relationship of hope to the specific situations of women in these traditions, and expressions of hope in the actual practice of Christianity in Hong Kong, the mainland China and Taiwan. The mainstream popular and common religious traditions in the Chinese-speaking world are also not included, but all of this leaves some good work for the future scholarship.

1

Threads of "Hope" in Traditional Chinese Religions

Judith A. Berling

Comparisons are fragile and dangerous exercises: fragile because identifying the object/concept to be compared is itself fraught with cultural and linguistic difficulties; dangerous because one often sets out on the trail only to have it crumble beneath one's feet.

I rather innocently accepted the assignment of this plenary, rejoicing that the topic was not "Christological" from start to finish. My initial joy began to fade when I realized that "hope" as such is not a construct within Chinese religion or philosophy; it is a virtue expressed in various forms in Chinese culture, some of them having something to do with "religion." But, as is often the case when the topic of a cross-cultural conference is defined in English, those of us who inhabit the world of Chinese texts find ourselves literally at a loss: our textual world offers no direct approach to the topic at hand.

Two Chinese Tales

Succumbing to the necessity for indirection, I begin this address in my textual world with two paradigmatic stories from traditional Chinese religions. As you listen, I invite you to join my wonderment about what these might tell us about "hope" in traditional Chinese religions.

The first story comes from Mencius (372?-289? BCE), the great disciple of Confucius, and co-shaper of the Confucian tradition. It is his tale of an encounter with King Xuan of Qi 齊宣王 (r. 319-301 BCE), who was very much a ruler of his times. An ambitious man, King Xuan sought to mobilize a strong army to compete with ruthless and aggressive neighbors, and to assert his authority and his prerogatives as a ruler over against his subjects. Mencius warned him:

> [Your desire] is to increase your territory, to summon the princes of Qin and Chu to your Court, to rule over the central states, and to impose vassalage upon the barbarians of the four quarters. If the means you adopt are those you now propose, if the aims you intend to pursue are those at present in your mind, then you are like a man who climbs a tree to catch a fish.[1]

Mencius instead recommended the way of the benevolent ruler:

> Let the five-acre homestead be planted with mulberry trees, and then those of fifty years of age and above might wear silk. Let the breeding of fowls, pigs, and dogs proceed in due season, and then those of seventy years of age and above might eat meat. On the hundred acre estates do not impress [into public service] the people at the times of sowing and reaping, and then large households need not starve. Take care as to the teaching in the schools, Let the curriculum be augmented with the justice of filial piety and fraternal duty, and then the gray-haired ones should not have to carry heavy loads on the roads. There has never been a state [with these policies] where the king was other than a True King.[2]

Mencius ideals for the ruler seemed to King Xuan far beyond his own abilities; he saw himself as a realist — a competitive, rather hard man of the world of whom the people were not too fond. He asked Mencius, "How do you know that I could be such a King?" Mencius replied:

> Hu Ho told me that your Majesty was sitting at the upper end of the audience chamber, and an ox was being led across the lower end. On seeing the ox, your Majesty asked where it was being taken, and was told that it was to be used in sacrifice at the dedication of a bell. Your Majesty ordered the release of the ox, observing that you could not bear to see it shuddering like a criminal being led to the execution yard. ... How can you allow that you have kindness for an animal, but not enough kindness to reach out to your people?[3]

Thus Mencius sought to persuade King Xuan that a king with sufficient compassion to spare an ox from the sacrifice could also show compassion to his subjects.

The second story comes from Zhuang Zi 莊子 (369?–86? BCE), the great Taoist raconteur, who played in "classical Taoism" a position more or less parallel to Mencius in "classical Confucianism."[4]

Master Si 子祀, Master Yu 子輿, Master Li 子犁, and Master Lai 子來 were all four talking together: "Who can look upon non-being as his head, on life as his back, and on death as his rump?" they said. "Who knows that life and death, existence and annihilation, are all a single body? I will be his friend."

The four men looked at each other and smiled. There was no disagreement in their hearts and so the four of them became friends.

All at once Master Yu fell ill, Master Si went to ask how he was. "Amazing!" said Master Yu. "The Creator is making me all crookedly like this! My back sticks up like a hunchback and my vital organs are on top of me. My chin is hidden in my navel, and my shoulders are up above my head, and my pigtail points at the sky. It must be some dislocation of yin and yang!"

Yet he seemed calm at heart and unconcerned. Dragging himself haltingly to the well, he looked at his reflection and said, "My, my! So the Creator is making me all crookedly like this!"

"Do you resent it?" asked Master Si.

"Why no, what would I resent? If the process continues, perhaps in time he'll transform my left arm into a rooster. In that case I'll keep watch on the night. Or perhaps in time he'll transform my right arm into a crossbow pellet and I'll shoot down an owl for roasting. Or perhaps in time he'll transform my buttocks into cartwheels. Then with my spirit for a horse, I'll climb up and go for a ride. What need will I ever have of a carriage again?"[5]

These tales from Mencius and Zhuang Zi represent or articulate fundamentally different orientations which shaped the Confucian and the Taoist traditions. But what, if anything, do they tell us about the interpretation of "hope" in Chinese religions?

Towards a Working Understanding of "Hope" as a Comparative Category

Standard Definitions: The OED Path

Since the topic for this conference was defined in terms which come from the Western tradition, I turned to Western sources for a working understanding of "hope" as a comparative category. Not wishing to replicate the research of my colleagues discussing, interpretations of "hope" in the Christian tradition, I began my investigations in the *Oxford English Dictionary(OED)*, which provided a basic definition: "expectation of something desired; desire combined with expectation." However, as one read through early definitive uses of "hope" cited by *OED*, an interesting split occurred between Christian statements about "hope" and non-Christian (philosophical) statements. The Christian statements on "hope" talked about "hope" in the midst of bitter experience; as in a statement by Cowper: "Hope, as an anchor firm and sure, holds fast the Christian vessel, and defies the blast." Thus, in many Christian statements, "hope" is an expectation in the midst of chaos or trouble, an expectation that runs against the grain or the surface appearance of affairs.

A philosophical statement cited from John Locke, however, is strikingly different. Locke spoke of "hope" as "a pleasure in the mind, the thought of a profitable future enjoyment of a thing apt to delight him." For Locke "hope" is pleasurable anticipation unthreatened by present circumstance. Locke's statement of "hope" suggested the *OED* definition of trust, which is a "confident expectation or hope."

Building solely on this evidence (which is by no means an adequate depiction of the place of Christian "hope" in the history of Western thought), I built a tentative working definition. Given the Christian examples in *OED*, "hope" requires a leap of faith, an ability to see beyond present troubles, bitterness or suffering to the expectation of the salvation or the coming of God's kingdom. It requires discontinuity, an overturning of or a radical change in present circumstances to fulfill the expectation.

In the *OED* "trust" is defined as confident expectation, a "hope" not threatened by perceived threats or barriers, so that there is a clear and unimpeded path toward the "future enjoyment." Trust suggests continuity, no radical change, simply an evolutionary unfolding of present circumstances.

Whether or not this dichotomy stands up to careful scrutiny of the history of Christianity and Western thought, it does help to highlight some aspects of the role of "hope" in native Chinese religions, and thus serves its purpose for my present analysis.

Another Reading of "Christian Faith and Hope"

In addition to consulting a standard dictionary in order to develop a basic definition of "hope," I also engaged in a number of conversations with Biblical scholars and Christian theologians in order to determine how they understood or situated the place of "hope" in Christianity.

Marian Meye Thompson of Fuller Theological Seminary shared an insight which opens up another path for reading the two Chinese tales in the light of "hope." Thompson remarked that the expressions of Biblical Christians that they have "overcome the world" were the courageous statements of a tiny, embattled minority religion. By no means a description of "reality" at the time of the writing of the Biblical accounts, they represented the "language of faith and hope." Building from Thompson's comment, I would add that the "language of faith and hope" was a proclamation of the promise and potential of the nascent Christian religious Community.

The early Christians proclaimed that they had overturned and transformed reality not because they had completed the task, but because they felt they had the answer, they keyed to such transformation in the presence and power of the risen Christ. Their confidence was that the power of the risen Christ was so great as to eclipse the fact that the actual transformation of the world was not yet complete.

Thus the focus of this "language of faith and hope" was not on the discontinuity, the radical transformation that would be required, but rather on the planted seed which would inevitably effect the transformation. "Hope and faith" enabled believers to see what others could not, to know the transformative or salvational vector of reality.

These two approaches to defining "hope" support two different readings of the tales of Mencius and Zhuang Zi, and two different readings of "hope" in traditional Chinese religions.

In this paper, I will tease out and follow threads of "hope," "trust" or "faith and hope" in tales and practices of the native Chinese religious traditions. Because they set up a polarity which constructed religious discourses (and options) throughout traditional Chinese history, I will begin with threads which characterize the Confucian and the Taoist traditions. However, recognizing that this polarity perhaps most accurately reflects two complementary aspects or dynamics of "native Chinese religions," I will turn to folk practices and beliefs which bring these two poles much closer together and illustrate the porous boundaries between them.

In the last section of the paper, I will reflect on the distinctive attitudes of "hope" or "trust" in Chinese religious traditions, and the nest of cultural patterns and themes in which they are embedded.

The Context for the Rise of Chinese Religious Thought (Confucianism, Taoism, and Other Streams)

Classical Chinese religious thought, shaping basic themes and patterns for over two millennia, took shape in a period of intense military strife, political intrigue, and ruthless ambition. As small states armed themselves for survival and larger states competed brutally for political and military hegemony, traditional social, political, and religious values crumbled before the advancing forces of realpolitik. The thinkers who shaped the so-called Confucian and Taoist traditions[6] emerged in this disenchanted world in which old ideals seemed hopelessly naive, and were being replaced by "realistic" strategies for ambition and political hegemony. It was not an environment friendly to religion or any form of idealism.

Judging the classical thinkers against this environment, we realize that the early Confucians and Taoists spoke profoundly and consistently against the grain of contemporary attitudes. They articulated positions which reclaimed and built upon core traditional values, retrieving what was best — indeed, in their views, foundational — in Chinese culture. It is not possible within the brief compass of this paper to do justice to even two of these positions, so I will restrict my discussion to a very few examples which may help to illumine the threads of "hope," "trust" or "faith and hope" in Chinese religious history.

Confucians
A Strategic Wager on Human Goodness

In the unsettled milieu of the Warring States period when traditional values were challenged by hard-headed realism and naked power, Confucius and his followers argued that stable, long-lasting power had to be founded in the values and practices of culture (*wenhua* 文化). Military power and political intrigue might prevail in a particular skirmish with one's enemies, but long-term stable rule required more: the respect of the people, their assent that the ruler embodied the values of the realm.

The Confucian vision of society suggested that harmony was based upon the achievement of civilization, civil culture in which the population shared basic values embodied in social arrangements and rituals and cultivated in education, Confucian civil culture required that leaders, parents, and heads of household modeled basic cultural virtues and inculcated them in citizens. Confucians believed that the virtuous model of rulers (and parents and other leaders) was more effective than force in creating good citizens, far better to nurture a person who knows how to do good rather than one who obeys only because he fears punishment.

The Confucian vision was founded on two assumptions which are at the core of their religio-philosophical vision: that the virtues are grounded in the natural order of things and backed by the principles of Heaven, and that humans fulfill their innate potential only as they understand and cultivate these virtues. Mencius in particular made clear the "wager" of the Confucian position: that human nature is basically and fundamentally good, despite a great deal of circumstantial evidence to the contrary. Mencius was not naive about prevailing ethos of his times, nor about the frailties and ambitions of the people he sought to influence. However, he recognized that appealing to cupidity and ambition only made people greedier and more ambitious. On what basis could one appeal to the higher instincts, to those fragile impulses for the good?

Mencius's response to this dilemma was quite striking, and laid the foundation for subsequent Confucian thinking. As evidence for the fundamental goodness of human nature, he sought to demonstrate to his audience that they contained within themselves the seeds (the beginnings) of such goodness. Such was the point of his famous example of the child falling into the well.

> All people have the mind which cannot bear [to see the suffering of] others. The ancient kings had this mind and therefore they had a government that could not bear to see the suffering of the people. Then the government cannot bear to see the suffering of the people is conducted from a mind that cannot bear to see the suffering of others, the government of the empire will be as easy as making something go round in the palm.

> When I say that all people have the mind which cannot bear to see the suffering of others, my meaning may be illustrated thus: Now, when a person suddenly sees a child about to fall into a well, he/she has a feeling of alarm and distress, not to gain friendship with the child's parents, nor to seek the praise of neighbors and friends, nor because he/she dislikes the reputation [of lack of humanity if they did not rescue the child]. From such a case, we see that a person without the feeling of commiseration is not a human being ... The feeling of commiseration is the beginning of humanity.[7]

This justly famous argument from example is striking in that it is based on rhetoric (persuasiveness) and not on logic per se. The example does not prove that everyone would have the instinct in his/her heart to save the child. What makes the argument powerful is that the reader inwardly assents: "Yes, I would feel a moment's compassion for the toddler about to fall into a well." That moment of assent is Mencius's moment of triumph, for he has demonstrated to every person making that assent that they in fact have a seed of virtue in their mind-and-heart.[8]

He attempted to do the same with King Xuan of Qi in the famous tale with which we began. King Xuan was not an easy case to crack. He was very much a man of his times, inviting Mencius to his court in the "hope" of learning something from him which will help him outwit his rivals, but deaf to the moral message Mencius seeks to convey. Mencius patiently circled this man, seeking an opening to convince him that he had the "right stuff" to be a virtuous ruler, King Xuan was quite rightly skeptical that he was generously endowed with virtue, but Mencius found a crack in his armor of ambition and disdain for the condition of his people in King Hsuan's compassion for the ox. Having found such a crack, he could move in to nurture actively the king's potential for good.

The Confucian wager, then, posited a spark of goodness within all human beings which rendered them open to positive persuasion, to good examples, and above all to education. It was a wager that positive programs can be more effective than force, punishments, and surveillance. It was a wager that humanizing efforts can in fact develop human potential, nurturing goodness from within instead of imposing a thin patina of acceptable behavior onto a basically brutish spirit.

Confucians and "Hope"

Marian Meye Thompson's notion of Christian "faith and hope" affirming the promise or potential of the early church long before such promise was actualized is a useful image for understanding the Confucian wager on human goodness. Like the early Christians, Mencius believed so strongly in the potential (the seed or beginning of goodness) of human nature that he acted on that faith in his appeals to King Xuan of Qi and others, despite overwhelming contrary evidence. The grounds of his faith were different from the grounds of faith for the early Christians. In developing his vision, Mencius could build on no recent and decisive event which confirmed the promise of the Confucian vision; there was no Confucian parallel to the resurrection of Jesus and the descent of the Holy Spirit at Pentecost. However, there was a ground for his faith in the lives of the ancient kings who built a government which could not bear to see the suffering of the people; those virtuous kings were the authors of Chinese civilization, and the ideal past to which the Confucians looked as their model. Mencius had "faith and hope" that the ideal age of the sage kings could be restored by means of the cultivation of virtue in every human mind-and-heart, supported and inspired by tbe model of wise and virtuous leaders. In some ways, then, the Confucian wager on human goodness was an act of "faith and hope."

However, there is another reading of the Confucian wager, which resonates with the definition of "trust" in the *OED* Confucians believed that appeals to virtue worked in tandem with the deepest essence of human nature and with the moral laws and principles which give order to the cosmos. Thus their approach to the improvement of the human world was evolutionary and continuous rather than radical and discontinuous. Such an approach suggests a strategy of "trust" (confident expectation) rather than "hope" (expectation in the face of enormous obstacles). The Confucian wager fueled humane and civilizing impulses in China: a strong focus on education, a strong sense of family values and tradition, a deep respect for the powers of the human mind-and-heart.

Even in the most straitened circumstances, Confucians put their trust in their mind-and-heart, believing that with sufficient sincerity and cultivation they would, as it were, see the light. An excellent example is that of Wang Yangming 王陽明 (1472-1529), whose youthful Confucian idealism met a severe test when he became embroiled in political controversies and was banished to Guizhou 貴州, a remote outpost where he was surrounded by exiled criminals, as well as minority peoples and low-class Chinese emigres who did not share his educational background. Bitterly lonely and isolated, he devoted himself to silent meditation, driving himself almost to the point of illness.

> Then late one night as he was pondering what a sage would do in such circumstances, he suddenly had a 'great enlightenment.' In it was revealed to him the real meaning of 'the investigation of things and extension of human knowledge'[9] which earlier had eluded him as he tried to apprehend the principle of things through the contemplation of the bamboo in his father's garden. Transported by his discovery; he called out exultantly and his feet danced for joy. His companions, awakened from sleep, were amazed at his behavior. Thus he first learned, it is said, 'that the way to sagehood lies in one's own nature.'[10]

Despite his hardship and suffering, Wang Yangming's enlightenment experience revealed to him his own nature. By not losing his trust in cultivation of the mind-and-heart, he gained a deeper insight into the full potential of his own nature. Although buffeted by events, Wang Yangming joined a long stream of Confucians who wagered on the innate goodness of the human mind-and-heart to help them achieve the thing expected — in this case the amelioration of the human mind-and-heart to fulfill its moral potential.

Taoists

Transcendence

If in the strife-filled tensions of the Warring States debates, the Confucians counseled a return to the tried and true accomplishments of human civilization, the Taoist rejected all man-made achievements, values, strategies, or powers in favor of a radical return to the Tao, "the way of Nature" — the natural rhythms and movements of the cosmos uncontaminated by human interference. The real power in the world, Taoist argued, was the natural, inevitable, and ineluctable power of all nature simply being itself, things unfolding as they will. Human beings are, with all things, small bit players in this vast natural order. In order to survive and thrive, humans must learn to move with, and not against, the flow of nature; human attempts at "improving" on nature through culture, civilization, learning, technology, or strategies of control are all doomed to failure — they create more problems than they solve.

However, since humans take undue pride in their individual and collective accomplishments, it is no easy task for them to see beyond the distortions of their own creation, to apprehend and appreciate the movements of the large forces of nature which are beyond the scope of human reasoning and intention. Such a move requires 1) radical imagination — an openness to unforeseen possibilities; and 2) radical adaptivity — seeing whatever happens as an opportunity for new adventures. Entailed in these virtues is an analysis of the constraints that normally keep humans from flourishing, primarily lack of imagination (narrow-mindedness) and rigidity (resistance to change). Taoist thinkers sought to shock, to tantalize, and to seduce their listeners toward imagination and receptivity, which — in their view — are the conditions of "hope."

The story of the four friends in Zhuang Zi is an example of shock and humor used to move listeners beyond their normal ways of thinking and acting. Zhuang Zi did not shy away from topics which make most humans "mean and trembly" — old age, death, crippling illness. The "changes" these four friends encountered were not whimsical or light, and yet they treated them as though they were. They saw the onset of illness, old age, and death as opportunities to explore new dimensions of existence. The tale of the four friends is a fascinating alternative to the story of the prince Siddhartha Gautama in Buddhism, in which the prince's encounters with disease, old age, and death impressed upon him the inevitability of suffering and led him to follow a path which led to Buddhist enlightenment. The Taoist friends' response to these same "sufferings" is to see them as a "game" — "What would I resent?"

The text of the Zhuang Zi is a delightful and powerful invitation to radical imaginative openness and receptivity, to imagining what has not been imagined. When pressed on how one achieves such a state, he told tales about "fasting of the mind," emptying the mind systematically of all the things that worry it until "heaven becomes one with heaven."

Later Taoists built on Zhuang Zi's themes in a number of directions, but one which weaves throughout the streams of Taoism is "transcendence" of the normal limitations of human existence: worries and troubles, attachments which erode our spiritual vitality, the limits of mobility, limits of imagination, mortality, illness, etc. The Taoist imagination sought a transcendent realm, power, or state of being, something discontinuous with ordinary life. For instance, Song Yu 宋玉 lost his post through political intrigue during the 3rd BCE Wandering in exile, he dreamt of an exuberant journey to heaven:

> In singleness of heart, I wished only to be loyal;
> But the jealous kept me apart and stood in my way.
>
> Just grant me my worthless body and let me go away,
> To set my wandering spirit soaring amidst the clouds;
> To ride the circling vapors of primordial ethos,
> Racing the myriad hosts of spirits;
> Bright rainbows darting swiftly in the trace,
> I pass through the thick throngs of the powers of air;
> On my left goes the Scarlet Bird with beating of wings;
> On my right the Green Dragon with undulating coils;
>
> The Lord of Thunder with rumblings brings up the rear;
> The rushing Wind God leads the way:
> In front, the light coaches, creaking as they go;
> Behind, the wagons, slowly trundling.
> We bear cloud banners that flap in the wind.
> A train of squadroned horsemen follow, file on file.
> My plans are firmly fixed and cannot now be altered;
> I will press forward and make them prosper.

Blessed with rich favors from the Lord of Heaven,
I shall return to see my lord free from all harm.[11]

Song Yu's lot was similar to that of Wang Yangming some eighteen centuries later; both were the victims of political intrigues which had unseated them not only from their posts but from their youthful idealism. Song Yu's response was quite different from Wang Yangming's. Song Yu did not stick with a curriculum of meditating and "wondering what a sage would do in this circumstances" until he finally realized that the potential for sagehood is in his own mind. Song Yu's mind and spirit rebelled and soared to heaven, transcending the swamps and mire of political intriguing, soaring with gods and cosmic powers, accruing heavenly strengths and virtues. This transcendence, he believed, would transform him and tip the balance of power when he returned: He ended the poem, "Blessed with rich favors from the Lord of Heaven/I shall return to my lord free from all harm."

Taoist images of transcendence included immortals, human beings who developed spiritual powers to such an extent that they could fly, heal illness, see for miles, and live extremely long lives. They also included ritual specialists who could engage the spirits of heaven to baffle illness or other enemies, protecting humans from life's harms. And they included a vast host of gods and spirits, an army of gods, who could be enlisted to fight the powers of evil.

Taoists and "Hope"

Taoist spirituality and Taoist religious imagination tended much more than the Confucian to envision humans as under siege from various forces externally and in internal bondage because of their lack of imagination and receptivity. In this major stream of Chinese spirituality, there was indeed a kind of "hope," but that "hope" rested on a) intervention by powerful deities or ritual specialists; b) the openness of humans to conceive of the "thing expected or desired" in terms not captive to ambition and materialism; c) receptivity to "blessings" in forms not remotely expected. All of these imply discontinuity with "normal" human activity, knowledge, and striving, and require an overturning of expectations to find their fulfillment.

Thus, in one respect, Taoists fit the *OED* definition of "hope" — expectation that the power of Tao prevails and will always prevail overall encumbrances, obstacles and opposing forces.

However, Taoist thought at a deeper level challenges the wisdom of "hope." If human constructs, plans, desires, and strategies inevitably fail to anticipate the movements of Nature in itself (Tao) and therefore run against or across the stream of its powerful flow, then it is counter—productive for humans to "hope for" anything. Humans need rather to "let go of" their "hopes" and instead practice radical openness and receptivity, like the four friends in Zhuang Zi's passage.

Yet, paradoxically, those who let go of normal, limited human "hopes" gain access to powers of Tao which will enable them to soar beyond normal human limitations, to transcend the constraints of human existence. The renunciation of normal "hopes and desires" leads to freedom and transcendence.

"Hope" in Chinese Religious Culture

I have painted in broad brush strokes two streams or poles of religious response to human yearning for a "good" world. Western writers have tended to think of these as two competing religions, but that construct does not fit Chinese religious culture, in which the normal expectation was that each individual and family would honor and practice many religious traditions in the course of their lifetime. Confucianism and Taoism structured a discourse or debate within Chinese religious culture, and featured religious options for the Chinese, but these options were part of a larger religious system.

In the lives of ordinary Chinese people, the Confucian option was practiced in their belief in moral retribution and in venerating their ancestors. The Chinese folk version of moral retribution was a sort of "enlightened" self-interest. In order to motivate people to do good, one could convince them that in the long run and for the sake of their families long-term flourishing, virtuous behaviors offered better pay-offs than selfish behaviors. Virtue creates few enemies who will try to undercut one's success; it creates habits of industriousness and reliability which will make one more successful; it builds up, as it were, "moral capital" of good will on which one can draw when needed. Such at least is the lesson of a 16th century novel about popular moral pedagogy, the *Sanjiao kaiming guizheng yanyi* 三教啟明歸真 (*Romance of the Three Teachings Clearing up the Deluded and Returning them to the True Way*).[12]

In this novel, three inexperienced masters of Confucianism, Buddhism, and Taoism deliver a dry and utterly ineffective lecture on morality in a town replete with examples of moral frailty in every generation. Not only is the lecture way above the heads of its intended audience, but in the course of the ceremonies the Buddhist, in an extravagant excess of compassion, inadvertently releases a throng of deluded souls from hell, who escape into the countryside possessing folks and exaggerating their moral foibles until they are pathetic caricatures of their worst selves. The chastened masters take responsibility for their gaff, and wander the countryside learning how to subdue these wayward spirits. In the process, they slowly develop skills in effective moral education. Such education builds upon enlightened self-interest and helps individuals to learn to take a very long-term view of the effects of their actions.

The novel does also recognize, however, that in some cases moral suasion will not be sufficient, and that is where ritual intervention of some sort enters in. Such intervention is the role of the Taoist master (and in some special cases the Buddhist). The intervention may involve shaping a person's dreams (that is, developing their imaginative capacities) or more direct intervention using the power of a deity (some external force) to break through the person's resistance to the moral lesson.

Thus the folk practice reinforces that the Confucian and the Taoist tales and teaching suggested: that the Chinese orientation toward the possibility of a better human condition is "hopeful," but it entails two distinct approaches: a) one which trusts the rational powers and moral potential of the human mind-and-heart to undergo evolutionary and continuous improvement; and b) one which recognizes that sometimes discontinuity is necessary, that there must be intervention or some radical overturning of selfish views and desires in order for "hope" to be realized.

Final Reflections

This paper has provided one portrait of how "hope" might be constructed in traditional Chinese religions. The Chinese orientation toward "hope" is striking for what it contains and for what it does not contain.

The most dramatic absence is any discussion of eschatological "hope" of the type associated with many forms of Christianity. For Confucians, there is "hope" for achievement of a "just kingdom or realm," but it is a "hope" based on the golden age of the sage rulers in past history, rather than of a promise of salvation and inauguration of a totally new realm. Some Taoist depictions of "isles of the immortals" suggest a land of perfection, but for Taoists such lands are transcendent, beyond the realm of time and space, beyond the normal rules of human society. Confucians consistently sought to perfect human society in every age, and Taoists dreamed of "hidden places" outside of normal space and time where an ideal world could exist. Neither held to a promise of a future-oriented world transformation.

Second, the "hope" of Chinese religions does not depend upon a single salvation event in the past (such as Christ's life, death, and resurrection). The Confucians' view of the past was the ground for their trust in a better world, but it was no single event, but rather a long history open to many interpretations (what was the secret of the sages?). The Taoists looked to a time before (or beyond) human memory, and found "hope" in what lay beyond the horizon of human imagination, the open possibilities of becoming.

Third, "hope" in the Chinese sense is embedded in a nest of concepts quite different from the nest of concepts associated with Christian concepts of "hope":

Taoist	Confucian
Imagination	Amenability[13]
Receptivity	Educability
Adaptability	Connections to Others

Fourth, and most challenging to the theme of this conference, Chinese constructs of "hope" are grounded (beginning to end) in the character of the human being and humanity's relation to the cosmic order. Although Taoists will call upon divine intervention as part of their "strategy of hope," the construction of "hope" is not "theological;" it is grounded in the structure of Being, not in the attributes of God.

That brings us back full circle to the fragility and complexity of the comparative enterprise. We have pulled out and followed some threads of "hope" through the fabric of Chinese religion. But since my methodology began with Chinese texts/narratives and allowed the Chinese tales and practices to develop these threads of "hope" with their attendant nested concepts, the results are quite distinctively Chinese. Those following the threads of "hope" through the Christian fabric will have highlighted distinctively Christian patterns. But on what ground can we step back to make a comparison? We shall have to proceed carefully, following slender threads to see if they suggest a pattern, a color, a texture which resonates across the lines of culture and history. We will perhaps succeed at least at complexifying our prior notions of "hope" and developing a more nuanced sense of what it means to have "hope" in our hearts.

Notes

1. The tale of Mencius and King Xuan is from Mencius, 1A: 7. The translation is from Mencins, *Mencius: A New Translation Arranged and Annotated for the General Reader, trans. W.A.C.H. Pobson* (Toronto: University of Toronto Press, 1963), p. 12.

2. Ibid., pp. 13-14.

3. Ibid., pp. 8-11.

4. As I will discuss later in the paper, Taoism and Confucianism are constructs used to classify lineages of texts and teachers and to structure certain rhetorics or options in Chinese religious history, but they are not to be seen as clearly independent and competing traditions.

5. Zhuangzi, *The Complete Works of Chuang Tzu, trans. Burton Waston* (New York: Columbia University Press, 1968), Chapter 6, pp. 83-84.

6. The Warring States period produced a number or philosophical schools and positions, of which Confucianism and Taoism represented only two. However, these two took deep roots in the culture and shaped or inspired many later streams and developments; their differences also shaped the structural polarities of much of mainstream Chinese religious life.

7. *Mencius*, 2A: 6. Translation from Wing-Tsit Chan, *A Source Book in Chinese Philosophy* (Princeton: Princeton University Press, 1963), p. 65. The brackets are included in Chan's translation. The translation has been adapted for inclusive language, since the Chinese "*ren*" 人 does not specify

gender.

8. The Chinese term "xin" 心 denotes both the mind (seat of reason and knowing) and the heart (seat of emotions); and Chinese religious philosophy never separates these two functions, as do many thinkers in the West. In order to avoid misunderstandings among English-speaking readers, it is important to make clear the conjunction and unity of mind-and-heart.

9. A phrase from the Confucian classic "Great Learning" which had become a key point in a Neo-Confucian "revival," serving as a guideline for self-cultivation of sagehood.

10. *Self and Society in Ming Thought*, by Wm. Theodore de Bary and the Conference on Ming Thought (New York: Columbia University Press, 1970), pp. 12-13; de Bary bases his account on the *nienpu* (life chronology) of Wang Yangming.

11. *Zhu Zi*, 118; cf. David Hawkes, *Ch'u Tz'u: Songs of the South* (Oxford: Clarendon Press, 1959), pp. 99-100; cited from Wolfgang Bauer, *China and the Search for Happiness: Recurring Themes in Four Thousand Years of Chinese Cultural History* (New York: Seabury Press, 1976), p. 184.

12. A novel was written by Pan Qingruo about 1615. For more about the novel, see my "Religion and Popular Culture: The Management or Moral Capital in The Romance of the Three Teachings," in *Popular Culture in Late Imperial China*, ed. David Johnson, Andrew J. Nathan, Evelyn S. Rawski (Berkeley: University of California Press, 1985), pp. 188-218.

13. By which I mean "openness to persuasion."

2

Natural Harmony of Human Societies: A Taoist Perspective of Hope

Xiaogan Liu

The paper is to discuss *ziran* 自然 (naturalness), the central value of Taoism, especially of Laozi's philosophy, from the perspective of hope, a concept borrowed from Christianity.[1] Although the Christian word gives the paper inspiration and reference, the author is basically interested in introducing Laozi's theories on naturalness supported by Tao as human's hope instead of a serious comparative studies. The word hope in this paper would be used in the usual sense, namely, a wish or desire accompanied by expectation of its fulfillment, or the object that is hoped for or desired, without any particular theological meaning.

Hope is a key term in Biblical tradition and especially in Christian eschatology. We find no literal counterpart of it in Chinese religions and philosophies. However, Chinese thinkers, Taoists, Confucians, or Buddhists, do have their hopes, or wishes, desires, expectations, faiths, like people in other cultures. Thus we find the foundation and possibility for scholars from different cultures to dialogue and exchange ideas about hope of human beings. As a student of Taoist philosophy, I found the key concept of Laozi's philosophical system, *ziran*, somehow similar or equivalent to Christian hope, and of significance, inspiration and enlightenment in the contemporary world.

The Meaning of *Ziran* [2]

The primary meaning of the Chinese word *ziran* is "so of itself," or "so on its own," and the same in Laozi's text (The *Laozi*). A common mistake of understanding *ziran* is to read it through its modern meaning, namely, to read *ziran* as natural world or Nature. However, in classic Chinese, Nature was not denoted by *ziran*, but by *tian* 天 (heaven), *tiandi* 天地 (heaven and earth), or *wanwu* 萬物 (ten thousand things). The meaning of *ziran* in the *Laozi* is descriptive or adjectival, even if it is used as a noun grammatically. In this paper when we use naturalness or spontaneity as counterparts of *ziran* for change or fluency, we just take them as tokens of the Chinese term without implying any specific meaning the terms may have in their Western context.

What is the general meaning of *ziran* in the *Laozi*? We may read it through chapter 17, which describes the high quality of the ideal ruler:

> The best rulers are those whose existence is merely known by
> the people,
> The next best are those who are loved and praised.
> The next are those who are feared.
> And the next are those who are reviled.
>
> (The great ruler) values his words highly.
> He accomplishes his task; he completes his work.
> Thus his people all say that he is *ziran* (natural).[3]

This chapter describes a gradation of the quality of rulership. Best of all is the ideal king of Taoism who just reigns without ruling, although Confucius has similar ideal about a sage king. People know of his existence but do not feel his interference, so they praise him for being "natural." Obviously "being natural" is highly valued. Laozi believes that the naturalness is the best art of rulership which brings societies natural life, peace and harmony.

Second comes the perfect ruler of the Confucian tradition, who bestows favors upon people and receives love and praise from them. He is optimal in the light of the common political standard, but not in the perspective of Taoism because even good rulers interrupt the people's natural activities. Rulers of the third group, next, are crude, thus the people dread to meet or mention them. Needless to say, they are bad sovereigns. The worst, finally, are the cruel tyrants who make people hate and insult them. This kind of monarch is often the cause of rebellions or revolutions.

While the last three kinds of rulers are graded in the light of general standards or traditional views, Laozi goes beyond these in his final evaluation. He does not reject the standards but places the ideal sovereign of Taoism above all, a sovereign who is first of all *ziran*. Thereby Laozi shows his concern with *ziran* as core value in his thought and high hope of people. Obviously the ideal ruler reigning without ruling is a Taoist sage who practices the principle of *wuwei* 無為 and takes no interruptive action.

In chapter 64, *ziran* appears next as the principle of handling affairs between sage and *wanwu*.

> Therefore the sage desires to have no desire.
> He does not value rare treasures.
> He learns to be unlearned, and returns to what the multitude has missed.
> Thus he supports all things in their *ziran* (natural state) but dares not take any action.

Here the sage is Taoist as opposed to mainstream Chinese or Confucian, since he has desires that go against the wishes of the ordinary people. He neither seeks to be rich nor fights for objects the multitude is fascinated with. Not preying on others or taking from them, he supports their naturalness or *ziran*, and expects the natural harmony and balance in general.[4]

Now we may conclude some points with regard to the meaning of *ziran* or naturalness. First of all, just as the term consists of the subject *zi* (self), and the adverbial suffix *ran* (such or so), naturalness in Laozi's philosophy indicates internal incentive, motive or dynamism without external interruption and interference. Draw upon the essential denotation of the word and the text of the *Laozi*, we can easily find connotations of *ziran*. Obviously, *ziran* or "so of itself" suggests that a thing is generated from itself, not by any others, also it exists and develops smoothly without sudden discontinuity or divergence from the original direction and track. This furthermore indicates that a natural thing will roughly be the same in future, thus it is predictable and not in danger.

According to Laozi, a sage helps all things in their natural development but dares not take any action to force them; he accomplishes his work but his people praise him for being natural. Obviously, a sage being natural and taking no action does not mean he does nothing or has no influence at all, on people and societies. What is the secret of being natural and meanwhile exerting influence on others? In fact it is very simple and plain: no forceful and interruptive action on others, no attempt to control the people and societies, and influence on others should be accepted voluntarily without any sign of reluctance. Thus naturalness does not necessarily and totally exclude external influence and effect, but some forms of them, such as direct interference, forced change, sudden discontinuity or divergence, and so on. When it emphasizes internal motives and dynamism, *ziran* demands that external effect be gentle and delicate, which is to realize the natural order and natural harmony of human societies.

Ziran and Tao (the Way)

Christian hope is closely associated with God. Similarly, Taoist hope for naturalness is directly justified and supported by Tao, the source and foundation of the universe. Here is Laozi's quasi-cosmology and ontology in chapter 25:

> There was something undifferentiated and yet complete,
> Which existed before heaven and earth.
> Soundless and formless, it depends on nothing and does not change.
>
> It operates everywhere and is free from danger.
> It may be considered the mother of the universe.
> I do not know its name; I call it Tao.
> If forced to give it a name, I shall call it Great.
>
> Therefore Tao is great.
> Heaven is great.
> Earth is great.
> And the king is also great.
> There are four great things in the universe,
> and the king is one of them.
>
> Man models himself after Earth.
> Earth models itself after Heaven.
> Heaven models itself after Tao.

And Tao models itself after *ziran* (naturalness).

There are three ways to read or translate the last line.[5] According to the authors' reading shown in the modified translation, we can see how Laozi in this chapter presents a full portrait of the Tao as unique, eternal, eminent, and magnanimous. It is at the top of the chain: man-earth-heaven-Tao. The Tao is the ultimate reality, the source of the universe — but even its greatness comes from *ziran*, spontaneity or naturalness.

Although this *ziran* is not a concrete entity, a real actuality, and is different from humanity, earth, heaven, and the Tao, it is yet the model of all. In other words, humanity, earth, heaven, and the Tao all follow the principle of *ziran* and are fully spontaneous and natural. Omitting, furthermore, the interim items of the chain, the ultimate message from Laozi becomes clear: ideally people, and especially rulers, should act in accordance with perfect naturalness. This naturalness is thus cardinal value in the system of Laozi's philosophy, and its significance is embodied by the Tao, the final metaphysical reality in the *Laozi*. In short "the Tao models itself after naturalness" articulates the key role of *ziran* that plays in Laozi's thought. Actually *ziran* or naturalness is the hope of humanity that Laozi revealed to us.

The greatness of Tao justified the naturalness as the highest value and hope of human being. Tao is almost God in terms of its effect and merit. Many words Christians used for God could also be used to portray Tao. For example, God is One, is pure Being, is wholeness. Tao is also one, also pure being, also wholeness. God is eternal, immortal, absolute and impervious. Similarly, Tao is also eternal, immortal, absolute and impervious. In addition, the words immanence, transcendent, the infinite abyss, often presented to God could also be used to describe Tao perfectly. Both God and Tao are ineffable. They could only be illustrated by analogical language and discussed in terms of what God or Tao is not.

However, Tao is quite different from God when we say that God is cosmic creator or designer. God is personal or person-like, purposive and willful, but Tao is not at all. The words omniscience, omnipotence that Christians use to praise God are not suitable for Tao. The feature of Tao is naturalness: it functions and accomplishes its work aimlessly and unconsciously. Laozi repeatedly says about Tao's purposelessness:

It gives them life and rears them,
It gives them life yet claims no possession;
It benefits them yet exacts no gratitude;
It is the steward yet exercises no authority.
Such is called profoundation and secret virtue (chap. 10). [6]

God loves people and expects gratitude, but Tao does not. Tao gives life to ten thousand things, but does not act as their master; it benefits people greatly, but seems unconsciously and randomly; it gives peace and harmony to societies, but not through control and rule. Tao's function, effect, merit and greatness are almost equal to God, Allah, or Buddha, but different from them who treat people with love and mercy and exert their will and emotion. Tao is the model and embodiment of the principle of naturalness because it works without interference and interruption letting ten thousand things and people develop spontaneously.

The message that Tao brings to us is clear and unique: natural order and harmony in human societies are superlative and peerless in comparison with chaos and disciplinary tranquillity. In the state of chaos, ordinary people could follow nothing and realize nothing. While few people will prefer a chaotic world, many people think order is desirable even under mastering and controlling. Laozi objects to the order under oppression with the concept of naturalness. He believes no one should or could be the master of the universe, although there is something so called Tao as the final source and foundation of the universe, our world, societies and individuals.

In fact, Tao is a concept in between the Christian God and modern scientific theories: Tao is a kind of ultimate concern and simultaneously, that explains about the source and basis of the universe coincidentally in the line of modern theoretical physics. A new trend in Christian theologies inclines to define God impersonally, and the latest science theories recognize the importance of intuition and the theories of harmony between oppositions rooted in Chinese tradition, which seem to indicate that theologies and sciences are developing toward the orientation of Laozi's Tao. Thus Tao makes us a dimension that combines the spirits of both religion and science. We may associate the hope of human beings with Tao which embodies the principle of both God and science.

The Philosophy of Naturalness

Philosophically speaking, naturalness in the Taoist context primarily means "so on its own." It indicates the condition when a thing is what it is by itself without any external impulse or interruption. "Tao is esteemed and virtue is honored without anyone's order" Laozi said. "They always come naturally." Naturalness thus clearly emphasizes that the esteem and the honor of the Tao and its virtue come from nowhere and nobody, but that they are esteemed and honored because of themselves.

Similarly, if a farmer gets up to work in the field in the morning, and comes back for dinner and sleeps in the evening without anyone's compulsion, he can be considered to be leading a natural life. If he is impelled to do this, it is not natural. So, if the government drafts farmers into military service, the farmer's natural life is interrupted, and the way of rulership is not natural. This is why Laozi said that "the best rulers are those whose existence is merely known by the people." A Taoist ruler does not do anything to push people or show off his existence, thus people only know there he is without feeling his existence, let alone his interference or threat. Vice versa, even the ruler is natural only as long as he is not pushed by his people or ministers to do something.

Again, a thing is what it is due to itself — this is the primary meaning of naturalness. If one's existence is forced or interfered with, he is not in naturalness; on the other hand, if someone forces or interferes with the existence of another, he also ruins that person's naturalness. The concept of naturalness thus postulates the independence and subjectivity of each individual, although it claims the harmony in general. Beyond that, the statement that a thing originates and exists by itself without external driving and interruption has the implication that the thing is what it is in itself now and will continue to be so in future.

Naturalness therefore comes with a continuity of its own. For example, if the farmer's son begins to help his father in farming in his early age and is expected to continue that later on in life, this would be perfectly natural. Natural life, life in naturalness, is predictable. On the contrary, if one day the farmer or his son suddenly decides to become a fisherman instead of farming for a living, he would no longer follow his naturalness. This is not because of the change in itself, but because of the suddenness, even if the decision was entirely, independently by the person himself. It thus becomes clear that naturalness excludes abrupt transformations or breaks in the continuity. As Laozi said, "[The sage] supports all things in their natural state but dares not take any action." The "natural state," whatever else it may be, is always steady, continuous, and predictable, and so the sage "dares not take any action" because he is afraid of any unexpected change or causing any harmful break. The principle of naturalness thus requires a smooth curve in movement and conversion.

In addition, it is now clear that naturalness means a balanced and harmonious situation without conflict and strife. If the farmer has to fight for his livelihood, his life would no longer be one of naturalness, despite the fact that there is no drastic change. Vice versa, if he discovers an improved way of making a living because of certain transformations in the society and pursued it without getting into conflict with others, the change would be conceived of as natural, despite the radical transition in his life. For this reason, the principle of naturalness is not necessarily opposed to any kind of transformation or reformation, but in all cases excludes conflict and strife. As Laozi said, "The sage accomplishes his task and completes his work; thus the people all say that he is natural." This is praiseworthy because the sage reaches a successful end without breaking the balanced and harmonious atmosphere of the world.

Ziran or naturalness in the *Laozi* therefore indicates the way a thing or living being is by itself and on its own, how it exists and develops smoothly without conflict or strife. It is manifested mostly in predictable and harmonious situations, devoid of sudden change or abrupt transformation. Obviously, to realize or keep a natural life of individuals and a harmony situation of the world, people will have to cancel or control certain actions, such as external enforcements, sudden internal whims, abrupt discontinuities, drastic divergences, strives, and conflicts. This is exactly the meaning and the significance of *wuwei*. The best social management should have a good effect yet feel as if nothing was happening at all.

While this holds true for the classical context, how can it be suitable or applicable in the contemporary world today?

Naturalness Today

Laozi's philosophy is the product of a primarily agricultural society, and there are thus obvious limits to its applicability in the industrialized and commercialized society we live in today. However, naturalness can still serve as a value in situations of modern life. For example, people still say that something is natural or unnatural, and in many cases prefer the natural to the unnatural. Why? Because naturalness is a constant value, even if only a subconscious one, and peace and harmony are lasting ideals of humanity. How, then, can and should one redefine the concept of naturalness to clarify its possible significance in the contemporary world?

Laozi's age and ours differ massively in terms of the rapidity and intensity of development and transformation, competition and stress. Obviously, classical Taoist naturalness had no need to deal with radical social change or severe competition, while we today cannot deny or avoid them. Nevertheless, even with these significant differences naturalness can still be relevant as a value. However, this is a different naturalness that needs a new definition. The new concept of naturalness, or modernized naturalness, must take into account rapid transformation and stressful competition.

The primary focus of the concept of naturalness, its emphasis on inner causes, is still central even today. "Inner causes" means voluntary decision-making, internal impulsion, personal motivation, and a continuous dynamism. If the farmer, to return to our example, realizes by himself the advantages of modern agricultural methods and decides to initiate a reform on his farm, this would be a natural development. If someone or something, on the contrary, forces him to buy and drive a tractor and combine harvester, this would not be a natural change, however much it actually might benefit him. External influence here is not excluded — there must be modernization, after all, for the farmer to realize its advantages — but it is clearly secondary to the voluntary acceptance of the transformation by the person in question. The principle of naturalness, therefore, prefers inner dynamism to external force. It does no longer merely mean that something is so on its own, but that something develops and transforms because of its own free will.

Another important part of naturalness also still applies today is the emphasis on smooth transformation. If the farmer erects some buildings to lease as guest houses, from which he receives rental income, then, inspired by his success and builds a motel, a hotel, or even a resort, and eventually gives up farming altogether to become a hotel manager, it would be a perfectly natural transition because it comes gradually and is on his own initiative. If, on the contrary, if he is forced to change his livelihood by war or natural disaster, because of a sudden inheritance or a surprise whim, it would not be in line with naturalness. Thus, naturalness does not exclude reformation or progress, but it implies a smooth development without sudden discontinuity, an easy progress without sharp turns from the direction of continuous movement.

Naturalness, therefore, means a balanced and harmonious state even within complicated movement and competition. This state, however, is not easily attained in modern industrialized and commercialized societies, where competitions are inevitable. Competitions provide efficiency and good production quality, but also cause tension, stress, and conflict. Thus, it is best to keep competition within limits and regulate it with the help of laws, to maintain an overall peace in society. So, in our example, if the farmer provides better products and services and thus beats his competitors without causing trouble to others, this would be acceptable as natural and would not break social harmony. If he fight and strive with other companies to win in competition, it would not be a natural success and thus go against the principle of *wuwei*. Yet again, if he ventures to break the law for extra profit, he would be a criminal and not only go against the principle of naturalness but also harm his fellow men.

In this context, then, do laws and regulations necessarily oppose *ziran* and *wuwei*? Yes, Laozi said, "The more laws and orders are made prominent, the more thieves and robbers there will be." That, however, does not mean that he denies the need for laws in general. While *ziran* prefers the internal course, naturalness motivation, and spontaneous dynamism, it does not negate external influences. As long as the external influence does not take the form of direct interference or massive disruption, it is acceptable. For this reason, there is enough room for laws to exercise their function. Laws, in fact, are inevitably necessary to keep the natural order and social harmony of the modern world.

Traffic regulations, to take an easy example, as much as the complex codes of civil and criminal law, are there to allow competitions among individuals while at the same time to keep social order and general harmony. Both the policeman regulating traffic in the center of an intersection and the intricate system of highways with its many signs, are forms of *youwei* 有為 (taking action) and thus interfere with the natural state. Nevertheless, they are necessary to make traffic flow smoothly, thus enabling a state of *wuwei* or natural order. On the other hand, there are also laws that bring oppression to societies and provoke rebellions, which is neither natural nor nonactive. Therefore, laws and law-makers, authorities, governments, and leaders have the important responsibilities to keep the natural order with the spirit of *wuwei*, lest they ruin natural harmony by overdoing their lawmaking.

Although Laozi promotes *ziran* and *wuwei* essentially for the sake of society and human begins, the spirit of these concepts is also useful to individuals. Let us take a college student as an example. If she chooses to go to medical school of her own free will because her family background and a will to help the sick, she is following the natural way and acting in non-action. If, on the other hand, she has no strong personal will to be a physician and just chooses medicine because of the high future income, she does not act naturally. Even worse, if she goes to medical school because her family or friends force her to do so, she is aggressively hurting both herself and the principle of naturalness. In all these cases, the key definition of naturalness is the first criterion of *ziran*, the inner impulse or cause. The more an action comes from internal sources, the more natural it is.

Another important criterion of *ziran* is the smooth development of events. If the student loves to perform on stage but gradually recognizes that she will never make a great actress and then finds herself drawn to a medical career, that is natural, no matter whether or not she will ultimately succeed in her goal. Supposing she loves art but is deserted by her artist boyfriend and chooses medicine out of spite, the degree of naturalness is significantly reduced. Any sudden discontinuity or sharp turn in development lessens the quality of *ziran*.

In addition, the principle of naturalness also rejects strives, fights, and conflicts. If the student's parents wish for her to pursue a legal career and she ends up fighting with them rather than persuading them of her superior suitability as a physician, it means a major breach in the spontaneous harmony of life and thus destruction of naturalness — however much the decision may be her own and may have grown gradually. Also, if the student ends up going to medical school but has to overwork herself for financial support, thus adding a great deal of strife to an already difficult curriculum, naturalness suffers.

This, however, does by no means imply that she is doing anything wrong. To be natural and follow the inherent course of oneself and of circumstances is better and more worthy of pursuit than to force things, but that does not mean that an unnatural act or situation is morally or even personally wrong. Sometimes, people feel that a narrow win is so much more exciting than an easy run, that a hard-won success is all the more laudable. Still, pragmatically, in the course of day-to-day life, people tend to prefer a natural achievement to an unnatural one, a steady growth to a superhuman effort. Obviously, in this context, practical, social, or historical perspectives one must remain clearly separate from moral or emotional considerations, but in all cases peace, harmony, and ease are concomitants of a natural process.

Ziran then applies both in general social situations and in individual conditions. For anyone, be he or she a farmer, student, or whatsoever, an action of internal impulse, peaceful movement, and freedom from struggle is natural or close to natural. A society, independent of its individual competition, with a smooth development and harmony, free from conflicts and external disruptions, is natural or close to naturalness. Otherwise it is not quite natural or unnatural.

Ziran, it becomes evident, can be graded: very natural, natural, almost natural, close to the natural, not natural, unnatural, and anti-natural. In addition, it can be analyzed: some of a course or process may be natural, while other elements are not. For example, an action may be natural as it is initiated by inner causes but it is not so natural because it involves a serious conflict. *Ziran*, therefore, can be described as a general and universal value, but it is certainly not an absolute one. Few values, in fact, are absolute. *Ziran*, as a result, can and should be joined with other values and used in balance with them. Even the value of naturalness should be accepted naturally, maintaining the spirit of naturalness itself.

Understanding its value correctly and applying it with these modifications and cautions, *ziran* can indeed serve as a valid concept of hope to guide human beings in the contemporary world. It stands for the smooth development and easy transformation that issue from a genuine inner motivation, for the spontaneous dynamism that allows competition among individuals but insists on an overall balance and social peace.

Notes

1. The author wishes to thank Dr. Archie Chi Chung Lee, for inviting me to the conference, which inspired me to study Taoist philosophy from a new perspective.

2. The discussion of *ziran* in this paper is based on the author's article: "Naturalness, the Core Value in Taoism: its Ancient Meaning and Significance Today," to be published in *Laozi and the Tao-te-ching*, edited by Livia Kohn and Michael LaFargue, by the State University of New York Press.

3. Translations of the *Laozi* are basically adapted from Wing-tsit Chan's book: *A Source Book in Chinese Philosophy* (Princeton, N.J.: Princeton University Press, 1963). His interpretation of the last line is "Nevertheless their people say that they simply follow Nature." In addition, D.C. Lau's translation is "The people all say, 'It happened to us naturally.'" See Lau's *Lao Tzu Tao Te Ching* (Hammondsworth: Penguin Books, 1963).

4. That Laozi "supports all things in their natural state but dares not take any action" should not be read of an environment protectionist, although Taoists could be the best possible companions of today's environmental protectionist. Preservation of natural resources in the environment was not a central topic in antique China.

5. The first reads it as Noun-Verb-Noun to mean "Tao models itself after nature," the second reading interprets the syntax to be Noun (possessive) — Noun-Adjective and renders: "The model of the Tao is natural," emphasizing that the Tao model itself on nothing. The third rendition matches both syntax and the correct meaning of *ziran*, using the term as a nominal object and keeping its classical definition as naturalness or spontaneity. The author adopts the latter one. For detailed argument, please see the paper mentioned in footnote 2.

6. Translation is adapted from Wing-tsit Chan and D.C. Lau.

3

The Nature of Hope in Pre-Buddhist Chinese Religion

Mu-chou Poo

Defining the Issue

The subject of this study is the nature of hope in pre-Buddhist Chinese popular religion. I choose this subject for the following reasons. In the study of Chinese religion, attention has for a long time been paid to Buddhism, Taoism, and, more recently, the so-called popular religion in the modern era. For the pre-Buddhist early China, however, only the state religion and the philosophical traditions that pertain to things religious have so far been studied in a more vigorous fashion. This situation has become increasingly inadequate, given our understanding of the fact that various elements in Taoism can be traced to the pre-imperial period. Its culmination in a distinct religion at the end of the Eastern Han was not only the result of a long historical development, but also the beginning of an enduring Taoist church; and both were intertwined with divergent elements of everyday religious life. Moreover, the recognition of this long root of Taoism, or indigenous Chinese religious belief, was vital to our understanding of not only Taoism, but also the development of religious culture, including Buddhism, in the subsequent era. For Buddhism did not enter a religious vacuum when it was first introduced into China, and its acceptance by Chinese society depended heavily upon its ability to cope with various elements of the indigenous religious culture. It is clear, therefore, that an understanding of ancient Chinese religion, in its everyday manifestations rather than the grandiose state rituals and intellectual discourses, is important not only for our comprehension of the nature of ancient Chinese society, but also for a sound assessment of later religious phenomena. Without such an understanding, any explanation of the successful spread of Buddhism and Taoism in the centuries after the Han, why both religions evolved the way they did, and why the so-called popular religion in modern China assumed its present shape would lack a firm foundation.

Another good reason for one to engage in this study is the appearance of a number of new archaeological materials in recent decades. These materials, including various funerary objects and texts, allow us to enter into the world of religious beliefs of the common people that has hitherto remained dark for the researchers.

The nature of a religious belief is characterized by the hope that this belief offers to the believers. An inquiry into the content and the nature of hope, therefore, amounts to an attempt at understanding the essence of the religious belief in question. How could one discuss the "nature" of something? It seems logical that one should first describe its physical shape, analyze its structure or components, and then compare the result with those of other similar things. Without comparison or contrast, it is often pointed out, one cannot have a firm understanding of one's subject. In the present paper, I shall try to approach the nature of hope in early China by examining two basic concepts: to seek happiness and to avoid misfortune. When describing the object of religious activities, i.e., the hope that people set forth in their belief systems, these are very often the standard replies. By examining these two concepts and their manifestations in early imperial China, this paper tries to probe one aspect of the nature of Chinese religious mentality before the rise of Buddhism.

Popular Religion in Early China

First we should discuss briefly the religious beliefs in people's lives in early China. In a recent study, I traced the development of religion in early China, from the Neolithic period to the end of Han, emphasizing the long neglected aspect of religious beliefs in daily life.[1] Here I would like to offer a brief characterization of the various belief systems. First, as expected, is the belief in the existence of extra-human powers, gods, demons, and ghosts. These extra-human powers could either be harmful or benevolent, depending on different situations.[2] There was also a belief in the relationship between man's fortune and fate and time, space, and directions. Here time is calculated in the sexagenary system, therefore a cyclical one. These relationships, furthermore, were believed to have been structured mechanically, that is, the relationships between certain kinds of fortune and corresponding time, space, or direction are fixed and therefore could be made known to human beings. The sexagenary system of time-reckoning was of course the backbone of this structure. The actions of the extra-human powers are partially conditioned by this mechanical structure, although some of them could act freely. Finally, and most importantly, although human beings may be vulnerable before the extra-human powers and helpless with regard to the progress of time and space, they nevertheless availed themselves to various methods to help them navigate through the numerous perils in life. These are nothing less than prayers, offerings, exorcistic acts, and the use of divination.

Although traditional texts could reveal a certain amount of information about the religious sentiments of the populace in pre- and early imperial period,[3] nothing can compare with that which a number of newly discovered texts have provided us. In particular, I refer to the Qin bamboo slips from Shui-hu-ti 睡虎地, Hupei province 河北, discovered in 1975.[4] Among the various finds are two versions of obviously one genre of texts, one of which the title "*Rishu* 日書 " or "Daybook." This text has received some attention in recent years, including two book-length studies,[5] due to its potential bearing on popular culture at the end of the Warring States period. Most of the studies, however, are concerned with philological problems and socio-political aspects, while relatively less attention has been paid to the religious dimensions. This is somewhat disappointing, since the *Rishu* is primarily a religious text, and should be treated as such. By stressing what we can learn from this text about the contemporary religious mentality, I hope to encourage more works in the future.

The *Rishu* stands for a whole genre of written divination techniques for determining auspicious days and hours. In effect it represented a kind of handbook, or almanac, for use by a variety of people probably outside the context of court ritual. We see this genre in circulation even today as *Tongshu* 通書, *Huangli* 黃曆, or *Nongminli* 農民曆. The pre-

Han and early-Han daybooks are the earliest extant evidence of this literature and of primary importance for the understanding of China's ancient religious practices. So far seven discoveries of daybooks have been made in tombs from the Warring-states period to Han Dynasty.[6] We can safely assume, therefore, that the contents of the daybooks should have been representative of the commonly received religious ideas in Qin-Han society. For our purpose, this is a good source to probe the hope and fear of the common people in this period.

The *Rishu* was, first of all, a collection of diverse treatises on choosing auspicious days. These in turn could be roughly divided into two categories: one is a type of general accounts of the auspiciousness of days in the entire year; the other can be described as special treatises that pertain to particular issues, such as "marriage", "child birth", "sickness," "constructions," etc.

What are the subjects that concerned the user of *Rishu* the most? When we examine four of the general treatises in the first category, namely Chu 除 (SHT 730-742), Qinchu 秦除 (SHT 743-754), Jichen 樱辰 (SHT 755-775), and Xing 星 (SHT 797-824), we find differences as well as similarities. For example, all four treatises are concerned with the proper days for sacrifice to deities or to ancestors. All are interested in finding out suitable days for conducting various constructions, whether to dig a well, or to build a house. All are concerned with wars or battles, and the escape of slaves. This is particularly so with Jichen. Marriage and childbirth are two important subjects that received much attention, although Qinchu has nothing on childbirth and Chu mentioned marriage only twice. Jichen in particular was concerned with finding proper days for burial; while Jichen and Qinchu are both interested in one's serving as *sefu* 嗇夫, or local bailiff. All except Xing mentioned proper days for having a party, i.e., to eat and drink freely. In terms of the number of different subjects mentioned, those in Qinchu only counted about half of those in Chu or Jichen. Yet only slightly more than half of the subjects mentioned in Chu are also mentioned in Jichen. About two-thirds of the subjects mentioned in Xing appeared in Chu. What this counting of the subjects means is that each treatise has its own emphasis. On the whole, such subjects as sacrifice, childbirth, marriage, constructions, business, and travel received more attention than other subjects. The entire range of subjects, however, covered almost everything in daily life: food, drink, clothing, housing, traveling, farming, hunting, business, sacrifice, childbirth, illness, funeral, official jobs, military operations, and even the catching of thieves and runaway slaves. As if these are not comprehensive enough, there is also one kind of expression in the rishu that is all-embracing: "(on this day,) everything is auspicious 百事吉" (SHT 732), or "everything is inauspicious 百事凶" (SHT 802, 803).

The subjects mentioned in the general treatises were then treated in the individual treatises in more detail. However, we should not pursue the logical connections between different treatises, for one can often detect inconsistencies.[7] One example is sufficient to illustrate my point. In Qinchu, in the Sixth month, the nature of the *wu* 午 (days) are "*bi* 閉" (SHT 748). According to the definition of "*bi*" given in the text (SHT 754), it is a day that is suitable for "intake of servants, horses, cattle, and other animals." However, when we turn to another treatise that deals with various prohibitions, it is stated categorically that "do not intake or sell servants, concubines, horses on the *wu— days*" (SHT 837). Obviously only one advice can be followed, although we do not know enough to make any suggestion. An anecdote of Han Emperor Wu's time mentioned that during a court gathering,

> ...the diviners were once gathered together and asked if a certain day was suitable for taking a wife. The *wuxing* 五行 diviner said "yes;" the geomancer said "no;" the *jianchu* 建除 diviner said "inauspicious;" the *congchen* 叢辰 diviner said "great disaster;" the *li* 曆 diviner said "minor disaster;" the *tianren* 天人 diviner said "somewhat auspicious;" the *taiyi* 太一 diviner said "highly auspicious." They could not come to a conclusion in their heated debate, and a petition was sent to the Emperor. The Emperor replied: "To avoid the various death taboos, follow the *wuxing* method in principle."[8]

Although this incident occurred in the Han dynasty, it certainly reflects the chaotic situation among diviners of earlier periods. Here the geomancer, *jianchu*, *congchen* (perhaps *jichen* in *jihshu*), and *li* diviners are listed as separate "schools." Yet they all appear in *Rishu*. This poses a question for us: are these different "schools" of divination methods originally part of a larger "school," represented by *Rishu*, or is *Rishu* only a collection of miscellaneous day-choosing (*zeri* 擇日) systems? In view of the contradictions among different methods and the inclusion of certain non-date-choosing material, I prefer to see the *Rishu as* a kind of "almanac" for day-choosing systems.

These subjects forcefully show us the concerns of the users of *Rishu* in their daily life. All are immediately related to the welfare of the person using the manuscript and his close relatives, parents and children. These concerns can be further divided into two categories according to the nature of the activities: one pertains to ordinary daily activities, the other deals with extra-human powers. When the text indicates that a certain day is inauspicious and that disaster would happen if things are not done according to the instructions provided in the text, however, the agents behind the disasters are usually not mentioned. When we read statements such as "do not cut big trees on the *wei-days* 危日, (otherwise) there will certainly be great disaster (SHT 838)", we do not know if the disaster would just happen by itself, or some extra-human power would cause the disaster to happen. I suspect both are possible, although this might not be of any importance or make any difference to the ancients.

In fact, in most of the treatises in Rishu, ghosts and spirits are rarely mentioned directly. Of all the 332 slips (including verso) that contain version A, only a handful of slips mention ghosts or gods of any sort. SHT 732 mentions sacrifice to the deities; SHT 819 mentions "sending the ghosts away;" SHT 830 warns against making divination on *zi-days* 子日 lest the "emperor on high (*shanghuang* 上皇)" be offended. In a treatise on traveling, the "red emperor (*chidi* 赤帝)" is mentioned (SHT 857). An "earth god (*tushen* 土神)" is mentioned in SHT 764, and a "god" is mentioned in SHT 748. The only exception is found with the treatise bearing the title "illness," which specifies the causes of diseases due to different ghosts: dead parents, grand parents, and other non-family ghosts (SHT 797-806). The coming of ghosts and the illnesses are related to the cardinal directions and time, therefore can still be seen as belonging to the general format of the Rishu genre. One treatise, however, seems to fall outside of the Rishu day-choosing style of composition. This is a treatise with the title "*jie* 詰," or "inquiry," which is actually a handbook for exorcism against various ghosts and demons (SHT 872-828).[9] About forty different "ghosts" are mentioned in this text. The text first describes the nature and behavior of the ghosts, then provides the user of Rishu with appropriate methods to exorcise each of them. This text is in fact not really compatible with other treatises contained in the Rishu, since the employment of the exorcistic methods has nothing to do with calendar systems. The reason that it is nevertheless included in the Rishu, I suppose, is probably to assist the users when it becomes necessary to "send away the ghosts."

When we use the two key concepts to examine the contents of *Rishu*, we find that both are represented. Thus, on one hand the user of *Rishu* needs to know what the auspicious days are so that whatever he does will be a positive gain. Examples include such expressions as "(on such and such day) it is auspicious to make sacrifice, conduct business, take in materials, all are auspicious" (SHT 739). On the other hand, he also needs to know the inauspicious days so as to avoid doing anything improper. On the same slip quoted above, immediately after the words "all are auspicious," the text adds, "(but) do not go out to the countryside." Similar examples can easily be multiplied.

The information given in the daybooks is geared toward the daily lives of the users. The principle guideline, therefore the main hope for the user, is to try to avoid the inauspicious and to follow what is prescribed as auspicious with the help of the daybook.

The *Rishu* could be seen as concrete evidence of people's hopes when alive, since it was made for the use of people in their daily lives. The use of *Rishu*, moreover, was relatively easy — one only needed to know the date to learn if certain actions were auspicious, or vice versa, if one needed to know a suitable date for certain actions — the answer could be found by simply flipping through the slips. No religious expertise was needed here. A more elaborate, and perhaps also more ancient, method to determine the auspiciousness of days and actions and future events, however, was divination by yarrow sticks and turtle shells.[10] The Shang royal practice of divination was made famous by their use of turtle shells. In general, only people with higher status could use both shell and yarrow stalks; those of lower status only used yarrow sticks. This explains why little physical evidence of the divination activities of the latter is preserved.[11] The recent discovery of a group of Chu bamboo texts from Pao Shan 包山, Hubei province, has provided us with some new information on the practice of divination. Although the writings on this text are difficult to decipher, their basic meaning is clear enough for us to make some observations. The subjects divined by the tomb owner fall into two categories: those related to personal health, and those related to his career.[12] Since the record we have pertains to the later years of the tomb owner, it is no surprise that the subject that interested him most would be his own health. Concerns with marriage and childbirth would be more appropriate for a man who is in the prime of his life. The text also mentions his inquires with regard to the auspiciousness of his having audience with the king, or whether he would be granted noble rank. When we remember the words of Confucius that "when one is old, and his physical powers declined, he should guard against covetousness," [13] the tomb owner was no doubt a man who did not follow Confucius' advice. Although the subject matters divined in the Pao Shan texts are limited, they nevertheless point to the fact that divination was still very much part of the lives of people at this time.

The prevalence of divination is also reflected by the negative criticism towards it. For example, the legalist philosopher Hanfei zi once attacked those who believed in the efficacy of divinations: "Those who employ the date-formula, serve the ghosts and spirits and believe in divinations and enjoy making sacrifices, are ill-fated."[14] He adds,

> When the shaman priests pray for someone, they say, "May you live a thousand autumns and ten thousand years!" But the "thousand autumns and ten thousand years" are only a noise dinning on the ear — no one has ever proved that such prayers add so much as a day to anyone's life. For this reason people despise the shaman priests.[15]

Toward the end of the Warring State period, the author of *Lushi chunqiu* 呂氏春秋 also made a pungent remark:

> Nowadays people consult oracles and pray and make sacrifice (to treat illness), which only incur more illnesses. This is like the archers who fixed the target when they missed it, which is of no avail for their marksmanship. It is also like adding hot soup to boiling water to stop the boiling, which only perpetuates the boiling. When one takes away the fire, however, the boiling will then stop. Therefore to employ *wu*-medicine man and to apply the poisonous drugs to expel the illness was despised by the

ancients, for it was not the proper way.[16]

Lushi chunqiu here exhorts the way of the sages for observing the proper relationships among nature and human destiny and physical well-being. The passage only demonstrates, however, the difficulty in rectifying an idea of everyday religions that was handed down through ancient traditions. The "ancients" most probably did not despise *wu*-medicine men but, on the contrary, believed in their abilities as the contemporary populace did. By the same token, Hanfei zi's comment that "people despise the shaman priests" was probably shared by a few "gentlemen" only.

Rishu* and divination methods of all sorts, as represented by the list of 190 "schools" and their "manuals" (totally 2528 *juans*), occupied a large portion of the existing writings of Pan Gu's 盤古 time (596 schools, 13269 *juans*) when he wrote *Hanshu* 漢書 or the *History of Han*.[17] This is also a very telling indication of the importance of such works in the daily life of the people then.

All these, however, are works for the use of the living to achieve their hope in life. There are also texts made for the use of the dead, representing another aspect of hope in people's religious life. Regarding the idea of life after death, we should be aware that there were those who aspired for nothing more than a hazy existence, side by side with those who had concrete visions of life in the nether world. Our evidence naturally concentrates on the latter, since only they would have left positive evidence for their visions. These include various so-called tomb-protecting texts (*Zhenmu wen* 鎮墓文), as well as texts that carry euphoric descriptions of an ideal nether world, as we shall see a little later.

Burial Styles and the Idea of the Nether World

Before dealing with texts related to life after death, however, we need to deal with archaeological materials. Tombs and funerary objects are expressions of people's hope with regard to the fate of the dead, and through the dead, the welfare of the living.

As I have suggested elsewhere, we can detect an increasing trend, more clearly from the Warring States period to the Han dynasty, in the concrete depiction of a life in the nether world.[18] Two points can be made in this regard: first, there was a gradual change of burial styles, i.e., from vertical pit wooden casket tomb burial to horizontal cave brick constructions. Second, the funerary objects changed from collections of ritual wares to objects of daily life. These are indications of an increasing tendency in society to imagine the world after death as somewhat similar to this world. I shall elaborate on these two points below.

The hope for a decent burial had been a central concern for Chinese since prehistoric times. The exact format of the coffins, caskets, and other paraphernalia varied according to the social and political status of the deceased, and may have followed various well-known rules during the Shang and Zhou dynasties.[19] Toward the end of the Warring States period, however, this burial system began to change. First, some tombs in the Chu area exhibit decorative motifs in the design of coffins and caskets that imitate or symbolize windows, doors, stairs, and upper and lower apartments. In a sense, they were models of the houses of the living.[20] Second, in the Central Plain area a new kind of tomb came into style. It used a horizontal cave as the burial chamber, and, instead of using wooden caskets as outer coffins, employed rock or clay bricks in the walls and ceilings of the chamber. As the burial chambers expanded from single to multiple, the whole structure came to resemble the houses of the living. This development continued throughout the Han dynasty and by the end of the Eastern Han finally replaced the vertical-pit wooden-casket tomb as the dominant burial style.[21]

Concurrent with changes in burial style, the funerary paraphernalia also underwent some transformation. Archeological and textual evidence show that the Zhou-era system of paraphernalia represented the socio-political status of the deceased. One example is the layers of coffins and caskets and another is the numbers and sets of bronze vessels: both were in accord with the status of the tomb owner.[22] Beginning around the middle of Eastern Zhou, however, the old burial system began to be violated, as powerful feudal lords sought privileges on par with those of the Zhou royal house. The gradual disintegration of the burial system was in fact symptomatic of the dismantling of the old socio-political order.[23] When Zhou society gradually turned into the despotic, bureaucratic, and merit-oriented society of the Warring States period, the burial system began to turn its focus on postmortem pleasures. Although old styles of funerary objects were still seen, the orientation of the entire ensemble became geared toward objects of daily use. The most obvious change was the disappearance of ritual bronze vessels, such as *ding* 鼎 and *gui* 簋; various everyday pottery items were supplied instead. In addition, all kinds of surrogate objects, representing servants, carriages, mansions, fields, and cattle, and the like, became the fashion of Han-era burials.[24]

Furthermore, brick tombs afforded new opportunities for wall and ceiling decoration. These included all kinds of scenes of daily activity in the private estates of the elite, as well as banquets and festivities, auspicious omens, animals, and immortals. It is possible that such devices distinguished the socio-political status of the tomb owner.[25] However once the tomb was sealed, these were intended to be seen by the deceased only. They had been similar to the functions of funerary objects: for use in the nether world. The deceased's postmortem life, presumably, was to be as happy as that depicted in the decorations, just as his movements were supposed to be enabled by the surrogate carriages.[26]

In sum, the developments in burial style and the material composition of funerary objects reveal a change in the concept of the nether world that had been in progress since the Warring States period. People began providing the deceased with a "living environment" that modeled his quotidian world. All the care taken to ensure a proper or splendid burial was on the one hand an expression of the hope of the deceased that he should be living in an agreeable place, and on the other hand a display of the wealth and social status of the family of the deceased.

Textual Evidence for Hope Regarding the Nether World

Given the concept of a life in the nether world, a number of textual evidences can be used to illustrate the hope of the people in the face of death. First there are some expressions found on tomb bricks, which include such short phrases as "Longevity, as Mount Tai," "Eternal life and old age," "Fortune and Prestige."[27] One cannot of course totally deny the possibility that these expressions are prayers for the fate of those still alive, but I think these expressions are here meant somehow to enable the deceased, after passing through the threshold of life and death and entered the nether world, to have a long and happy existence. On many bronze mirrors that often accompany the deceased, we find a variety of longer inscriptions. For example:

> There is happiness daily, and fortune monthly. There is joy without (bad) events, fit for having wine and food. Living leisurely, being free from anxiety. Being accompanied by flute and zither, with contentment of heart. Years of happiness are secure and lasting.[28]

Such descriptions no doubt are portraying an ideal life hereafter, but they can also be seen as expressions of the ambiguous. In either case, the mundane world was the model behind the portraiture. Some inscriptions, moreover, even aspired for life as an immortal:

> If you climb Mount Tai, you may see immortal beings. They feed on the purest jade, they drink from the springs of elixir. They yoke the scaly dragons to their carriage, they mount floating clouds. The white tiger leads them straight to heaven. May you receive a never ending span, long life that lasts for ten thousand years, with a fit place in office and safety for your children and grandchildren.[29]

It is somewhat uncertain as to whether the text refers to life in the nether world or life of the immortals. The mention of the immortals in a funerary setting suggests that the two worlds, i.e., the nether world and the world of the immortals, are confounded in the mind of people. This may have something to do with the concept of *shijie* 尸解, i.e., the dissolving of the corpse after the deceased has attained immortality.[30]

The above textual and archaeological material could be seen as evidence of hope for happiness after death. This hope of course did not necessarily mean that people believed that the nether world would be a pleasant place to stay. The Eastern Han thinker Wang Chong 王充 once described what he considered as a common conception of life after death:

> Thus ordinary people ... imagine that the dead are like the living. They commiserate with them, [thinking] that in their graves they are lonely, that their souls are solitary and without companions,

that their tombs and mounds are closed and devoid of grain and other things.[31]

Here we do not see any positive aspects regarding the fate of the dead. Since people believed that life after death basically resembled life on earth. For the ordinary, relatively poor families, this meant that the deceased would continue to encounter problems. An obvious problem for the common people was the tax and corvee burdens and the incessant harassment of associated officials. One tomb-protection text (*Zhenmu wen*) reads words:

> Today is an auspicious day. It is for no other reason but the deceased Chang Shujing 張叔敬, who unfortunately died prematurely, is scheduled to descend into the grave. The Yellow God, who produced the Five Mountains, is in charge of the roster of the deceased, recalling the *hun* 魂 and *po* 魄 , and in charge of the list of the dead. The living may build a high tower; the dead returns and is buried deeply underneath. Eyebrows and beards having fallen, they drop and became dirt and dust. Now therefore I (the Messenger of Heavenly Emperor) present the medicine for removing poll-tax and corvee conscription, so that the descendants will not die. Nine pieces of *renshen* 人蔘 from Shang-dang 上黨 substitute for the living. The lead-man (*qianren* 鉛人) is intended to substitute for the dead. The soybeans and melon-seeds are for the dead to pay for the taxation underneath. Hereby I establish a decree to remove the earthly evil, so that no disaster will occur. When this decree arrives, restrict the officer of the Underworld (*dili* 地吏), and do not disturb the Chang family again. Doubly urgent as prescribed by the laws and ordinances.[32]

Texts such as these are written on small clay bottles, the so-called "tomb protecting bottles" (*zhenmu ping* 鎮墓瓶). Inside some of the bottles are found small lead figurines, obviously the lead-man mentioned in the text. According to the text, these figurines were, presumably after proper magical spells had been cast on them, able to substitute for the deceased in nether world corvee. Another text describes the function of the lead-man: "Use the lead-man to substitute for oneself. The lead-man is versatile. He can grind grain and cook, he can drive a carriage and write letters."[33] The function of the lead figurines, contrary to the surrogate servants (*yong* 俑) usually found among funerary objects, especially in the richer tombs, was not to serve the deceased in the nether world, but to substitute for him should he be summoned to perform hard labor. It is no wonder that they are usually found in poorer tombs, for the underprivileged naturally would worry about such impositions by the state.[34] This can be seen as an expression of the deceased's hope to avoid misfortune. From a comparative perspective, however, the custom of burying surrogate servants or lead-men was not unique in the ancient world. The ancient Egyptians, for example, provided two kinds of funerary figurine in their tombs. The first was a wooden replica of various household servants in action: in the kitchen, in the fields, catching fish, or spinning and weaving.[35] These figurines were usually placed in the tombs of persons with considerable social and political status. Their function, as with other funerary objects, was to be of service to the dead in the nether world, and their counterparts are also common among the rich tombs of Han China. Another kind of figurine, however, serves a different function. The so-called "*ushabti*" figures are of a standard form, a standing mummy. On the figurine was written a standardized spell:

> *Ye ushabti*, if N. is counted off, (if N. is assigned) to any work that is wont to be done yonder in the god's domain (lo, obstacles have been set up for him yonder) as a man to his duties, to cultivate the fields, to irrigate the shores, to transport sand of the east to the west, "I will do (it); here am I ," shall ye say.[36]

The *ushabti*, therefore, were substitutes for the dead for the forced labor in the nether world, just as the lead-men in the Han tombs were. Unlike the lead-men, however, the ushabtis are found not only in tombs of commoners, but also in those of the nobles, while the lead-men so far are found only in poorer tombs. In the imagination of the ancient Egyptians, it seems, even people with high status could be asked to do hard labor in the nether world.[37]

In China, besides taxes and forced labor, the entombed dead also needed protection against disasters and malfeasance. One of the major functions of the tomb-protection texts was to provide this security, thus the phrase, quoted earlier, "to release the culpability, so that no disaster will occur." Similar expressions are found in other texts. For example,

> The Messenger of the Heavenly Emperor hereby reverently establishes safety and security for the tombs of the Yang family. It is reverently done, using lead-men, gold and jade, to release culpability for the dead and to dismiss wrong doings for the living. After this bottle reaches (the tomb), it is decreed that the people should be relieved. The deceased should enjoy his own rent-income underneath, which amounts to twenty million per year. It is decreed that generations of sons and grandsons shall serve in offices and be promoted to the ranks of duke and marquis, with fortune and prestige as marshals and ministers without end. (This decree) is to be dispatched to the Minister of Grave Mound and the Governor of the Grave, to be employed accordingly, as decreed by the law and ordinance.[38]

The term "to release culpability (*jiezhe* 解謫)" originated from legal practice and means to remove the crime committed by a person when proper amendment was made. The text, therefore, serves as a magical spell to relieve whatever wrong doings a person might have committed while alive. Another text reads:

> May the deceased in the tomb not be disturbed or have fear, and stay tranquil as before. It is decreed that the descendants shall increase in wealth and number, without disasters for thousands of years. He is hereby reverently provided with a thousand jin of gold, to fill the gate of the grave mound, and to eliminate the names (of the descendants?) on the roster of the dead underneath, without other calamity, and with harmony among the people (?), and to use this essence of the five kinds of stone to secure the grave, to benefit posterity. Thus the sacred bottle is used to guard the gate of the grave, as decreed by the law and ordinance.[39]

The "stones" were a surrogate funerary object, often in the form of clay ingots or cakes, which represented gold. This gold was obviously meant to bribe the underworld official who was in charge of the roster of the dead. In the text quoted above, we also see the use of *renshen* to substitute for the living, presumably to allow their names be eliminated from the roster of dead. The power of the spell, together with the power of the lead-man and the offering of gold and jade, also ensured the good fortune of the descendants of the deceased. This included preventing premature death,[40] or to ward off evil spirits that haunted the living. It cannot be over emphasized, therefore, that the tomb-protection texts were written not only for the dead, but also for the survivors. By protecting the dead, the descendants were expected to lead prosperous lives.

Thus burial and funerary equipment, no matter how shabby, was not exclusively for the benefit of the dead. In choosing burial sites, for example, the principle for determining the appropriateness of a site was whether the site would be auspicious for descendants. We see amazingly little concern with the deceased himself when it comes to decide his final resting place.[41]

On the whole, except for literary evidence with special views, especially the philosophical Taoist ones, of life and death,[42] the impression one gains from *in situ* funerary texts are that of fear and repulsion toward death. One text reads:

> How hurting and sad, concerning Xu A'qu 許阿瞿, who was just five years old, and yet left the bright world to join the long night, without seeing the sun and stars. His soul dwells by itself, returning down to the darkness, separated forever from his family, with no hope of seeing his (?) face.[43]

Yet although the living mourned the dead, they preferred to have no more contact with the dead, except through sacrifices and offerings. A tomb-protection text reads: "The living and the dead go different ways; they should not become obstacles to each other."[44] Death as a long, dark journey of no return is seen in such expressions as: "The hun of the dead returns to the coffin. ... After ten thousand years, (we) shall reunite."[45] On a wooden slip, a spell for expelling ghosts is as follows:

> He who died on the i-ssu day has the ghost-name "heavenly light" (*tianguang* 天光). The Heavenly Emperor and Sacred Teacher already know your name. Quickly go away 3,000 miles. If you do not go immediately, the ... (monster ?) of the South Mountain is ordered to eat you. Hurry, as prescribed by the law and ordinance.[46]

There is no hint that this ghost is malicious to the living, yet he was obviously unwelcome. On the other hand, although the living did not want to be close to the dead, they nevertheless wished that the dead, their ancestors, could somehow bring them good fortune, as the tomb protection texts testify. An inscription found on a stone tomb-brick from Shantung gives us a revealing perspective:

> The scholar shall be promoted to high offices and decorated with seals and cordons. The one managing business shall earn ten thousand times of profit daily. He who is forever to stay in the darkness shall be separated. The grave pit shall be closed and not be opened again.[47]

It seems, therefore, that we detect two divergent attitudes: an optimistic attitude toward postmortem life, and an attitude of fear of death and repulsion from the dead. How could these two attitudes be reconciled? That our evidence is from tombs of different social strata is certainly worth considering. Rich tombs, with abundant funerary equipment and colorful decoration, may give the impression that life in the nether world is a happy one. The tomb-protection texts from poorer tombs, on the other hand, present another perspective. However, one should perhaps not try to reconcile or to separate these attitudes, for it is perfectly possible that the two could co-exist even in the same social stratum; there is no rules probiting the ancient mentality, or even modern ones, from operating along mutually contradictory lines. If we may speculate a little further, it can also be argued that, paradoxically, rich tombs presented an optimistic attitude exactly because people fundamentally held a pessimistic or skeptical view of life after death. Abundant equipment for the deceased allowed a happy and comfortable postmortem existence. But it could also be explained as the result of a fear of hardship. Seen in this perspective, then, the rich funerary equipment may have originated from the same mentality that produced tomb-protecting texts, wherein the poorer dead were equipped with soybeans to pay tax in the nether world.

Concluding Remarks: Some Comparative Perspectives

So far my discussion has been focused on China, yet a brief comparison with some other ancient cultures may bring out even clearer the characteristics of the nature of hope in Chinese religious life. I would like to mention the religions of ancient Egypt, Mesopotamia, and Greece.

In ancient Egyptian religion, man's attitude toward the greatest event in life, i.e., death, was that of aversion. Abundant evidence has shown that "the Egyptian — despite his anticipation of the hereafter based on equation with Osiris — never seems to have been seized by a yearning for death in joyous hope (not despair) such as was experienced by the early Christians during the age of the martyrs."[48] This aversion from death is comparable to the Chinese attitude discussed above. An example may illustrate this point: "He who liked to drink is in the land which has no water; the lord of many granaries, he has hastened thither. ... Woe for you who are rich in people. He passed by all his kinsmen, he has hastened to the land of eternity and darkness, in which is no light."[49] The nether world is also a place where one sleeps forever:

> The west, it is a land of sleep, darkness weighs on the dwelling place, those who are there sleep in their mummy-forms. They wake not to see their brothers, they see not their fathers, their mothers, their hearts forgot their wives, their children. ... As for death, "Come!" is his name. All those that he calls to him come to him immediately. Their hearts are afraid through dread of him.[50]

Different from the Chinese in dealing with this sentiment, the Egyptians constructed a life hereafter and represented it in various ways: the dead may exist in the western land of the dead under the protection of Osiris, rise up in the sky with the northern stars, or ride in the bark of the sun god *Re*.[51] In short, his hope was to conquer death with the gaining of an eternal life.[52] Except in a very few special cases, moreover, no dead person was worshiped by people; ancestors certainly do not become deity-like figures who could protect the living descendants. Another aspect separates Egypt and China: we rarely see explicit hope for an Egyptian to gain worldly happiness. All the cheering expectations are directed toward life hereafter, one can hardly find prayers of the dead bestowing happiness to those still living. The closest things are admonitions and advices for the living to lead a pious life in order to reach a blessed life after death.[53] For an Egyptian, life on earth was a preparatory stage for the next life. Most of the biographical texts found in funerary settings were written with the intention to confirm the integrity of the dead, so that he could have a blessed next life.

The ancient Mesopotamian religion offers another perspective. As the divine world was imagined as the reflection of the human world, and people were believed to have been created by gods to serve the gods, just as they had to serve their earthly rulers, the religious activities of the Mesopotamian people were basically to perform service to the gods, to pay obedience to the gods, and to accept their sanctions.[54] Evil suffered by man was prescribed by the gods for his offenses — even though he might not realize it himself. Man's hope in life, therefore, was trying to survive under the heavy burden of having to serve his worldly and divine masters. This is expressed in a prayer to the goddess Ishtar:

> What have I done, O my god and my goddess?
> As one not fearing my god and my goddess I am treated!
> Sickness, headache, loss and destruction have befallen me,
> Terrors, (people) averting (their) faces (from me), swelling with
> anger (at me) have befallen me.
> Wrath, rage, and resentment of gods and men.[55]

Religiously, this means that he had to resort to self-protecting rituals or exorcism against all imaginable evils. These include "physical and 'moral' diseases, disgraces, catastrophes, worries and inconveniences of any kind."[56] Unlike the Chinese who had created the idea of the immortals, to the ancient Mesopotamians death, the inevitable fate of man, was never thought to be avoidable,[57] and life in the nether world, an immense, dark, silent and sad cavern, was nothing but a gloomy and torpid existence.[58]

The Greek religion, especially the aspect practiced by the common people, handles the desire to seek for happiness and to avoid misfortune similar to that taken by the ancient Chinese: if the gods are sufficiently appeased, all kinds of blessings would come about, including rich harvests, healthy children, and civic order. By paying proper sacrifices and prayers, it was hoped that such misfortunes as bad harvests, diseases of men and cattle, barrenness of women and abnormal offspring, civil wars and defeats by foreign enemy could somehow be avoided.[59] The gods' will could be influenced by human effort. Only philosophically refined religious sensibility would consider praying for the Good and leave the rest to the gods. Plato, for example, questions strongly the idea that gods can be influenced by gifts and sacrifices as anything close to justice.[60] Yet such sublimated piety could never become the general rule.[61] The question here, as with the Chinese, lies in how popular piety in the worship of deities could be alleviated to a moral plane that espouse blessing for the just, but not vise versa. Similar to the Mesopotamians, however, is the Greek idea of the nether world. Although we hear of the Elysian Fields, a pure and peaceful place where only a few could ever have the chance to go there after death, the common idea of the world of the dead was a dark and cold place where shadowy figures of the dead lead an obscure existence.[62]

The above rather cursory look at the manifestations of hope in the religion of ancient Egypt, Mesopotamia and Greek societies provides us with a background against which we could assess our findings in the Chinese case. We see that in each of the religious traditions, earlier and more primitive notions survived alongside the more advanced and sophisticated views of the intellectuals, and continued to exercise a powerful influence over men's minds in later eras.

To return to China, our previous discussion has shown part of the manifestations of hope in the religious life of early China. It seems clear that people had similar hopes for a happy life: to keep away from sickness, fear, and hunger. This is reflected in the common saying: "Happiness is to have no misfortunes and illnesses (*wuzhai wubing bianshi fu* 無災無病便是福)." Happiness was the conditions of life that one finds acceptable; while misfortune was the unacceptable situations. In this sense, to seek for happiness is to avoid misfortune. There are of course more to happiness than merely avoiding misfortune: for the dead in the nether world, happiness meant a life abundantly provided with all the necessities of life; for the living descendants, longevity, wealth, and high social positions.

All these considerations, as it should be clear, are centered on the human self. There was no divine commandment for the people to follow, but they put forth hope for happiness and expect the deities and ancestors to help them. Except for perhaps a few, happiness was expected to be found not in heaven but on earth. As we have seen, life after death was not really an ideal option; people held proper burials for the deceased not only for the welfare of the dead, but even more for the benefit of the living.

We have not dealt with the view of the elite, since our attention was on the religious mentality of the wider populace. However, some observations can be offered to compliment the impression gained above. As expected, the intellectuals, especially those with Confucian inclination, proclaimed that one's happiness or misfortune rests on one's virtue, behavior, and fate, but not on material offerings toward the supernatural beings. Thus says the Eastern Han scholar Wang Fu 王符:

> Concerning one's happiness or misfortune, it mainly depends on his conduct, but eventually decided by fate. Behavior is the manifestation of one's own character, fate is what heaven controls. One can certainly improve on what lies in himself, he can not know what lies in heaven. The prayers of *wu*-shamens could also help a person, yet not without his having virtue. ... Thus only when one's virtue and justice are installed, would ghosts and gods accept his offering. When ghosts and gods accept the offering, one's happiness and fortune would then become abundant.[63]

Similar opinions could be multiplied easily.[64] Even the Eastern Jin scholar Ge Hong, who propagated the art of immortality in *Baopuzi* 抱朴子, expressed a disdain toward those "superstitious" worship of demons and insisted that virtue was as important as physical nurturing:

> As for those commoners, deficient in virtue, and unnurtured in body, who wished to seek a prolongation of years through the sacrifice of three animals and wine and food, and imprecations directed toward the ghosts and gods, what misconception could be greater than this![65]

Thus we see that the means to achieve happiness propagated by the elite differs from that upheld by the common populace. Yet the nature of hope itself seems to have been the same in both cases. Excepting those related to the grandiose idea of promoting the welfare of society and state, the personal benefit that an intellectual hoped to gain from religious activities differed little from the common people. The Eastern Han scholar Cui Shi 崔寔 was a good example. In the *Simin yueling* 四民月令 *(the Monthly Ordinance for the Four Classes of People)*, a work by Cui, he listed various religious activities around the seasons, to be participated by elite and farmers alike, presumably in his own manor.[66]

From the above observations, it seems that the hopes of the ancient Chinese reflected in religious activities were fundamentally this-worldly oriented. The question is, was there unconditional devotion in such beliefs? By this I mean the devotee had complete trust in the divine efficacy and benevolence of his/her god, and as a believer he/she was not in a state of mind to bargain for personal welfare. This involves their conceptions of the relationship between religious piety and the gaining of happiness. It is clear that not everyone who made sacrifices and offered prayers could be blessed by the deities. How did they explain the "injustice" they suffered, given the fact that they had performed the proper rituals and maintained honorable conduct? Before the introduction of the Buddhist idea of karma, or the idea of *chengfu* 承負 (inherited evil) introduced in the *Taiping jing* 太平經 *(Scripture of Supreme Peace)*,[67] various ideas relating to theodicy might have solved some of the problems, but perhaps not entirely.[68]

In sum, complete devotion may not be difficult to achieve, but devotion without underlying *do ut des* relationship between the human and the divine was something that needs to be discovered in ancient China.

Reflecting upon our understanding of the religious activities in the above mentioned cultures, one common theme can be established: the hope of the people in a religious tradition more or less defines the nature of that religion. Yet the pictures we draw for each of the religious traditions could also be liable to the danger of falling into the trap of post facto rationalization. Our depiction of the religious activities, and our explanation of the hope of religious activities as seeking for happiness and avoiding misfortune, one may question, seems to assume that religious activities are the result of mostly rational choices.

It is commonly accepted that the fear of the unknown might have contributed to the origin of religions, and to alleviate this fear involved certain actions. These actions, such as propitiating the deities and ghosts, choosing auspicious days for proper activities, are usually defined as religious activities, and can all be seen as manifestations of "hope." Yet can we explain these actions as simply rational calculations of the relationship between human and the spiritual beings? When people worship a certain deity out of fear for the deity's retribution, is it an act of rational choice? Or is it precisely because the act of worship is out of fear, therefore emotional and irrational? Further, it is often argued that religious activities in a traditional society are mostly experienced by the members as a form of living. Sacrifices are awesome experiences, and festivals are joyous. What one needs and hopes for in life is not much different from one's fellowmen; one's worship can only be seen as one wave amidst the current: they are neither rational, nor blind faith, but a way of life. This, however, must remain an open issue.

Notes

1. Poo Mu-chou, *Zhuixun yiji zhi fu: Zhongguo gudai de xingyang shijie* 追尋一己之福 — 中國古代的信仰世界 (Taibei: Yunchen wenhua, 1995); *In Search of Personal Welfare: A View of Ancient Chinese Religion* (English ed.; Albany: State University of New York Press, 1997).

2. For my use of the term "extra-human power," see Poo, *Zhuixun yiji zhi fu*, Chapter 1.

3. Poo, *Zhuixun yiji zhi fu*, Chapter 3.

4. The main publication is Yunmeng shuihu qinmu bianxie zu 雲夢睡虎秦墓編寫組, *Yunmeng shuihu di qinmu* 雲夢睡虎地秦墓 (Beijing: Wenwu chuban she, 1981). The slip numbers quoted are from this work, henceforth abbreviated as SHT. A more recent transcription of all the texts with commentary is Shuihu di qinmu zhujian zheng li xiao zu, 睡虎地秦墓竹簡整理小組 ed., *Shui hu di qin mu zhu jian* 睡虎地秦墓竹簡 (Beijing: Wenwu chuban she, 1990). For bibliography, see Jue yi 堀毅, "Youguan yunmeng shuihu qinjian de ziliao he zhushu mulu 有關雲夢睡虎秦簡的資料和著述目錄," *Qinhan fazhi shi lunkao* 秦漢法制史論考 (Beijing: Falu chuban she, 1988), pp. 438-42, and Gansu shen wenwu kaogu yanjiu shuo 甘肅省文物考古研究所 ed., *Qinhan jiandu lunwen ji* 秦漢簡牘論文集 (Gansu renming chuban she, 1989), pp. 314-330.

5. Rao Zhongyi 饒宗頤 & Zheng Xiantong 曾憲通, *Yunmeng qinjian rishu yanjiu* 雲夢秦簡日書研究 (Hong Kong: Chinese University, 1982); Liu Lexian 劉樂賢, *Shuihu di qinjian rishu yanjiu* 睡虎地秦簡日書研究 (Taibei: Wenchin chuban she, 1994). See also Poo Mu-chou, "Shuihu di qinjian de shjie 睡虎地秦簡的世界," Lishi *yu yan* yanjiusuo jikan 歷史語言研究所集刊, 62, 4 (1992): 623-675. Idem, "Popular Religion in Early Imperial China:

Observations on the Almanacs of *Shuihu di*," *T'oung Pao*, 79 (1993): 225-248; idem, *Zhuixun yiji zhifu*, Chapter IV; M. Loewe, "The Almanacs (*jihshu*) from *Shuihu di*," *Asia Major*, n.s. 1, 2 (1988):1-28; Li Ling 李零, *Zhongguo fangshu kao* 中國方術考 (Beijing: Renmin zhongguo, 1993), pp. 39-43.

6. M. Loewe, "The Almanacs (*jihshu*) from *Shuihu di*"; Li Ling, *Zhongguo fangshu kao*, pp. 39-43.

7. The relationship between the general and the individual treatises, therefore, was not that of "abstract principle" and "practical application" as suggested by some scholars, such as *Rishu* yandu ban 《日書》研讀班, "*Rishu* — Qinguo shehui de yimian jingzi 《日書》— 秦國社會的一面鏡子," *Wenbo* 文博, 1986, 5: 8-17. See also Liu Lexian, *Shuihu di qinjian rishu yanjiu*, pp. 415-418.

8. *Shiji* 史記, 127: 3222. Among these divination systems, the *jianchu, congchen* and *li* are found in the Shuihu di daybooks, while others are not explicitly mentioned. This may indicate that a number of the divination systems contained in the daybook later became independent, if they were not so from the beginning.

9. See D. Harper, "A Chinese Demonography of the Third Century BC," *HJAS*, 4S (1985): 459-498.

10. For a general treatment of this subject, see M. Loewe, "Divination by Shells, Bones, and Stalks during the Han Period," *T'oung Pao*, 74 (1988): 81-118.

11. The major finds of the late Warring States are those from T'ianxing guan tomb no. 1, and Baoshan tomb no. 2. See "Jiangling tianxing yihao chumu 江陵天星一號楚墓," *Kaogu xuebao* 考古學報, 1982, 1; Hubei sheng jingsha tielu kaogu dui 湖北省荊沙鐵路考古隊, *Baoshan Chumu* 包山楚墓 (Beijing: Wenwu chuban she, 1991). See also Michael Loewe, "Divination by Shells, Bones, and Stalks during the Han Period," *Tóung Bao*, 74 (1988): 81-118.

12. Hubei sheng chingsha tielu kaogu dui, *Baoshan chujian*, p. 12. For a study of the Baoshan text, see Peng Hao 彭浩, "Baoshan erhao chumu pushi he qidao zhujian de chubu yanjiu 包山二號楚墓卜筮和祈禱竹簡的初步研究," in *Baoshan chujian* 包山楚簡, pp. 555-563.

13. Cf. J. Legge, *The Chinese Classics, vol. I: Confucian Analects* (reprint; Taibei: Southern Materials, 1985), p. 313.

14. Wang Xianshen 王先慎, "Wangzheng 亡徵," *Han Feizi jijie* 韓非子集解 " (Taibei: Shijie shuju, 1962), 5/ 78.

15. Wang Xianshen, "Xianxue 顯學," *Han Feizi jijie*. 19/356; Watson, *Han Feizi*

(N.Y.: Columbia University Press, 1964), p. 127.

16. *Lüshi chunqiu* 呂氏春秋 (Taibei: Zhonghua shuju, 1972), 3/5a.

17. "Yiwen zhi 藝文志" *Hanshu* 漢書 (Beijing: Zhonghua shuju, 1965), 30/1775, 1781.

18. See Poo Mu-chou, *Muzang yu shengsi: Zhongguo gudai zongjiao zhi xingsi* 墓葬與生死 — 中國古代宗教之省思 (Taibei: Lianjing chuban she, 1993), chapter 7.

19. Poo, *Muzang yu shengsi*, chapter 2.

20. Ibid., chapter 3.

21. Ibid., chapter 5; also Wang Zhongshu, *Han Civilization* (New Haven: Yale University Press, 1982), pp. 175-183.

22. Chen Gongrou 陳公柔, "Shi sangli jixi lizhong shuo jizhai de shangzhang zhidu 士喪禮既夕禮中所記載的喪葬制度," *Kaogu xuebao* 1956, 4: 67-84, Yu Weichao 俞偉超, "Zhoudai yongding zhidu yanjiu 周代用鼎制度研究" *Xianqin lianghan kaogu lunji* 先秦兩漢考古論集 (Beijing: Wenwu chuban she, 1985), pp. 62-107; Wang Fei 王飛, "Yongding zhidu xingshuai yiyi 用鼎制度興衰異議," 1986, 6: 29-33; De Zhengsheng 杜正勝, "*Zhouli shenfen zhi zhi queding ji qi liubian* 周禮身份制之確定及其流變," (Taibei: Academia Sinica, 1989); Poo, *Muzang yu shengsi*, chapter 2.

23. See Cho-yun Hsu, *Ancient China in Transition*, pp. 78-106.

24. Wang Zhongshu, *Han Civilization*, pp. 175 ff. ; Poo, *Muzang yu shengsi*, chapter 6.

25. See *Powers, Art and Political Expression in Early China* (New Haven: Yale University Press, 1991); Wu Hung, *The Wu Liang Shrine, the Ideology of Early Chinese Pictorial Art* (Stanford: Stanford University Press, 1989).

26. See Poo, *Muzang yu shengsi*, chapter 7.

27. *Kaogu tongxun* 考古通訊, 1956, 3: 58; 1958, 3: 1-4; *Guangzhou hanmu* 廣州漢墓, nos. 5015, 5041.

28. *Wenwu* 文物, 1987, 6: 44. Similar mirror inscriptions, *Wenwu*, 1989, 1: 42; Kong Xingxiang 孔星祥 & Liu Yiman 劉一曼, *Zhongguo gudai tongjing* 中國古代銅鏡 (Beijing: Wenwu chuban she, 1984), p. 70; Bernard Karlgren, "Early Chinese Mirror Inscriptions," *BMFEA* (1934): 79-82.

29. See Loewe, *Ways to Paradise*, p. 200; Karlgren, "Early Chinese Mirror Inscriptions," pp. 92-96.

30. See Miyakawa Hisayuki 宮川尚志, *Chûgoku shûkyôshi kenkyû* 中國宗教史研究(一) (Kyoto: Dôhôsha, 1983), chapter 13.

31. Liu Panshui 劉盼遂, "Pao zang 薄葬," *Lunheng jijie* 論衡集解, 23, p. 461;

Forke, *Lunheng* (N.Y.: Paragon Book Gallery, 1962), part II, p. 369.

32. Ikeda 池田溫, "Chugoku rekidai boken riakuko 中國歷代墓券略考," Tôyôbuka kenkyûjo kiyô 東洋文化研究所紀要, 86, no. 6: 273. For discussions see A. Seidel, "Traces of Han Religion in Funeral Texts Found in Tombs," in Akitsuki Kan'ei 秋月觀暎, ed., *Dôkyô to shûkyô bunka* 道教と宗教文化 (Tokyo: Hirakawa, 1987), pp. 21-57; T. F. Kleeman, "Land Contracts and Related Documents," in *Chûgoku no shûkyô shiso to kagaku* 中國の宗教思想と科學, *Makio Ryokai Festschrift* (Tokyo: Kokusho Kankokai), pp. 1-34.

33 Ikeda, "Chugoku rekidai boken riakuko," p. 270, no. 2.

34. See Zhuo Zhenxi 禚振西, "Shanxi huxian di liang zuo hanmu 陝西戶縣的兩座漢墓," *Kaogu yu wenwu* 考古與文物, 1980, 1: 48.

35. For examples, see M. Saleh & H. Sourouzian, *The Egyptian Museum Cairo, Official Catalogue* (Mainz: Philipp von Zabem, 1987), pp. 74-78.

36. T.G. Allen, *The Book of the Dead, or Going Forth by Day* (Chicago: University of Chicago Press, 1974), p. 150. For specimens of *ushabti*, see Saleh & Sourouzian, *The Egyptian Museum Cairo*, nos. 150, 151, 172, 182.

37. For an overview of the problem of *ushabti*, see "Uschebti" in *Lexikon der Aegyptologie*, vol. 6 (Wiesbaden: Otto Harrassowitz, 1986), pp. 896-899.

38. Ikeda, "Chugoku rekidai boken riakuko," p. 275, no. 12.

39. Ikeda, "Chugoku rekidai boken riakuko," p. 273, no. 8.

40. Ikeda, "Chugoku rekidai boken riakuko," p. 270, no. 2; p. 271, no. 3.

41. For references, see Poo, *Muzang yu shengsi*, p. 96.

42. See Poo, "Ideas Concerning Death and Burial in Pre-Han and Han China," idem, *Muzang yu shengsi*, pp. 254-268.

43. *Wenwu* 1974, 8: 73-75.

44. Ikeda, "Chugoku rekidai boken riakuko," p. 222, no. 17 = *Wangtu Erhao Hanmu* (Beijing: Wenwu, 1959), p. 13. Similar phrases, Ikeda, "Chugoku rekidai boken riakuko," p. 223, no. 21; p. 224, no. 22; p. 270, no. 1.

45. *Wenwu* 1977, 9: 93.

46. *Kaogu*, 1960, 10: 18.

47. Ikeda, "Chugoku rekidai boken riakuko," p. 214, no. 5.

48. Sigfried Morenz, *Egyptian Religion* (Ithaca: Cornell University Press, 1973), p. 190. See, in general, J. Zandee, *Death as an Enemy* (Leiden: Brill, 1960).

49. Morenz, *Egyptian Religion*, p. 188, with slight change.

50. M. Lichtheim, *Ancient Egyptian Literature*, vol. III (Berkeley: University of California Press, 1980), p. 63.

51. H. Frankfort, *Ancient Egyptian Religion* (New York: Harper, 1961), pp. 108-110.

52. Morenz, *Egyptian Religion*, pp. 210-213.

53. The classic on this subject is Fr. W. von Bissing, *Altägyptische Lebensweisheit* (Zurich, 1955). A recent discussion is M. Lichtheim, *Late Egyptian Wisdom Literature in the International Context: A Study of Demotic Instructions* (Freiburg: Universitatsverlag, 1983), p. 20.

54. See J. Bottero, *Mesopotamia: Writing, Reasoning, and the Gods* (Chicago: University of Chicago Press, 1992), pp. 221-229.

55. Thorkild Jacobsen, *The Treasures of Darkness: A History of Mesopotamian Religion* (New Haven: Yale University Press, 1976), p. 149.

56. Bottero, *Mesopotamia*, p. 230.

57. The theme of death is explored in the Epic of Gilgarmesh, see Jacobsen, *The Treasures of Darkness*, pp. 202-208.

58. See Jacobsen, *The Treasures of Darkness*, p. 52; Bottero, *Mesopotamia*, pp. 230-231.

59. W. Burkert, *Greek Religion* (Cambridge: Harvard University Press, 1985), p. 264.

60. Plato, *Republic*, 364b-365a; see E. Hamilton & H. Cairns, eds., *Plato, the Collected Dialogues* (Princeton: Princeton Uriiversity Press, 1963), pp. 611-612.

61. Burkert, *Greek Religion*, p. 75; pp. 305 ff.

62. G. S. Kirk, *The Nature of Greek Myths* (N.Y.: The Overlook Press, 1975), p. 260; R. Garland, *The Greek Way of Death* (Ithaca: Cornell University Press, 1985), pp. 48-76; E. Verrneule, *Aspects of Death in Early Greek Art and Poetry* (Berkeley: University of California Press, 1979), pp. 33 ff.; N. J. Richardson, "Early Greek views about life after death," in P. E. Easterling & J. V. Muir, eds., *Greek Religion and Society* (Cambridge: Cambridge University Press, 1985), pp. 50-66.

63. Wang Fu 王符, "Wulie 巫列," *Qianfu lun* 潛夫論 (reprint; Taibei: Zhonghua shuju, 1971), 6/6 a-b.

64. For example, *Shiji* 史記, (Beijing: Zhonghua, 1971), 24 /1235 : "Therefore heaven grants happiness to those who did benevolent deeds, and inflicts misfortune on those who did evil deeds."

65. Wang Ming 王明, *Baopuzi neipian jiaoshi* 抱朴子內篇校釋 (Beijing: Zhonghua shuju, 1985), p. 256; cf. James R. Ware, *Alchemy, Medicine, Religion in the China of A.D. 320: The Nei P'ien of Ko Hung (Pao-p'u tzu)*

(Cambridge: The MIT Press, 1966), p. 234.

66. Cui Shi 崔寔, *Simin yueling* 四民月令, ed. by Shi Hansheng 石漢聲, *Simin yueling jiaozhu* 四民月令校注 (Beijing: Zhonghua shuju, 1965). For his life and work, see Shi, *Simin yueling jiaozhu*, pp. 79-108. See Poo, *In Search of Personal Welfare*, chapter 6.

67. B. Hendrischke, "The Concept of Inherited Evil in the *Taiping jing*," *East Asian History*, 2 (1991): 1-30.

68. Chen Ning, "The Problem of Theodicy in Ancient China," *Journal of Chinese Religions*, 22 (1994), pp. 51-73.

4

Hope in the Early Taoist Experience of Sins and Repentance

Chi-tim Lai

Introduction

To be sure, many religions, including Taoism, contain both a diagnosis of inner evil and prescriptions for therapy. More specifically, confession of "sins"[1] is a basic feature of religious quest to overcome the consciousness of guilt within one's own heart as well as the shadow of punishment. According to Paul Ricoeur, confession of sins begins as an experience of fault, a crucial experience of the threat of suffering and punishment.[2] But, more than an experience of fear, terror, or negativity, the language of confession also resides in an anticipation it evokes. It is a movement which re-affirms a religious view of life in the senses of happiness, future, and hope.[3] In Ricoeur's words, "[b]y negation, order reaffirms itself" and "punishment results in happiness."[4]

The religious practices of "confession of sins" (*shouguo* 首過), "reflection upon transgressions" (*siguo* 思過), and "self-accusation" (*zize* 自責) are commonly known as a prerequisite of early Taoist believers in their religious life to rid themselves of sins, in a sense of moral inadequacy. From the beginning of the Taoist sects of the Great Peace (*Taiping dao* 太平道) and the Celestial Masters (*Tianshi dao* 天師道) in the late second century CE, a main component in their healing of diseases was a requirement of confession of sins by the patient. In a brief account, the dynastic history of the late Han, the *Houhan shu* 後漢書, depicts that "the patients were asked [by the Taoist sect] to kneel, make obeisance, and confess their offenses."[5] Given that this was a common practice continued in the Taoist life during the period of Six

Dynasties, other references to the practices of confession of sins by penitents are scattered in the *Taotsang*, the vast Taoist Canon, and other official histories.[6]

However, since most of the historical and literary accounts of Taoist experiences of confession are tantalizingly brief and often only emphasize its practical or material function and effect in faith-healing, the religious consciousness of guilt in the depth of penitents' language of self-accusation and confession has not yet been sufficiently understood and developed. As a result, experts on Chinese religions sometimes prefer to stipulate that the Taoist rite of confession of sins was probably borrowed from the Buddhist rite of confession, called *uposathsa* (*chanhui* 懺悔) in Sanskrit. Indeed, we can trace this Buddhist rite to the fourth century CE because *uposathsa* was evidently observed by all Chinese monastic organizations.[7]

Despite a lack of sufficient textual evidence preserved in the Taoist Canon which could be identified as reflection of some immediate expressions of remorse or self-disclosure instanced by Taoist penitents, the extant text of the *Taiping jing* 太平經 (*The Book of Great Peace*) consists of a corpus of texts written in the form of a penitential appeal to divinities. According to Wu Pei-yi, there is a particular category of writings in Chinese religious tradition called self-stricture, in which the authors disclose their experience of sins, confessions of inner evil, self-accusation, feeling of repentance, and promise of reform.[8] Based upon Wu's definition, the penitential texts in the *Taiping jing* can likely be treated as another example of the writing of "self stricture."

The *Taiping jing* is believed to have been produced and transmitted since the second century CE and then finally edited in the sixth century CE[9] From the chapters 1-10 to 1-14 in the extant version, a Taoist adept is depicted who has spent years of practicing Taoist techniques and moral behavior. Despite that, he overwhelmingly feels a deep awareness of the human proclivity to evil, a deep anguish over his afflictions, and an unshakable will to abolish his inheritance of sins (*chengfu* 承負). At the end, he hopes for transcendence (*dushi* 度世).

Similar to what Ricoeur has noted as "the rich source of interrogate thought," self-disclosure of one's sins registered in the *Taiping jing* specifically takes the form of interrogative conversations among a student of Taoism, named Sheng 生, a Great Deity (*dashen* 大神), and the Heavenly Lord (*tianjun* 天君).

Yoshikawa Tadao consistently argues that the depth of the Taoist view of life in the early medieval China was actually represented in the instances of Taoist's authentic acknowledgment of inner evil of which one is oneself capable.[10] In this view, Taoist practices of self-accusation, self-disclosure, confession of sins and self-mortification are linked to its specific religiousness.

By linking the Taoist consciousness of evil to the *Taiping jing*, the goal of this paper is twofold. Firstly, it aims at a re-reading of the text and a deeper, if not an "authentic," understanding of the religious meaning of such a particular Taoist response to the fear and terror of death that resonated in the common experience and life of Chinese people in the early medieval period. Secondly, the religious study of the *Taiping jing* undertaken in this paper can be seen as a contribution to the theme about the relation between religion and hope. It can be seen as a case study that attempts to reveal the religious meaning of Taoist confessions of sins, which, we contend, not only reside in a sense of moral guilt but also constitute a religious discourse of hope. It includes a kind of Taoist hope for 1) the abolition of the inheritability of evil as well as the punishment of it and 2) a long life (*changsheng* 長生), or transcendence.

The Popular Beliefs of Afterlife and Inheritance of Sins in the Late Han Period

On the religion of the Chinese common people during the Han period (206 BCE - 220 CE), recent excavation of funerary texts from Han tombs, such as the *zhenmu wen* 鎮墓文 (celestial ordinances for the dead) and *jiezhu ping* 解注瓶 (pottery jars for the exorcism of punishment [of the dead]), provides a different understanding of the Han people's religion from some official reports made by court historiographers or Confucian literati.

It is a commonly accepted historical fact that Han people were greatly concerned with the ways of burial practices, as instanced by their highly respected social custom of rich burials (*houzang* 厚葬). Based upon the edicts of those Han emperors, the discussions of the literati, and the information from those Han tombs, excavated, for example, at Mawang dui 馬王堆, in Chang sha, Hunan, it is testified that in the Han period popular religious belief generally holds that one's way of burying the dead would have an effect upon the condition of the dead in the life hereafter and upon living descendants.[11]

A decree issued by Emperor Guang wu 光武 (r. 26-57 CE) in the late Han period attributed the custom of rich burial to competition among families for an exhibition of one's higher social status:

> All the world thinks that rich burials are honorable and thrifty funerals disgraceful. Thus the rich vie with each other in their extravagance, whereas the poor spend their entire fortune. Law and regulations cannot prohibit them; proprieties and justice cannot stop them.[12]

In addition, in the *Yantie lun* 鹽鐵論 (*Discourses on Salt and Iron*), we find that burial ritual was conceived as a realization of Confucian values of *li* 禮. If the living could offer the "proper" li to the dead as well to the living,[13] the family of the deceased could be made known to the world because of successfully realizing the Confucian value of filial piety (*kao* 孝). The text says,

> Nowadays people cannot respect the living; [they only vie with each other] in the luxurious gifts [displayed in the funeral] when [their parents] die. Although no sorrow or grief is expressed, as long as rich burial and abundant funerary goods are furnished, it is called filial piety. His name will be known to the world, his fame remembered by the folk. So the people all emulate and follow this kind of example, even to the extent of selling their houses and properties [to furnish the funeral].[14]

Concerning the socio-ethical justification of Han burial practice, Poo Mu-chou writes, "The *Yantie lun* pointed out that in the eyes of ordinary folk the proper expression of filial piety was identified directly with elaborate burial and rich funerary goods."[15]

Basically, the above explanations of the Han's custom of rich burial only elucidate the socio-economic and ethical consequences of these ritual activities. Further interpretation involving the religious values and beliefs of afterlife is much needed. You Yingshi, in his famous essay "O Soul, Come Back!" strives to suggest a seemingly religious interpretation of the Han-era Chinese ritual of lavish burial in accordance with a "unifying" system of Chinese belief concerning the human souls, *hun* 魂 and *po* 魄, as well as the survival of them after death.[16]

According to Yu, the Han fundamental belief in afterlife includes: 1) When the *hun*-soul separates from the *po*-soul and leaves the human body, life comes to an end;[17] 2) at death the heavenly *hun*-soul immediately returns to heaven and the earthly *po*-soul returns to earth or the so-called underworld below.[18] Based upon this dualistic concept of the souls, Yu shows that burial objects like silk prints, for example, which were found well-preserved in the tombs at Mawang dui, either functioned to summon the departed *hun*-soul of the dead or depicted the hun-soul's journey to Heaven.[19]

Furthermore, in order to account for the general practices of lavish burial, Yu explains that because of the Han people's association of the *po*-soul with the physical body, life of the po in the underworld depends very much on the condition of the body when buried. He claims,

> If the body was well-preserved and properly buried, then the *po* soul would not only rest in peace and remain close to the body but probably also last longer. Lavish interment and body preservation thus are quite characteristic of Han tombs belonging to families of some means.[20]

To a great extent, Yu's analysis depends very much on the assumption that there is a coherent Han belief-system "shared by the elite and popular cultures."[21] However, his account of the origin and development of a dualistic structure of the souls after one's death has been challenged.[22] Informed by her own study of funerary texts of *Zhenmu wen*, for example, as seen in the one written for the dead man Zhang Shujing 張 叔敬 in 173 CE, Anna Seidel says, "We are far from the literati theories about the spirit soul (魂) soaring up into space while the vitality of lingering with the corpse descends into the tomb." In contrast to this literati view, Seidel, based upon funerary texts, finds that the souls do not become separate at death but *hun* and *po* together descend into the mountain netherworld.[23]

For a further understanding of the religious character and meaning of funeral ritual in the Han period, one needs first to know that one of the important aspects or symbolism of the "corpse," called the *Jiu* 柩

when it is put into the coffin,[24] actually signifies "the body in its permanent home."[25] Corresponding to this symbolism, the Chinese word 柩 depicts a (wooden) encasement with the graph *jiu* 久 inside it, suggesting the meaning of "forever" or "eternal."[26] Therefore, as Wu Hung maintains, "[t]he safest place for the dead was his tomb, just as the safest place for a living person was his home."[27] Speaking in this way, the degree of the "safest" condition of the deceased in the *jhiu*-coffin or "permanent home" therefore relates to his/her existence in the afterlife. Logically, the hope of the living when engaged in the activities of graceful death ritual, such as the construction of the tomb, preparations of burial furnishings, and the purification and wrapping of the corpse, was that their deceased would finally resume his/her existence in his/her underworld "happy" and "permanent" home.

However, there was more than a mere concern for the dead. Kominami Ichiro rightly points out that the people of the late Han lived in a religious world view which widely accepted that the souls of the dead in the netherworld would influence, or even intervene in, the fate and fortune of the living.[28] The funerary texts of *Zhenmu wen* on jars demonstrate such beliefs as well as the related feelings of anxiety and fear. The common people of Han believed that the souls of the departed could inflict many misfortunes and suffering upon their living family members. This was the case especially if the deceased's misdeeds and evils during life could not be successfully spared from the punishment determined by the Celestial god (*tiandi* 天帝) or his Envoys, namely, *tiandi shizhe* 天帝使者 or *huangshen* 黃神 (Yellow god).[29]

One of the common misfortunes presumably inflicted upon the living by the souls of the dead, when they are indicted in the netherworld, is the suffering of the living from a terrifying array of diseases and epidemics.[30] The sickness caused and transmitted by the "corpse" (*shizhu* 尸注), the [evil] spirits (*jingzhu* 精注), or the demons (*guizhu* 鬼注) is interpreted as the return and activity of those unsettled souls of the dead.[31] Relating to this type of belief, the *Taiping jing* says, "corpse demons 尸鬼 furnish and bring diseases and harm to the human, and inflicts many strange or calamitous phenomena 災變怪異."[32]

To release the living from such an emotional state of fear and anxiety about the possible affliction of misfortune by the souls of the dead, most of the *Zhenmu wen* funeral texts very much emphasize a dualistic separation of the two worlds, saying "there was a strict separation between the living and the dead 生死各自異路" .[33] A *zhenmu wen* written for the dead person Xu Wentai 胥文臺 sharply demonstrates this idea of separation between the two worlds:

> Heaven above is blue,
> Limitless is the underworld.
> The dead belong to the realm of Yin,
> The living belong to the Yang.
> [The living have] their village home,
> The dead have their hamlets.
> The living are under the jurisdiction of Changan[34] in the West,
> The dead are under the jurisdiction of Mount Tai [in the East].
> In joy they do not [remember] each other,
> [In grief] they do not think of one another.
>
> 上天蒼(蒼)倉(蒼)，地下芒芒，死人歸陰，生人歸陽。
> [生人有]里，死人有鄉。生人屬西長安，死人屬太(泰)山。
> 樂無相[念]，[苦]無相思。 [35]

Beyond expressing the idea of the separation to be enforced between the living and the dead, the further and existential purpose of the funerary texts is twofold: "to exorcise malefic influence on behalf of the living, and to gain release from culpability on behalf of the dead 為生人除殃，為死人解適(謫)."[36] Simply speaking, these two purposes converge to the same end, namely: to ward off evil influence from the netherworld of the dead on the living, or, to ward off evil from the tomb.[37]

To pardon the dead from indictment and punishment for his/her earthly offenses after their souls were subjected to a subterranean spirit administration, a *Zhenmu wen* funerary text suggests the following method:

> Respectfully we offer lead figurines (鉛人) , gold and jade, in order to gain release from culpability for the dead and elimination of misdeeds for the living.[38]

The offer of lead figurines in tombs is undoubtedly used to substitute for the dead when they are punished in the netherworld.[39] But, what underlies such an offer is a kind of wish (or, indeed, anxiety) of the living, namely that the evils and misdeeds committed by the dead during their life-time would then be absolved (*jiezhe* 解謫) through this symbolic act. Ultimately, it is hoped that after such a symbolic ritual of elimination, the punishment enforced by the Celestial god for the mistakes of the dead would not be passed to the living.[40]

The religious belief of the transmission of the evils of the dead to the living, which dominates the world-view of the *Zhenmu wen* funerary texts, is also found in the *Taiping jing*. As its central idea, this early Taoist text maintains that the "inheritance of sins" continues and grows over generations.[41] Accordingly, the doctrine of *chengfu* is defined as follows,

> *Cheng* refers to "before" and fu refers to "after." *Cheng* is the original action of the ancestors who first received (*cheng*) the will of Heaven (*tianxin* 天心) and then slowly lost it. Since they have not realized such loss, day after day, the loss accumulates and gains a lot. [By carrying such loads] the descendants inherit their ancestors' sins (*guo* 過) and culpability (*zhe* 謫). In consequence, they are continuously inflicted with calamity.[42]

In this regard, the doctrine of *chengfu* is used to account for the connection of the misery, suffering and calamities received by the current generation with the evil deeds committed by their ancestors, who put the load on the backs of their descendants.[43]

Although the *Taiping jing* accounts for the genesis of the inheritance of evils by saying that it is as old as heaven and earth and leads to continuously accumulating misery and suffering, the origin of *chengfu* is primarily linked to intra-family transmission.[44]

Despite the communal aspects of the inheritance of evils, Barbara Hendrischke rightly points out that *chengfu* as an explanation of reception and transmission of sins of the past does not simply lay all the blame at the feet of previous generations, but more importantly, it reminds the listeners of their individual responsibility, become "individual behavior will increase the load of misery transmitted to the latter generations [as well as to the previous generation]."[45]

Finally, relating to the idea of the separation between the living and the dead, the doctrine of *chengfu* assumes a moral system of examination sustained by the law of heaven (天之法). Underlying this judicial system is a day and night examination of one's merit and misdeeds during one's lifetime. Thus, "crimes are punished by Heaven just as they are punished by the human sovereign."[46] Echoing this moral principle, the *Taiping jing* says that Heaven is angry (*nu* 怒) and *chengfu* results.[47]

Based upon this view of supernatural judicature, for the Han people there is a Heavenly director of destiny (*siming shen* 司命神), given many different names and controls the registers (*luji* 錄籍) of the living or/and the dead. Such registers show a mortal's fate and destiny, for example, the exact time and dates when he/she is due to die and be summoned to the underworld.[48] As we see in the Zhang Shujing funerary text of 173 CE:

> The Yellow god 黃神[49] [governs] the Five Marchmounts, He controls the registers of the living (主生人錄); summoning spirit souls and vital souls (主死人籍), He controls the files of the dead.[50]

In sum, Han people believed that when a newly dead person descended to the netherworld, he/she would continuously be under the jurisdiction of the envoy of the Heavenly god. Believing so, the *Taiping jing* says,

> When the god of underground receives the newly dead, the latter will be checked in accordance with their deeds.... [B]ased upon this examination, their register is determined [in the netherworld]; and on account of their transgressions, [the god] will accordingly punish the dead.[51]

Probably, it is due to the combination of the religious speculation about the fate of the dead, his/her culpability in the netherworld, and also the belief in the inheritance of the sins of ancestors that various constructions and objects are introduced in Han burial ritual. They are used to abolish the possible infliction of the misfortune on the living family members. By so understanding, we can conclude that the richness of the religious symbolism as seen in many archaeological discoveries in Han tombs, e.g., the construction of tomb, structure of coffin, the funeral texts of land contracts and *Zhenmu wen*, and lead figurines, is principally of the protection of the surviving members of the family from the terror of calamities possibly inflicted by the dead's influence in the netherworld. After all, and most importantly, the religious therapy effected in rich burial ritual helps to release the psychological anxiety and fear of the living from their terrifying experience of the death of family members as well as from their worry about the horrifying state of the unknown netherworld.

The Rite of Confession of Sins in the Sect of the Celestial Master

The earliest recorded practice of confession of sins in Chinese religious history is connected with the earliest Taoist sects of the Great Peace and the Celestial Masters.[52] Both Taoist movements are widely considered to be the beginning of a "new" religious revolution in the second century CE, not related to Confucianism and Buddhism.[53] Above all, one of the central religious practice formulated by them is faith-healing through the method of confession of sins by the patient.

From the *Houhan shu*, we have the following account of the Sect of the Great Peace headed by Zhang Jiao 張角:

> Zhang Jiao of Shu-lu 蜀魯 styled himself the Great Sage and Good Teacher. He followed the way of Huang di and Lao-zi (黃老道 Huang Lao Dao), collecting around himself a number of disciples. They were taught by him to practice healing. The patients were asked to kneel, make obeisance 叩頭, and reflect their sins 思過. This procedure, together with Zhang's spells, holy water, and incantations cured a great number of the sick.[54] [emphasis is mine]

From the *Dian lue* 典略 (third century CE), quoted in Pei Songzhi's 裴松之 commentary on the biography of Zhang Lu 張魯, the primary concern of the priests of the Sect of the Celestial Masters is equally said to have been the curing of disease. It depicts,

> Zhang Xiu's 張修 method was similar to Zhang Jiao's, except that he had silent chambers (*jingshi* 靜室) provided for the sick in which they would reflect on their transgression (*siguo* 思過). ... He appointed "demon deputies" who appealed to the gods through prayers on behalf of the sick. For each patient the demon-deputy would write down his name and announced his repentance of his sins 說服罪之意. Three copies of the document were made: one was to be placed on a mountain peak for presentation to Heaven, one was to be buried underground, and one sunk into water. These were called the dispatches to the Three Offices.[55]

One detail in the above accounts is of great significance for our purpose: the method of confession of sins is a main component in the healing of diseases. The accounts respectively express two different discourses concerning the rite of confessions of sins. Namely that, "*shou*"-*guo* refers to a self-disclosure of one's sins and "*si*"-*guo* refers to a self-reproach over one's wrongdoings. Despite that, both accounts actually point to a consciousness of guilt within one's heart and a readiness for repentance felt by the patients.[56]

Relating to this significant point in the accounts is the Taoist interpretation of the origin of sickness associated with transgression — whether one's own or that of one's ancestry. Firstly, no doubt, in connection with the beliefs held by the people of Han before and outside of Taoism the Taoist interpretation inherits the religious conception of disease considered by itself as the punishment for one's evil deeds by supernatural authority. The *zhenmu wen* funerary texts and the doctrine of *chengfu* exemplify this religious world view. Because of this commonality, Anna Seidel has long before claimed that "Taoism was a certain combination of Han beliefs."[57]

However, what was new in Taoism? What is the religious character of the healing of disease combined with confession of sins in the "new" form of religious practice of Taoism? What is the religious meaning of confession of sins as a therapeutic method to account for the fear and anxiety felt by the people of late Han concerning the fate and culpability of the souls of deceased ancestors (of the sick) in the subterranean world and their malefic influence on behalf of the living?

In Taoism, instead of simply emphasizing the practice of rich burial and the magic of grave goods for absolving the dead from their guilt, it is quite clear that the method of confessions of sin basically signifies a kind of internalization, or rationalization, of one's individual moral responsibility in the consciousness of guilt within one's own heart. Evolving from such a moral consciousness, the Taoist rite of confession progressively resolves the Han-era Chinese psychological anxiety over the perennial question of the link between the suffering of the living and the fate of deceased ancestors in the netherworld.[58] Against this background, our contention is squarely opposed to some scholars who see the rite of self-accusation only a "standard procedure in early [Chinese] religious ritual" without further noticing its specific religious character.[59]

Developing from its beginning in the second century CE and until the fifth century, the believers of the Sect of the Celestial Masters were acquainted with a rite of repentance enacted in a so-called "silent chamber" (靜室) — whether in the Taoist church (治) or in the believer's own house, wherein the patient was asked to disclose and to reproach all his sins to the divine order.[60] For instance, a fifth-century Taoist scripture says,

> If a sick person eschews all concoctions, medicines, acupuncture, and moxibustion, and only relies on talisman water for his cure, furthermore recollects and repents all the sins and wrongdoings he has committed throughout his life, then be his sin even so severe that it merits death, it will yet be pardoned from its foundations, and there will be no more pains, hardships or diseases.[61]

The following episode about Wang Zijing 王子敬 similarly demonstrates this specific Taoist practice in the context of realizing one's moral responsibility towards human suffering. When Wang was stricken with illness, his relatives, who were believers in the Sect of the Celestial Masters, decided to present a written appeal on his behalf to the Taoist Divinity. He was asked to reveal his wrongdoings in the course of his life. Wang replied, "I'm not aware of anything else, except only that I remember being divorced from my wife of the Chi family 郗."[62]

In summary, we can find that the Taoist's acknowledgment of interior evil or moral consciousness of guilt was taken as a response, or "therapeutic method,"[63] to overcome the "prison" of suffering of the living conceived as the punishment of transgression — whether one's own or that of one's deceased ancestors. A Taoist, in his endeavor to seek the healing of disease, writes "petitions for the confession of sins, the ransom of crimes and the release from [subterranean] captivity of deceased ancestors (of the sick person) 為亡人首悔贖罪解謫章."[64]

Hope in the Consciousness of Guilt: A Self-stricture in the *Taiping jing* Chapters 110-114

Although the Taoist rite of confession of sins is a method to overcome one's inheritance of sins, to which it would be linked to the penitent's suffering, sickness, calamity, death, failure, very few of the penitential texts written by Taoists themselves can be glimpsed in the present Taoist Canon. As a result, there is a lack of Taoist records, insofar as I have read, that reveal the self-disclosures and self-reproach of the Taoist penitents in the rite of confession of sins. Owing to this limit, the religious depth of the consciousness of guilt and its rationalization in Taoism continue to remain unclear.

Against this background, it is my suggestion that the sections identified as the *Taiping jing*-C text, consisting of chapters 110-114 of the extant *Taiping jing*, stand out as a unique source for introducing the rite of repentance and the deep consciousness of sins expressed by Taoists.[65] The C-text includes dialogues between a Heavenly Lord (*tianjun* 天君), a Great Deity (*dashen* 大神) and a Taoist believer (Sheng 生). Recently, Takahashi Tadahiko has further authenticated the twelve dialogue passages in the C-text.[66]

In the C-text dialogue passages, Sheng is depicted as one who has spent years practicing moral behavior, for instance, loyalty (忠), filial piety (孝), and faithfulness (順).[67] Despite that, he constantly experiences a threat of faults committed (不敢犯禁),[68] a fear of violating the will of Heaven (恐負天心),[69] and a dread of losing his allotment of life (不竟年命之壽) at the end.[70] Believing the connection of evil with misfortune, Sheng admits himself to be "frequently in (a psychological state of) fear and trembling. Day and night, [I] feel miserable and terrified, and dare not to be at peace with myself (日夜愁怖，不敢自安)."[71]

In regard to the origin of the consciousness of guilt, Riceour has rightly stated that "Man enters into the ethical world through fear and not through love."[72] Likewise, it is mainly because of Sheng's dread of vengeance that a consciousness of guilt falls upon the Taoist penitent. He confesses that "[I] often feel overwhelmed by a feeling of fear, [thus] haven't yet any moment that I have been self-satisfied, but only keep myself to seek the commandments of the Lord of Heaven in a hope of completing my allotment of life" (常懷怖心，未曾自安，思得太上之戒，以全其命).[73] Out of dread, Sheng is advised to constantly observe the Taoist rite of confession, to retreat to the silent chamber to reproach himself and to reflect upon his faults.[74]

To a great extent, the connection between vengeance with disobedience to divine commands and suffering in the C-text quite coincides with the common belief in a heavenly examination system cherished in the other parts of the *Taiping jing* as well as in the *zhenmu wen* funerary texts. The Heavenly Lord is said to send the deities who control the registers of the living (生錄籍之神), day and night to keep an account of one's *chengfu* (日夜占之) as they do of his/her merits and failure.[75] However, for our Taoist penitent, the danger of carrying the load of evils received and transmitted by his ancestors and the impact of his own misdeeds has been internalized as a moral foundation to form a consciousness of guilt and to ask for the confession of it. So he proclaims, "[I] discipline myself to reflect upon my evils and the misery they carried. I am most worried about whether they can be eliminated; if not, in the end these evils would been counted by those deities."[76] In a word, the penitent's feeling of fear and remorse is primarily established upon a belief system with a strong foreusic meaning. Most terrifying for him, the vengeance with the retribution of *chengfu* would finally doom him to the punishment of death. Death was conceived as the greatest misery by the common people of Han.[77]

Furthermore, although the C-type penitential text, in line with other A and B parts of the *Taiping jing*, equally recognizes the doctrine of the hereditary moral evils and punishments, comparatively speaking, the C-text more emphasizes personal sin that one commits after he/she has begun to exist as a person. So, Hendrischke maintains that the text "attempt[s] to adjust *chengfu* to individualist aims."[78] Relating to this adjustment, one detail of great significance for our thesis is that the penitential texts state that the proper method to rid oneself of sins and the evils received and transmitted by one's ancestors is 自責 (self-reproach), 自悔 (repentance), 思過 (reflection upon one's evils), and 悔過 (remorse). Being so instructed, the Taoist penitent Sheng many times confesses himself that he never ceases to reflect upon his own transgressions, saying,

> [To achieve that], I do my best to fulfill the duty of loyalty and faithfulness, [in a way that] I dare not to release myself. From day and night I also dare not to waste any time so as I can reflect upon my evil deeds and condemn myself (生誠貪生，故盡其忠誠，于敢解息，思過自責，何敢失日夜).[79] (emphasis is mine)
>
> I am always worried that I cannot not repay the [heavenly] grace.

> Sins twist my whole body and I am afraid that they can not be eliminated. [If so], I can only mourn for it. If [my sins] can be pardoned, I will continue to reflect upon the evils committed and the sins I carry (常獨念恩不報，罪還著身，恐不辭解，但惻怛而已，雖見原省，使得自思念所負). [80]

Viewing from the above accounts, the Taoist penitential text is not very much concerned with metaphysical conceptualization about a universal human propensity to evil, in a Christian theistic sense, although it likewise endorses a transmission of hereditary sins. In the dialogue passages, the religious motivation lying behind the internalized consciousness of one's wrongdoing and the emphasis upon the confession of sins basically arise from the ultimate concern for the elimination of vengeance for transgressions. By striving so, long life will be gained. So, it is equally important to know that for Sheng as well as for other Taoists, "[t]he desire for life and the hatred for death (貪生惡死)" ultimately rationalizes the Taoist consciousness of sins and the rite of repentance. So, Sheng confesses:

> The deities maintain the law [of Heaven], and unceasingly check human evils and wrongdoings. [For the one] who cultivates his own body and examines himself, he can earn long life (修身自省，既得生耳). On the other hand, since I am destined to fixed years of life, it is impossible for me to live comfortably. By thinking of this fact, my heart is in pain, and tears wet through my clothes (念之心痛，淚下沾衣). Such misery happens for a long time. Now, I more and more treasure my given life-span, and am afraid of not being able to gain longevity (日惜年命，恐不得壽). [81]

Conclusion

To conclude this study, we contend that the Taoist guilty conscience and confessions of sins fundamentally express a kind of internalized religiousness induced by a threat of punishment for transgression. Firstly, the Taoist rite of confession of inner evil aims to save believers from the mischievousness of ancestors. Secondly, Taoists hope that by confessing sins within one's own heart they will achieve a transcendent state of long life and deathlessness (使得長生，在不死之籍). [82] In the *Taiping jing*, this discourse of religious hope is symbolically conferred by the Heavenly Lord, who would righteously permit successful believers to join the immortals by issuing a decree to minor deities to free them from their load of *chengfu*.[83]

Notes

1. In this paper, the meaning of sin will not be understood within the limit of Christian theistic perspective. Sin is interchangeably used to refer to evil deeds and violation of the will of heaven in a moral sense.

2. Paul Ricoeur, *The Symbolism of Evil* (Boston: Beacon Press, 1967), p. 27.

3. Ibid., pp. 44-45.

4. Ibid., p. 43.

5. *Houhan shu* 後漢書 (Beijing: Zhonghua shuju, 1964; hereafter *HHS*), chapters 71, p. 2299.

6. Masayoshi Kobayashi 小林正美, "The Celestial Masters under the Eastern Jin and Liu-Song Dynasties," *Taoist Resources* 3 (1992), p. 23.

7. Wu Pei-yi, "Self-Examination and Confession of Sins in Traditional China," *Harvard Journal of Asiatic Studies* 39 (1979), p. 10; E. Zurcher, "'Prince Moonlight':Messianism and eschatology in early medieval Chinese Buddhism," *T'oung Pao* 68 (1982), pp. 2-75.

8. Wu Pei-yi, "Self-Examination and Confession of Sins in Traditional China," p. 5. For the discussion of the writings of self-stricture in the Chinese tradition of Confucianism, see Wu Pei-yi, *The Confucian's Progress: Autobiographical Writings in Traditional China* (Princeton, New Jersey: Princeton University Press, 1990).

9. For the discussions of the date of the extant copy of the *Taiping Jing* in the Daozang, see Yoshioka Yoshitoyo, "Tonkoben Taibeikyo ni tsuite" 敦煌本太平經 について ,*Toyo bunka kenkyusho kiyo* 22 (1961), pp. 1-103; B. J. Mansvelt Beck, "The Date of the *T'ai-ping ching*," *T'oung Pao* 66 (1980), pp. 149-32; Lai Chi Tim 黎志添 "Shiping zhongguo xueze guanyu taiping jing de yanjiu" 試評中國學者關於太平經的研究, *Zhongwen daxue zhongguo wenhua yanjiu suo xuebao* 中國文化研究所學報 No. 5 (1996): 297-318.

10. Yoshikawa Tadao 吉川忠夫, "Chugoku rikucho jidai ni okeru shukyo no mondai," 中國六朝時代 における 宗教の問題, *Shiso* (1994), pp. 99-118.

11. For the discussion of the Mawangdui's Han tombs related to Han people's burial practice, see Yu Weichao 俞偉超, "Mawangdui yihao Han-mu bohua

neirong kao" 馬王堆一號漢墓帛畫內容考, in Yu Weichao, *Xianqin lianghan kaogu xue lunji* 先秦兩漢考古學論集 (Beijing: Wenwu chuban she, 1985).

12. *HHS,* chapter 1, p. 51. The translation is based on Poo Mu-chou, "Ideas Concerning Death and Burial in Pre-Han and Han China," *Asia Major* (3rd. series) No. 3 (1990): 42.

13. Xunzi 荀子 says that only if one could "serve the dead as he would serve the living" 事死如事生 would society function well according to li; see *Xunzi jijie*, ed. Wang Xianqian (Beijing: Zhonghau shuju, 1988), p. 378.

14. *Yantie lun* 鹽鐵論, ed. Wang Liqi (Beijing: Zhonghua shuju). The translation is based upon that of Poo Mu-chou.

15. Poo Mu-chou, "Ideas Concerning Death and Burial in Pre-Han and Han China," in *Asia Major* (3rd Serics) 3, 2 (1990): p. 46.

16. Yu Yingshi 余英時, "'O Soul, Come Back! A Study in the Changing Conceptions of the Soul and Afterlife in Pre-Buddhist China," *Harvard Journal of Asiatic Studies* 47 (1987): 363-395.

17. Ibid., p. 365. Cf. Wang Chong 王充, *Lunheng* 論衡 ("Lunsi" 論死), ed. Huang Hui (Beijing: Zhonghua shuju, 1990), p. 871; Ge Hong: *Baopuzi neipian* 抱樸子內篇, ed. Wang Ming (Beijing: Zhonghua shuju, 1985), pp. 125-6.

18. Yu Yingshih, "'O Soul, Come Back!' A Study in the Changing Conceptions of the Soul and Afterlife in Pre-Buddhist China," pp. 374, 384.

19. Ibid., pp. 368, 382. Cf. Wu Hung, "Art in a Ritual Context: Rethinking Mawangdui" *Early China* 17 (1992), pp. 111-143, argues against Yu Yingshih's view by stipulating that the ritual of the "summons of the soul" functioned as a "final [healing] effort of the living to revive the life of a family member who had just ceased to breathe and seemed to be dead" (p. 113).

20. Yu Yingshih, p. 385.

21. Ibid., p. 363.

22. Cf. Wu Hung, "Art in a Ritual Context: Rethinking Mawangdui," pp. 112-5.

23. Anna Seidel, "Traces of Han Religion in Funeral Texts Found in Tombs," in Akizuki Kan'ei ed., *Dokyo to shukyo bunka* 道教と宗教文化 (Tokyo: Hirakawa, 1987), p. 705.

24. According to the *Record of Rites* 禮記, it is said that "(The corpse) on the couch is called a *shi* 尸 (the laid out); when it is put into the coffin, it is called a *jiu* 柩." Cf. Wu Hung, "Art in a Ritual Context: Rethinking

Mawangdui," pp. 117-8.

25. Wu Hung, "Art in a Ritual Context: Rethinking Mawangdui," p. 117.

26. Ibid., p. 118; cf., Bai gu 班固, *Baihu tongyi* 白虎通義 (Beijing: Zhonghua shuju).

27. Ibid., p. 124.

28. Kominami Ichiro 小南一郎, "Kandai no sorei kennen" 漢代の祖靈觀念, *Toho gakuho* 東方學報 66 (1994), pp. 17, 19. Cf. Wang Chong, *Lunheng* 論衡, "*Lunsi*" 論死 and "*Dinggui*" 訂鬼.

29. For a detailed discussion of the Huangshen in the context of Taoism, see Liu Zhaorui 劉昭瑞, "Gianlun 'huangshen yuezhang' — wjianlun huangjin kouhao de yiyi ji xiangguan wenti," 簡論 "黃神越章" — 兼論黃巾口號的意義及相關問題, *Lishi yanjiu* 歷史研究 (1996): 125-132.

30. For research on the religious conception of the cause of diseases in the late Han, see Lin Fushi 林富士, "shilun taiping jing de jibing guannian," 試論太平經的疾病觀念, *Zhongyang yanjiu yuan lishi yuyan yanjiu suo jikan* 中央研究院歷史語言研究所集刊 62 (1993), pp. 225-263.

31. Liu Zhaorui, "Taiping jing yu kaogu faxian de donghan zhenmu wen" 太平經與考古發現的東漢鎮墓文, *Shijie zongjiao yanjiu* 世界宗教研究 Vol. 63 (1994): pp. 115-6.

32. Wang Ming, *Taiping jing hejiao* 太平經合校 (hereafter *TPC*; Beijing: Zhonghua shuju, 1960), p. 51.

33. Liu Zhaorui, "Chengfu shuo yuanqi lun" 承負說緣起論, *Shijie zongjian yanjiu* Vol. 64 (1995): 103-4.

34. According to Liu Zhaorui, "Changan" 長安 should not literally refer to the geographical location of the Han capital of Changan, but to the place wherein there is no death. See his "Chengfu shuo yuanqi lun," p. 103.

35. The translation is based on Anna Seidel, "Traces of Han Religion in Funeral Texts Found in Tombs," p. 704.

36. Ibid., p. 693; Liu Zhaorui, "Taiping jing yu kaogu faxian de donghan zhenmu wen," p. 111; Wu Rongzeng 吳榮曾, "Zhenmu wen zhong suojian de donghan daowu guanxi 鎮墓文中所見的東漢道巫關係," in his *Xianqin Lianghan shi yanjiu* 先秦兩漢史研究 (Beijing: Zhonghua shuju, 1995), p. 362.

37. Kominami Ichro, p. 26.

38. The translation is based on Anna Seidel, p. 692.

39. Liu Zhaorui, "Taiping jing yu kaogu faxian de donghan *Zhenmu wen*," p. 112.

40. Anna Seidel, pp. 690-694.

41. Liu Zhaorui, "Chengfu shuo yuanqi lun," pp. 103-4.

42. *TPC*, chapter 70.

43. On the discussion of the doctrine of chengfu in the *Taiping jing*, see Kamitsuka Yoshiko, "Taibeikyo no shofu to taibei no riron ni tsuite" (太平經の承負と太平の理論について), *Nagoya daikyoyobu kiyo* A-32 (1988), pp. 41-75.

44. *TPC*, chapter 67: "The children will receive and transmit (何承負) the misdeeds of their parents in excess and will sometimes be called children of thieves and of robbers or meet with their own ruin," p. 251.

45. Barbara Hendrischke, "The Concept of Inherited Evil in the *Taiping jing*," *East Asian History* 2 (1991), p. 11.

46. *Lunheng*, chapter 6, p. 273.

47. *TPC*, chapter 37, p. 55

48. Cf. *Shiji* 史記 (天官書) and *Huainan honglie jijie* 淮南鴻烈集解, chapters 3, 8.

49. For the study of the Yellow god, as the representative of the Heavenly god, see Kominami Ichro, "Kandai no sorei kennen," pp. 53-54; Liu Zhaorui, "Gian lun 'huangshen yezhang' — jianlun huangjin kouhao de yiyi ji xiangguan wenti," *Lishi yanjiu* (1996), pp. 125-132.

50. The translation is based on Anna Seidel, "Traces of Han Religion," p. 30.

51. *TPC*, p. 72.

52. Wu Pei-yi, "Self-Examination and Confession of Sins in Traditional China," p. 6.

53. Michel Strickmann, "On the Alchemy of T'ao Hung-ching," in Holmes Welch and Anna Seidel eds., *Facets of Taoism: Essays in Chinese Religion* (New Haven: Yale University Press, 1979), pp. 165-6.

54. *HHS*, chapters 71, p. 2299.

55. *Sanguo zhi* 三國志, "*Wei zhi* 魏志," chapter 8, p. 264.

56. Yoshikawa Tadao, "Chugoku rikucho jidai ni okeru shukyo no mondai," p. 102.

57. Anna Seidel, "Traces of Han Religion," p. 633; cf. her "Imperial Treasures and Taoist Sacraments — Taoist Roots in the Apocrypha," in Michel Strickmann ed., *Tantric and Taoist Studies*, vol. 2 (Bruxelles: Institut Belge des Hautes Etudes Chinoises, 1983), pp. 291-371.

58. Kominami Ichro, "Kandai no sogen kennen," pp. 55-9.

59. Barbara Hendrischke, "The Concept of Inherited Evil in the *Taiping jing*," p. 22.

60. Cf. *Yaoxiu keyi jielu chao* 要修科儀戒律鈔 chapter 10; *Lu xiansheng daomen kelue* 陸先生道門科略 (TT 761); *Zhengao* 真誥 (TT 637), chapter 18. For

details on the structure of silent chamber and the procedure of the rite of repentance in it, see Yoshikswa Tadao, "Seishitsu ko" 靜室考, *Toho gakuho* 59 (1987), pp. 125-162.

61. *Lu xiansheng daomen kelue* 陸先生道門科略, 1b-2a.

62. *Shishuo xinyu* 世說新語, chapter 1. Cf. Richard B. Mather (trans.), *A New Account of Tales of the World* (Minneapolis: University of Minnesota Press, 1976), p. 19.

63. Michel Strickmann, "On the Alchemy of Tao Hung-jing," p. 168.

64. Anna Seidel, "Traces of Han Religion," p. 689.

65. The division of three strata or layers contained in the extant version of the *Taiping jing* was first established by Xiong Deji 熊德基, "Taiping jing de zuozhe he sixiang jiqi he tianshi dao de guanxi" 太平經的作者和思想及其和天師道的關係, *Lishi yanjiu* 4 (1962), pp. 8-25. For detailed analysis of the C type-stratum, see Takahashi Tadahiko 赤塚忠, "Taiheikyo no kaiwatai no seikaku ni tsuite" 太平經の會話體性格について, *Yoyo bunka kenkyujo kiyo* 105 (1988), pp. 243-81; and Barbara Hendrischke, "The Concept of Inherited Evil in the *Taiping Jing*," pp. 3-5, 22-25.

66. see n.58. The division of the twelve dialogue passages by Takahashi Tadahiko is as follows: pp. 529-530; 531-532; 533-534; 535-536a; 536b-538a; 538b-540; 549b-552; 554-556a; 556b-558a; 559b-562a; 606b-609; 610-612.

67. *TPC*, p. 538.

68. Ibid., p. 528.

69. Ibid.

70. Ibid., p. 537.

71. Ibid., p. 607.

72. Paul Ricoeur, *The Symbolism of Evil*, p. 30.

73. *TPC*, p. 560.

74. Ibid., p. 536.

75. Ibid., pp. 526, 534, 544, 546.

76. Ibid., p. 610.

77. Ibid. : "It therefore says a separation of the dead and the living, which are incommensurable" 故言死生異路，安得相比, p. 554.

78. Barbara Hendrischke, "The Concept of Inherited Evil in the *Taiping Jing*," p. 23.

79. *TPC*, p. 558.

80. Ibid., p. 555.

81. Ibid., p. 550.

82. Ibid., p. 554.

83. Ibid., p. 561.

5

Early Taoist Messianism: A Survey[1]

John Lagerwey

The earliest known Chinese "soteriological religion"[2] involves the Western Queen Mother (Xiwang mu 西王母); a severe drought in the year 3 BCE seems to have been the immediate cause, but the movement also coincided with the appearance of a comet: "In the area east of the pass, the people transmitted stalks of the Queen Mother of the West as they moved. They went through commanderies and kingdoms until they crossed the pass to the West and entered the capital. The people also assembled to sacrifice to the Queen Mother, and some went up at night on the housetops with torches to beat drums, call out, and frighten each other." Related passages add that some people went barefoot and dishevelled, or carried manikins made of straw or hemp; "they held services and set up gaming boards for a lucky throw, and they sang and danced in worship of the Queen Mother of the West. They also passed around a written message, saying, "The Mother tells the people that those who wear this talisman will not die."[3] However we are to interpret these all-too brief passages, the student of later Chinese popular religion cannot but be struck by a whole series of the elements encountered here: "barefoot and dishevelled" calls to mind shamans (*wu* 巫), as does song and dance in worship; "manikins of straw" suggest "substitute bodies" (*tishen* 替身), and the use of "gaming boards for a lucky throw" the role of gambling in the context of the *Jiao* 醮 (communal sacrifice).[4] The talisman that procures immortality reminds us not only of later popular Taoism, but also justifies calling this a "soteriological" movement. This, in turn, obliges us to see the worship of the Queen Mother of the West already at this early date in the context of the search for immortality and, of particular interest for us here, in the context of salvation from apocalyptic disaster.

We might gloss the whole event in this manner: attacked by drought demons and warned by astral manifestations, the people set out to meet their goddess bearing protective talismans and other tokens which prove they belong to her, but also substitute bodies on to which to deflect the harmful pneuma abounding at such a dangerous moment; as they advance toward the fateful encounter, they "roll the dice" to see whether the conjuncture is lucky or, on the contrary, potentially disastrous. We have here, in short, a uniquely Chinese soteriological pattern: a cosmic conjuncture — in whose definition the political, the natural, and the social all have a part — is a moment at once fraught with danger and opportunity, a time when demons abound, but also a time when a passageway to immortality suddenly opens. It is up to the individual to "read the signs" and seize the opportunity.

Anna Seidel's "The Image of the Perfect Ruler in Early Taoist Messianism" was first presented to the fall 1968 Bellagio Conference on Taoist Studies and then published the following year in the acts of that conference. It is divided into two parts, the first being on "the perfect ruler in the Taiping ideology of the Han" and the second on "the perfect ruler in the popular movements of the Six Dynasties." From the very beginning, Taoist messianism is associated with the notion of the "great peace" (*taiping* 太平): as early as 5 BCE, a book of that name having been presented to the throne, Aidi 哀帝 assumes the title "Emperor of Great Peace." Shortly thereafter, during the reign of Wang Mang 王莽, a prophecy that the Han would be restored with the help of a Mr. Li 李 leads Wang to set up one Li Shen 李琴 as commander-in-chief and give him the title "sage" (*sheng* 聖). But a second prophecy having explicitly linked the Li family to the return to power of the Lius 劉氏, one Li Tong 李通 rallies to the cause of Guangwu Di and is rewarded with the title "coadjutor of the Han" and marriage to the emperor's younger sister. This set a precedent for the same "peculiar link" between the Lius and the Lis in the Liu-Song dynasty in the early fifth century, but even more importantly it is the first known instance of a Li who appears as a kind of political saviour to help restore order in decadent times. Later Lis will become universal saviours, incarnations of the god Laozi, whose putative family name was Li.

Most Taoist-inspired rebellions of the second century CE, including the famous Yellow Turban rebellion of the year 184, worshipped Laozi as the supreme god. One text is of particular interest, the *Laozi bianhua jing* 老子變化經 (*Scripture of the Transformations of Laozi*), in which Laozi is portrayed as having regularly appeared in the world, first as "counselor to the holy sovereigns of old"[5] and then, no fewer than five times in Sichuan between the years 132 and 155, as "perfect man" (*zhenren* 真人): "In this present age I will choose the good people, " the text concludes, "The people are in deep distress, epidemics and famine are everywhere. (In order to) turn your destiny I will shake the Han reign."[6] Here we have all the ingredients of a messianic text: a saviour god who comes in time of great tribulation to save "the good people."

The second part of Seidel's article treats first of "rebels and rulers from the Li clan" and then, specifically, of Li Hong 李弘, whose name is usually written as a rebus: *muzi gongkou* 木子弓口. As her chief sources are precisely those dealt with by Robinet, Strickmann and Mollier, we shall turn now to them, beginning with the "list of the main Taoist apocalyptic texts of the Six Dynasties" established by Mollier:[7]

Heavenly Master Texts

1. *Nuqing guilü* 女青鬼律 (*The Blue Woman's Penal Code for Demons*; DZ 790): "Prior to the fourth century. It describes the golden age, the degeneration of humanity, cosmological disorder, and the loss of moral order, predicts calamities of demonic origin, the extermination of sinners, the advent of an era of the Dao (*daoyun*) and Great Peace, the salvation of the elect (*zhongmin* 種民), the return of the faithful to their original lands (the reconquest of the barbarian-held north?), and the appearance of Li Hong (*muzu santai*)."

2. *Laojun bianhua wuji jing* 老子變化無極經 (*Scripture of the Infinite Transformations of Lord Lao*; DZ 1195): "Long poem (6 *juan* 卷) in heptasyllabic verse; prior to the year 360. It describes the imminent advent of Li Hong the Perfect Lord (*muzi gongkou*), the salvation of the elect (*zhongmin* 種民), and the advent of an era of Great Peace."

3. *Zhengyi tianshi gao Zhao Sheng koujue* 正一天師告趙昇口訣 (*Oral Instructions Revealed by the Heavenly Master of Orthodox Unity,*

Zhao Sheng; DZ 1273): "Dates probably to the fourth century... It predicts the imminence of the Great Kalpa (*dajie* 大劫), the flood of the year jiashen 甲申, the end of the Metal Horse (*jinma* 金馬: rebus for the Sima 司馬 lineage of the Jin dynasty, which ruled by virtue of metal), demonic invasions which bring disorder and illness, the coming of Lord Li, sent by the Most High Lord Lao to save the elect, resurrect the dead, and usher in an era of Great Peace."

Shangqing Texts

4. *Shanqing housheng Daojun lieji* 上請後聖道君列紀 (see below).
5. *Taishang santian zhengfa jing* 太上三天正法經 (*Scripture of the Most High on the Orthodox Methods of the Three Heavens*; DZ 1203): "It describes the end of the cosmic era and cosmological disturbances, signs of the imminence of the end of time, and the diffusion of a sacred book, saviour of humanity; it predicts the extermination of the evil, the appearance of the Most High in the year *renchen* 壬辰, the advent of the Metal family, that is, the Liu-Song dynasty."[8]

Lingbao Texts

6. *Taishang lingbao tiandi yundu ziran miaojing* 太上靈寶天地運動自然妙經 (see below).
7. *Dongxuan lingbao ziran jiutian shengshen zhangjing* 洞玄靈寶自然九天生神章經 (see below).

Texts from Marginal Movements

8. *Dongzhen taiji beidi ziwei shenzhou miaojing* 洞真太極北帝紫微神咒妙經 (*Marvelous Dongzhen Scripture of the Divine Incantations of the Purple Empyrean of the Northern Emperor of the Great Pole*; DZ 49): "Most likely dates to the end of the fourth or beginning of the fifth century, as it refers (9b) to 'the era of the great Jin dynasty.' By the mouth of the Venerable Worthy of the Primordial Beginning, it predicts disasters and calamities propagated by demons and victimizing 'people of the last cosmic cycle' — the last nine years of the 60-year cycle — was well as the imminence of the Great Kalpa which will be accompanied by a massive flood."

9. *Taishang lingbao Laozi huahu miaojing* 太上靈寶老子
華胡妙經 *(Marvelous Lingbao Scripture of the Most
High Concerning the Conversion of the Barbarians
by Laozi*; Tunhuang manuscript, Stein 2081): "According to Anna
Seidel, it dates to the Six Dynasties. ... It is, as she states, a 'Buddho-
Taoist' scripture. Two saviours are awaited: the Perfect Lord and
Maitreya. The other messianic themes are those of the previous
works: prediction of the end of a cosmic era, moral degeneracy, a
world turned upside down, massive invasion of demons, salvation
of the elect, advent of the reign of Great Peace under the Buddho-
Taoist messianic couple, Maitreya and the Perfect Lord."[9]

Shangqing Messianism

According to Robinet,[10] the now-lost *Santian zhengfa jing*, as seen in
quotations primarily in the *Wushang biyao* 無上秘要, "set forth a theory
of cosmic cycles and the ends of the world based on *Hanshu* 21: the six-
Yin and the nine-Yang ends of the world mark the end of either great
or small *kalpas* (*jie* 劫) and are caused either by fire or by water. At
that time, mythical animals appear — the Heavenly Horse, the Great
Bird, and the Mother of Waters; the world is turned upside down, the
stars are darkened, the seas and mountains levelled, and the six
directions fused in one: it is the return to Original Chaos. One of the
cosmic ends will occur in the 46th *dinghai* year after the reign of Yao;
the renewal will begin in the following *renchen* year 壬辰, when a red
star and a white comet will appear above the moon. Those whose names
are written on the celestial registers will be saved. The *Santian zhengfa
jing* was probably the text which gave the means to escape from the
cataclysms at the end of the world."

To this may be added a few details from my paraphrase of the
Wushang biyao quotations:[11] "At the end of a cycle of the Nine Heavens,
the energies of the Six Heavens return to the upper Three Heavens;
after one measure, the Mother of Waters encounters the King of
Dragons. At the time of the crisis of a small kalpa on earth, the nine
sources overflow, the Mother of Waters clears the courses of the five
rivers, the mountains collapse, and a great bird halts at the Dragon
Gate. In the heavens, the Five Emperors gather in the Capital of

Mystery, the nine energies are renewed, and the myriad emperors change positions. All that is evil is destroyed; only the good and the pure survive. Toward the end of a great *kalpa*, the numbers of the Nine Heavens reach their limit and, when the cycle of the Six Heavens is exhausted, all that is perverse and evil flourishes, heaven and earth are turned upside down, gold and jade fuses, and the six directions become utterly obscure." Two other citations from this text tell the adept how to prepare himself for entering a mountain[12] and state that a thousand recitations of the present text will enable the adept "to communicate with the gods and see the future. After ten thousand recitations, he will be able to communicate with the Perfected, see the Venerable Worthy, and survive calamities of water and fire".[13]

Robinet is, thus, right to suggest that the *Santian zhengfa jing* enabled its practitioner to survive the final cataclysm. He did so, apparently, by entering the mountains and reciting this text. The encounter of the Mother of Waters with the Dragon King is also intriguing, as it recalls that of the Queen Mother of the West and the Heavenly King of the Primordial Beginning (Yuanshi tianwang 元始天王) in the *Renniao shan zhenxing tu* 人鳥山真形圖 (*Diagram of the True Form of Bird-Man Mountain;* DZ 424), which in turn bring us back to the Latter Han relationship between the Queen Mother and the Royal Father of the East (Dongwang gong 東王公): "On Kunlun there rests a copper pillar which reaches heaven and which is thus called the Pillar of Heaven. It is 3000 *li* wide in girth and it curls around like a crooked knife. Below there are the meandering houses, the establishments of the nine courts of the immortal beings. Above there is the great bird whose name is Seldom Seen. The bird faces south; he stretches his left wing to cover the King Father of the East and his right wing to cover the Queen Mother of the West. On the back of the bird there is a small spot that has no feathers and that is one myriad and 9000 *li* large. Once each year the Queen Mother of the West climbs upon the wing to go to the King Father of the East... Yin and Yang are then partnered together. "[14] And this tale, in turn, reminds us of the annual encounter of the Cowherd and the Weaving Girl: dimly, behind salvation by recitation, we can still catch a glimpse of salvation by cosmic copulation.

The primary Shangqing messianic text is the *Shangqing housheng Daojun lieji* (*Annals of the Lord of the Way, the Latter-Day Saint of*

Shangqing Heaven; *DZ* 442). Robinet[15] shows this text to be closely linked to the *Huangtian shangqing jinque dijun lingshu ziwen shangjing* 皇天上清金闕帝君靈書紫文上經 (*Superior Scripture of the Purple Text and Magic Writ of the Imperial Lord of the Metal Gate of the Sovereign Heaven of High Purity;* DZ 639), which "replaces sexual practices by the evocation of Taokang, a god of the embryo and source of life mentioned earlier in a sexual manual of the Heavenly Masters. We have, in this text, a first hint of the interiorization of sexual practices begun in the Shangqing revelation and given its mature expression in internal alchemy." In her presentation of the *Lingshu ziwen*,[16] Robinet says the following of its exercise for "swallowing the essence of the sun": "When the adept has pronounced the formula, he must visualize the 'purple energy' of the sun, called 'Flying Root, Mother of Waters.'" Had only the parallel exercise — for the absorption of the essence of the moon — involved visualizing the Dragon King...! Curiously, another related text, the *Langgan huadan shenzhen shangjing* 琅玕華丹神真上經 (*Superior Scripture of the Gods and the Perfected of the Flowering Elixir Langgan*; DZ 255), includes an invocation of the Weaving Girl.[17]

Strickmann, in his introduction to the translation of the *Housheng lieji*,[18] calls it "the basic text" of the entire Shangqing revelation, whose social and political background he had already so masterfully described in his article "The Mao Shan Revelations." We will only recall here his central thesis, that these revelations, which occurred in the years 364-70, represented to the aristocratic southerners who received them a kind of sweet revenge on the northerners who had so recently imposed their political will and religious preferences on them.

As its title suggests, this text is a spiritual history of the Saint-who-will-come-again to judge the living and save the elect: conceived immaculately when his mother dreamed of the sun and the moon wrapping her round under the cover of a dark cloud, he has no earthly father and so takes his mother's surname Li. "At the age of five," says the text, "he already loved the Tao and took pleasure in perfection" (1b). After fifteen years of Taoist practice at home, he decides to "leave his family and kin" to lead the life of a Taoist hermit. The text does not say how long it took, but eventually his assiduity leads to "the descent of the Heavenly Emperor to instruct him" (2a). The Emperor gives him, among other things, the Langgan elixir and the hymns for the absorption of the sun's essence, and he then "retires to fast, recite the scriptures, and practice the 24 items in them." Renewed practice provokes a second celestial descent, of a luminous chariot sent by the Most Perfect Heavenly Emperor of the Purple Empyrean to "welcome the Holy Lord to the Palace of High Purity" (2b). This time, he receives a seal of office, vestments, and the title by which he will thenceforth be known, Imperial Lord and Latter-Day Saint of the Metal Gate of High Purity.

In a blaze of *Chuci*-style poetry, the text turns now to the "second coming": "Behold the Holy Lord's progress: riding in a coral chariot with wheels of precious stones..., he is preceded by nine male phoenixes singing in unison and followed by eight female phoenixes crying out together. From below, divine tigers look up and roar, while flying dragons look down from above and call.....Numinous spouses sing hymns of praise; immortal guests clear the way. Divine women spread purple vapors to clear the air, while jade lads spin solar precipitate to eliminate the night. The cloudy ranks sound a never-ending song, and there is neither day nor night" (3a). Such will be, "when the time comes" (*danger shiye*), the royal progress of the Holy Lord.

The Holy Lord reigns over all the universe, from High Purity above and the Great Pole (*Taiji* 太極) in the middle, to the ten heavens where dwell the myriad people below and the cave-heavens in the Yin-underworld. "The two energies now separate, now join, and there is a time for the ordering of all things," pursues the text. ... "In the year *jiashen*, neither before nor after, he will plant the good folk and uproot the deficient; epidemics and floods will come pell-mell from above, and wars and fires break out uncontrollably below. Every form of evil will be obliterated, and all that is no good destroyed. Those who love the Tao will hide on dry land, and the good will take refuge in the hills. The dissolute will disintegrate and be driven into the abyss. All will be clearly distinguished.[19] In the *renchen* year, on the sixth day of the third moon, the Holy Lord will descend; he will approach the myriad people. In that time, the Holy Lord will set forth from the western mountain of the Blue City. ... (He will tour the universe) and destroy the evil with floods and fires, and he will save as his planted people the compassionate and the good. Those who are at the beginning of their apprenticeship will become immortal angels, and those who have obtained the Tao immortal officials. If they can perform (a whole series of Shangqing practices), they will be able to traverse all disasters without harm, and they will assuredly witness the cosmic renewal of the Great Peace" (3b-4a).

A bit farther on we read that the Holy Lord will further select those worthy to "assist the Saint in teaching the people, ordering energies, and spreading virtue. Some will be put in charge of a city; to others will be confided the government of a principality. ...The Holy Lord will give offices in accord with ability, there will be small feudal lords and great, each with an appropriate rank, so as to govern the planted people" (5a-b). A whole spiritual bureaucracy will thus be built up around the Saint and his book. The major portion of the second half of the text is devoted to describing how difficult it is even so much as to see the titles of this book transmitted but three times every seven centuries. "Those who receive the book must swear an oath before the gods never to divulge it. To instruct those with the bones of destiny and those who study immortality with a concentrated mind and utter sincerity, I herewith send down Ma Ming, Zhang Ling..., 24 persons in all... The Holy Lord of the Latter-Days ordered Lord Wang to direct these 24 Perfected and decide the roles of each in the instruction of adepts. Each of them received his instructions from the Blue Lad of Fangzhu and the list of their adepts from Lord Wang" (8a). The Blue Lad is one of the chief revealing divinities of the Shangqing movement; Lord Wang is here stated to be the only person to have received the present text. It is the source of his power.

By incorporating such famous early Taoists as Zhang Ling into his teaching staff, the Holy Lord, as Strickmann so skillfully showed, staked a claim for those who possessed his book to signal spiritual and terrestrial honors: the predicted apocalypse of the year *jiashen*, to be followed by the second coming of the year *renchen*, became arguments for conversion to the Shangqing Way, receiving its scriptures — especially the "Annals of the Saint" — and practicing its techniques. In other words, while waiting for the return of the Latter-Day Saint, the adept could do no better than to receive and recite the book which, by telling his story, substituted for the Saint: the revealed book, transmitted with great precautions, became the actual vehicle of salvation insofar as it enabled the adept to prepare for "that time."

Lingbao Messianism

As we saw above, Mollier includes two texts from the Lingbao canon in her list of apocalyptic texts: the *Taishang lingbao tiandi yundu ziran miaojing* (*Marvelous Scripture of the Lingbao Canon of the Most High Concerning the Spontaneity of the Cyclical Periods of Heaven and Earth*; DZ 322) and the *Dongxuan lingbao ziran jiutian shengshen zhangjing* (*Scripture of the Hymns of the Dongxuan Lingbao Canon for the Birth of the Gods of the Spontaneous Nine Heavens*; DZ 318). The first, which probably does not belong to the older strata of the Lingbao revelation, [20] presents an extremely complex account of cosmic eras and, like the Santian zhengfa, looks to the coming of Li Hong (*gongkou shiba zi*) in a *renchen* year, the founding of the Liu-Song dynasty, and the advent of an era of Great Peace. "It describes the signs of the end — barbarian invasions, floods, fires, 'Venus leaving its normal orbit' — and predicts the imminence of the nine-Yang and hundred-Six crises, of the *jiashen* year of the Blue Dragon, or conjuncture of the Aquatic Dragon, that is, the end of the cosmic era, and the world turned upside down."[21]

The Hymns of the Birth of the Gods "predict the imminence of the Great Kalpa and the jiashen year, as well as the salvation of the elect (*zhongmin*)."[22]

An early commentary on the central text of the Lingbao canon, the *Lingbao wuliang duren shangpin miaojing* 靈寶無量度人上品妙經 (*Marvelous Scripture of the Upper Category for Incommensurable Salvation of Humankind by the Magic Treasure*; DZ 1, *juan* 1), states that it, too, is to be recited in order to survive the apocalypse: "The above are the four heavens of the Realm Without Sexual Attraction (*wuse jie* 無色界). [23] The Yin and the Yang have forms, their bodies are hundreds of li tall, but this does not hamper them. They can hide their forms and enter the infinitely small, for neither desire nor attraction exist anymore. They have knowledge of each other only in the perfect mode, and they live for accumulated kalpas. Although they do not focus on practice, they are capable of doing good: this is a karmic recompense of purely good fortune. But as for the demon-kings whose study of the Tao has not reached the end, they also wander in these heavens, incapable of transcending the Three Realms or avoiding the calamitous flood. When the cycle comes to the conflagration and the 28 heavens are scrambled into one, those who have practiced perfection will be worthy to be among the elect (*zhongmin*) welcomed by the Queen Mother to ascend... to the four supreme heavens. Those who have practiced the ways of saintliness, perfection, or immortality of the Three Realms will fall back to the path of humans. Those who, in suffering the three punishments, manage to transcend and progress, will be promoted in accord with their merit" (*Wushang biyao* 4.2a-b). This introduction is followed by the hymns of the demon-kings of the Three Realms (4. 2b-3b). Found also in the original *Duren jing* (1.11b-13a), they are sung to this day when the Taoist high priest makes his ascent to highest heaven to present a memorial[24] "Whoever recites them 100 times," says the text (1.13a), "will see his name transferred to the Southern Palace, who a thousand times will be protected and welcomed by the demon-kings, and who ten thousand times will accomplish the Tao and fly up to the Great Void, transcend the Three Realms, and take up a position as Immortal Duke."

A bit farther on, we read: "The Tao says, the cyclical degrees of heaven and earth also come to an end; the sun, the moon, and the five planets wax and wane; the most saintly of divine persons encounter negation; adepts of the latter days get sick and die. Whoever has these disasters, if they belong to the same energy, they should unite their hearts and perform a fast. Six times in the day they should spread incense and recite this scripture ten times. Then good fortune and health will descend immediately and obliterate all that is inauspicious. The incommensurable text saves all without limits" (1.13b-14a).

The concrete meaning of "incommensurable salvation" is given, in fact, at the beginning of the *Duren jing*, where we read that each of the ten successive recitations summons the gods of a corresponding direction. When the ten recitations are completed and the entire celestial assembly has gathered, "for seven days and seven nights, all the stars in heaven, the sun, the moon, and the Dipper, all cease to turn; the divine wind falls silent, and the mountains and hills retain their clouds. There is nary a cloud in the sky, and the atmosphere is crystal clear. The land, hills, rivers, and forests are all levelled, there is no longer high or low, and the earth is all of a perfectly uniform green jade. When all the perfected had taken their seats, the Heavenly Worthy of the Primordial

Beginning, suspended in midspace on his five-colored lion, recited the text once through. As one person, all the assembled great saints uttered their admiration, and all the deaf men and women of the entire country heard and understood" (1a-b). Each successive recitation heals another kind of disease or handicap, from barrenness to death: thus does the recitation of the Scripture of Salvation save all the persons of that land.

These recitations cause such a massive gathering of gods and people that the earth gives way under their weight. The Heavenly Worthy then draws all the gods into a "pearl the size of a grain of rice," causing the people to disperse and the earth to regain its flatness. From within the pearl, he now recites the text once again, thus transmitting it, under the watchful eye of the divine assembly, to the "ego" (*wo* 我) of the text, that is, the Tao. This recitation-cum-transmission causes a mass conversion of its auditors and hence an end to all evil-doing: "The land was at peace, the people enjoyed abundance, and all took joy in the Great Peace"(1.3a). The Tao then explains the secret of the scripture's power — it is entirely composed of secret divine names — and also when and how to recite it. The actual text of the *Duren jing* is given after these instructions, which ends with the standard ritual opening known as the "lighting of the incense burner" (*falu*).

If, in the Shangqing revelation, the book and its recitation had played an important part in the salvation of the elect, Shangqing texts nonetheless also required of their adepts that they engage in exercises that Robinet rightly calls the forerunners of internal alchemy. In the Lingbao canon, by contrast, the only mode of practice is recitation: it is recitation, on a regular basis and in community, that heals even death and triggers the Great Peace. Ritual time is the time of the apocalypse, when the adept rides up on the wings of the demon-king hymns to the safe haven of the Queen Mother. That safe haven, we learn in other Lingbao texts, is the Metropolis of Mystery on the mountain of the Jade Capital.

Shenzhou Messianism

The basic text of this school, the *Taishang dongyuan shenzhou jing* 太上洞淵神咒經 (*Scripture of Divine Incantations of the Cave-Abyss of the Most High*; DZ 335) has a complicated textual history we need not go into here. Suffice it to say that students of the *Shenzhou jing* generally accept the first ten *juan* as belonging to the Six Dynasties and at least some of these chapters as dating to the fifth century because of references to Liu Yü (363-442) as the "fifth generation son of the Liu clan who helps govern the world."[25] Clearly written after the Lingbao revelation, the Shenzhou texts share much of its general ethos and ideology. What makes this work unique, however, and central to any study of Taoist messianism in this formative period, is the graphic, not to say virulent, character of its descriptions, and its almost single-minded focus on the real world, both political and ecclesiastical. It owes these qualities, I suspect, to its roots in the movement of the Heavenly Masters.

Much of this is clear from the opening lines: "The Tao stated: When, from above the three heavens, I recited the *Incommensurable Scripture* to all men and women in order to convert all creatures, the Perfected from the lower world, such as Wei Mingluo, and the masses of all the worlds — 490,000 in all — came to the three heavens to listen to the recital, and all, within and without, was peaceful and quiet."[26] We have here the neo-Buddhist Lingbao context and consequences of the revelation of a scripture whose very name has been cribbed from the *Duren jing*: we know already that the answer to the gathering tide of disaster and disease in this time of the "imminent great kalpa" will be to receive and recite this scripture. But the audience of this new "incommensurable scripture" is not a celestial one which "utters its admiration" (*chengshan*) at the end, as in the *Duren jing*; it is the people of China (*Zhongguo* 中國),[27] men and women, and they are meant to be converted (*jiaohua* 教化) by its hearing, to "believe in the Tao and its methods" (1. la), and join the *Shenzhou* church.

As we will see, that church is the only real refuge in the face of the coming crisis, but let us look first at the apocalyptic context: as in the Lingbao texts, the demon-kings (*mowang* 魔王) are at once the cause of the disorder in the world and the key to its salvation. When told they are "spreading poison and killing the good people" (1.1b), the Tao promises to "send 49 myriads of interdicting officials (*jinguan*) to arrest the demon-kings of the 36 heavens and oblige them to take an oath: 'Henceforth, if anyone in China is the victim of unjust death, critical illness, imprisonment, or exile, the demon-kings will be blamed for not preventing the lower demons from preying on the elect (*zhongmin*) ...

If they do not interdict the lower demons, they will be beheaded without mercy"' (1.2a-b). The Most High then sends out his hosts to hail the demon-kings et al.before him and listen to the following most remarkable harangue: "From the time of Fuxi to the end of the Han, the people lived in great joy. Most did not believe in the Tao: they were all endowed with the energies of heaven, which are natural. The devious demons did not know there was a Tao, nor did they know of Its methods or scriptures: they worshipped only what was natural. In these latter days, there are some who believe in the scriptures, but not many. Only among the people of the Song is it common to take refuge in the Tao" (1.3a).[28] Thus, if the scripture, the church, and its rituals are the answer to the crisis, their very existence is a sign of that crisis!

A little farther on, the text speaks of how, "at the end of the Han and the Wei, the people were obliged to flee, and half of them died. Until a fifth-generation descendant of the Liu clan continues the work of his ancestors, the people of China will live in an unsafe and dangerous world. There will be no dwelling in peace for the people under heaven: they will be driven out by the six barbarians and forced to take refuge on the left bank of the River. The Liu clan, too, will hide its traces by taking refuge in the area between the sea and the *Huai* 淮 river. In the *jiawu* year 甲午, the Liu clan will return to China and rule from Chang'an. Qinchuan (Gansu-Shanxi) will be overjoyed, and the six barbarians will submit and go off to live in the mountains and marshes, not in the central valleys. The Tao and its methods will flourish, and Muzu Gongkou (Li Hong) will rise again" (1.3b-4a).

But for now, "the great kalpa is imminent," and there will be nothing but bad crops and evil-hearted men who revolt, rob, and murder; there will be epidemics of all kinds, and only Taoists and ritual masters who receive and recite the *Shenzhou jing*, with its myriads of divine protectors, will escape these horrible fates. Naturally, all who hear these words of the Tao "wish to receive this scripture" (1.4b), and the Tao approvingly tells them: "The time has come; most people are evil. Those who believe in the Tao and worship the scriptures are the people of Heaven; they are not the fools of this world" (1.5a). "The great kalpa is near; the waters will wash across China, and all under heaven will be purged, the people will all die. Only Taoists — those who receive this scripture — will be greeted by the nine dragons" (1.8a). "If you receive the ten chapters of this book, if you worship it and practice it, whether at home or while traveling, all your illnesses will be cured, officials will receive good promotions, you will have everything your heart desires, and you will be able to see the advent of the Perfect Lord. He is not far off: in the year jiashen there will be catastrophes, all the world will be in turmoil, there will be a great purge, and then a new heaven and earth, and then the Perfect Lord will come forth. When the Perfect Lord comes, all saints, sages, and immortals, as well as those who have received this scripture, will come to help him. From all sides, the Taoists will come to assist him; there will be no fools. You people of the world, all you have to do is receive this book, and without doing a thing you will see the Perfect Lord. The Tao says: the Perfect Lord is Muzi Gongkou" (1.10a-b).

The anti-barbarian virulence of the *Shenzhou jing* extends to the barbarian's religion—Buddhism—as well. Some of the negative references to Buddhism were removed from the text in the Taoist canon, but they have been retrieved from Tunhuang: "The Buddhist doctrine will return to the Western lands, for that is its place. That which alone the Chinese of the Great Plain should possess is Taoism. The Taoist scriptures of the Three Caverns will be legion, and the Buddhist scriptures will disappear. The *sramanas* will put back on the white clothes of a layman and will be despised. The Taoists will perpetuate the nobility (of the tradition), and distinguished people will all become Taoists."[29]

Clearly, Buddhism is rejected in the first place because it is non-Chinese, an attitude which must be placed in historical context: "The demonic nature which the *Shenzhou jing* attributes to these (barbarian) populations is readily explained by the pervasive xenophobia in the society of South China, still profoundly marked by the terrible traumatism, already a century old, of the invasion of Central Asian tribes, the collapse of the Western Jin, and the retreat of the Chinese south of the Yangzi. Permanently threatened by incursions of the barbarians from the north, the people in the south saw in them the most awful demonic incarnations."[30] And a bit farther: "The nationalism of the *Shenzhou jing* express without pulling any punches in the following passage: 'Only the Chinese have rites and justice.[31] From east to west and north to south, China stretches 140,000 *li*. Everyone there knows the Law and studies the great Way ... Other countries have nothing of the kind.'"

Mollier's study of the "religious community"[32] shows it to be a close (but rival) sister to that of the Heavenly Masters: "The faithful of the *Shenzhou jing* receive the same sacraments of initiation as those of the Zhengyi church and observe the same ritual calendar. They also define themselves as the 'seed-people' (*zhongmin*)."[33] They must avoid all participation in "the cults of ordinary people" (*susi*): "People do not adhere to the Tao; worse, they have plebeian masters beat drums, (brandish) swords and bells, and sacrifice to the divinities by killing by threes, pigs, dogs, chickens, and suckling pigs. By the waterside, they invoke the hundred demons and make offerings to gods from the margins."[34] Adepts of this movement are supposed to sacrifice only to the domestic divinities approved in the *Liji* 禮記: the gods of the stove, the well, and the soil. "The most dangerous of all are dead military or political heroes who have been divinized. Like the popular gods, they are but maleficent demons who cause calamities, illness, torments of all kinds, and premature death. For the Shenzhou jing, the origin of evil lies in the perpetuation of the cults of the Way of demons (*guidao* 鬼道)".[35]

The solution is entry into the Church and participation in its rituals. Entry into the Church usually occurs after a Shenzhou master has healed a family member. An altar to the Five Emperors is set up in the mountains, and the new adept swears an oath of allegiance: "On this day, I drink the cinnabar and receive the scripture. Without failing, until my death, I will honor it. For the sick and the afflicted, for those who suffer from family tensions, who are victims of calumnies, of official punishment or imprisonment, I will recite it and perform fasts (*zhai* 齋) in conformity with the liturgical codes. During these fasts, only vegetarian food will be eaten. We will neither eat meat nor drink alcohol."[36] Once a member of the community, the Shenzhou adept received the same sequence of registers — of one, ten, and then 75 generals — as the Zhengyi adept, except that the last layman's register — that obtained by a ritual of sexual union — as called *jiashen guodu* ("passage of the *jiashen* year") as opposed to *huangshu guodu*.[37] The Shenzhou church had a complete liturgical panoply[38]: therapeutic rituals, with their "oral supplications" (*kouzhang* 口章); "grand communal rituals" that took place on the 15th days of the first, seventh, and tenth months and involved written supplications, worship of the Five

Emperors, and a *Jiao* on the last day; and funeral rituals, with a "ten-fold refining of the spirits of the body" to replace the "five-fold refining" done in Lingbao funeral ritual.

Some idea may be had of the theological content of this work by looking at the section titles of Mollier's fourth and final chapter, entitled "Theological Structures and Apocalyptic Themes": the sacred book; Laozi and Li Hong; cosmology and dualism; the eschatalogical pantheon — half-gods and demons; the end of the world — degeneration, destruction, purification; salvation — the elect and the evil; sins and sickness; paradise and purgatory; the perfect kingdom — egalitarianism and integration. It is in its description of the terminal pathology of the endtimes that the *Shenzhou jing* is unique: "The predictions of the *Shenzhou jing* concern almost exclusively the raids of monstrous spirits, their misdeeds, and the torments they inflict. They spread throughout the earth in uncountable numbers, kidnap children and old people, suck the blood of people and domestic animals. Armed with clubs, daggers, and ropes, they break into houses and kill the innocent as well as the wicked. They are everywhere. ... They take all forms. ...They cause brutal death and atrocious illness, which they propagate with their toxic drugs and venomous breath... ."[39] Total destruction is the condition for renewal: "The creation of a state of absolute happiness and peace must paradoxically be realized by violence, the extermination of the infidels, and the destruction of the world."[40]

Patterns

Some of the patterns are obvious enough and even quite familiar from other religious contexts: a dramatic increase in violence, disease and famine as the prelude to a final cataclysm, which is at once a time of judgment and salvation; the idea of a "great peace," in which even the earth becomes level; the yearning for a "once and future king," in the books we have examined concentrated to a remarkable degree on the Liu clan and the dream of restoring something akin to the Han dynasty (cf. the role of the Roman empire in the Western imagination).[41] The time scale on which all this is to happen, although it has been influenced by the Buddhist notion of kalpas, remains fundamentally Chinese: *jiashen* is the standard year for the final cataclysm, renchen for the coming of the Perfect Lord. There is also general agreement on the identity of the Perfect Lord — Li Hong — an agreement which, as Seidel puts it, "lived on in the people."[42] Seidel then quotes Woodbridge Gingham on the revolt by one Tang Bi in 614 CE that led to the collapse of the Sui dynasty: "Tang Bi did not take supreme command himself, but set up a man named Li Hong as emperor instead."

As interesting — and as important politically — as these patterns may be there are others which I think even more fundamental. The first might be formulated as a kind of sociological law: the more "popular" a text is the more political it is (the inverse is not necessarily true). Beginning with the *Laozi bianhua jing* 老子變化經 and ending with the *Shenzhou jing*, texts which refer to actual historical events, either in retrospect or in prospect, that is, texts which situate their messianic hopes right here on earth — that talk of "shaking the Han reign" or the "fifth generation son of the Liu clan who helps govern the world" — are also texts which identify the Perfect Lord with a physical person and show concern for the "deep distress" of the people or with organizing the "seed-people" into a church. The rank nationalism of the *Shenzhou jing* is likewise symptomatic of its clearly popular character. Salvation, in short, is both sociologically and politically "physical" in popular texts. By contrast, in more elite texts like those of the Shangqing and Lingbao canons, both the Perfect Lord and salvation are at once individual and cosmic: "spiritual," "mental."

Movements can also be graded along a popular/elite axis by the degree to which they depend on oral or written texts: the first movement we examined, that involving "barefoot and dishevelled" people dancing and singing in worship of the Queen Mother, like the later Heavenly Masters movement of the second century, left no texts at all. Texts like the *Laozi bianhua jing* were clearly meant for recitation from memory and had, in themselves, no talismanic virtue whatsoever. The *Shenzhou jing* has absorbed the elite Shangqing and Lingbao cult of the book, but it also allows for "oral supplications" in the context of therapeutic rituals. More generally, and in marked contrast with the Shangqing and Lingbao canons, its helter-skelter form — not to mention its lurid imagination — is also a telltale sign of its more popular origins. The central place, in Lingbao ideology and practice, of ritual recitation of the book, as well as its much simpler language when compared with Shangqing texts, reveals the Lingbao canon to be midway between Shangqing and Shenzhou on the popular/elite scale.

But perhaps the most interesting pattern of all is the recurrent idea, in texts both popular and elite, of a "ritual soteriological union" as the means to save the "planted people" from the apocalypse. This is clearest in the Shangqing and the Shenzhou movements: in the latter, the "ritual of passage of the *jiashen* year" is at once the final step of initiation into the church and the way to escape the *jiashen* cataclysm; in the former, we saw the interiorization of those very sexual practices. We find here, in short, the same physical-spiritual contrast just discussed, but in the context of the central rites of salvation.

What I would suggest is that all the references we have encountered to the (Western Queen) Mother, and the echoes of her regular meetings with the (Eastern King) Father, are also to be understood in this context. Already in the movement of 3 BCE, the "Mother tells the people that those who wear her talisman will not die." In the *Shangqing Santian zhenfa jing*, it is the Mother of Waters who encounters the King of Dragons; in the *Housheng lieji*, the adept visualizes the purple energy of the sun, called "Flying Root, Mother of Waters." In the *Lingbao Duren jing*, the Queen Mother welcomes the planted people into the four supreme heavens beyond the Three Realms. Sometimes, only her eastern counterpart is mentioned: the Lingbao canon's *Tiandi yundu ziran miaojing* refers to the "*jiashen* year of the Blue Dragon;"[43] in the *Shenzhou jing*, adepts "will be greeted by the nine dragons"; and in the *Housheng lieji*, the 24 assistants of the Saint are taught by the "blue lad of Fangzhu."

Is there anything hidden in these scattered references, or is our selection of them simply tendentious? It may be. But a number of factors incline me to think not: the first is the Mother herself, so central in much later popular religion;[44] the second is the importance of the "arts of the bedchamber" (*fangzhong shu* 房中術) in obtaining immortality, already in the proto-Taoism of the pre-imperial period. Among those said in the Han dynasty *Liexian zhuan* 列仙傳 (*Biographies of Immortals*) to have practised these arts is Laozi himself, and Laozi is of course the ultimate identity of Li Hong, as is clear enough in the tale of his immaculate conception and adoption of his mother's surname in the *Housheng lieji*. The End of the world, in other words, is a return to the Beginning: to the womb of time, the Mother, the Tao. And ritual recitation is a kind of "embryonic respiration" (*taixi* 胎息).

Notes

1   I wish to begin by stating clearly that I am not a specialist of the question and intend therefore only to summarize what others have written, principally Anna Seidel, Isabelle Robinet, Michel Strickmann, and Christine Mollier. The reader will find no reference here to the work of their great Japanese predecessors, in particular Ofuchi Ninji and Yoshioka Yoshitoyo, but will find ample evidence thereof in the relevant writings of the four Western scholars I do cite. The greatest use of this paper may lie in its introduction to a wider audience of the work of Mollier, whose excellent study and summaries of the *Shenzhou jing*, that most lurid of all Chinese apocalyptic literature, deserves more attention than it has received.

2   Homer H. Dubs trans., *The History of the Former Han Dynasty: A Critical Translation* (Baltimore: Waverly, 1938-1955), p. 3.34.

3   The first passage is my own translation; Michael Loewe, *Ways to Paradise: The Chinese Quest for Immortality* (London: Allen & Unwin, 1979), p. 98, refers to "people exchanging tokens in preparation" for the advent of the Queen Mother of the West"; on p. 99, he again translates, "preparing for the royal advent and worshipping the Queen Mother of the West." Although it seems fairly clear that the people are heading west to meet the Queen Mother of the West, it is also possible they are simply going west to the capital; in any case, the Chinese text contains no term comparable to the theologically laden word "advent," and it therefore seems best to avoid it in the translation.

4   This is not something widely written about, but in recent fieldwork throughout the Hakka areas of Fujian, Jiangxi, and Guangdong, it is proving to be a virtually universal feature of such *Jiao*.

5   Anna Seidel, "The Image of the Perfect Ruler in Early Taoist Messianism: Lao-tzu and Li Hung," *History of Religions* vol. 9, no. 2-3 (1970): 223.

6   Ibid., p. 225.

7   Christine Mollier, *Une Apocalypse Taoiste du Ve Siecle: Le Livre des Incantations Divines des Grottes Abyssales* (Paris: Institut des Hautes Etudes Chinoises, 1990), pp. 22-25.

8   Isabelle Robinet, *La Revelation du Shangqing dans L'histoire du Taoisme*, 2 vols (Paris: Ecole francaise d'Extreme-Orient, 1984), pp. 87-91 shows that this text is not the original Shangqing text, now lost except for quotations found in such works as the *Wushang biyao*; cf. John Lagerwey, *Wushang biyao, Somme Taoiste du Vie siecle* (Paris: Ecole francaise d'Extreme-Orient, 1981), p. 261. We will look briefly below at some of the quotations from the original text.

9   As she notes, Mollier bases her summary on the article by Anna Seidel, "Le Sutra Merveilleux du Ling-pao Supreme Traitant de Lao-tseu qui Convertit les Barbares," *Contributions aux Etudes de Touen-houang*, ed. Michel Soymie (Paris: Ecole francaise d'Extreme-Orient, 1984), pp. 306-52.

10 Robinet, *La Revelation du Shangqing dans L'histoire du Taoisme*, vol. 2, p. 90.

11 Lagerwey, *Wushang biyao, Somme Taoiste du Vie Siecle*, pp. 81f.

12 Ibid., pp. 172f.

13 Ibid., p. 143.

14 The *Shenyi jing*, as translated by Wu Hung, *The Wu Liang Shrine: The Ideology of Early Chinese Pictorial Art* (Stanford: Stanford University Press, 1989), pp. 125f.

15 Robinet, *La Revelation du Shangqing dans L'histoire du Taoisme*, vol. 2 (Paris: Ecole francaise d'Extreme-Orient, 1984), p. 109.

16 Ibid., vol. 2, p. 104.

17 Ibid., vol. 2, p. 106.

18 Michel Strickmann, *Le Taoisme du Mao Chan: Chronique d'une Revelation* (Paris: Institut des Hautes Etudes Chinoises, 1980), p. 209.

19 Ibid. Strickmann translates, rightly, I think, "And thus will be executed the last judgment." If I have given the sentence what might be called a Cartesian twist, it is because fenbie is also a technical term in Taoist ritual: when the Taoist priest has, in the context of the "review of his register" (*yuelu*), "exteriorized his officials" (*chuguan*), he must proceed to fenbie them, so that each may be de- or promoted in accord with his merit (cf. Du Guangting). The term thus clearly refers to a judgment, but one which is based on a kind of 'discernment," in which the Holy Lord—or the Taoist priest—sees with utter clarity the true nature of each and all: the "last judgment" is a time of total transparency.

20 Lagerwey, *Wushang biyao, Somme Taoiste du Vie Siecle*, p. 207.

21 Mollier, *Une Apocalypse Taoiste du Ve siecle: Le Livre des Incantations Divines des Grottes Abyssales*, p. 23.

22 Ibid., p. 24.

23 In the *Duren jing's* scheme, the first six heavens belong to the Realm of Desire (*yujie* 欲界), where "the Yin and the Yang are born in the womb and live ten thousand years;" the next 18 heavens belong to the Realm of Sexual Attraction (*sejie* 色界), where "the Yin and the Yang are sexually attracted, just as in the Realm of Desire, but they do not copulate. People are born by transformation and live for billions of years" (quoted in John Lagerwey, *Wushang biyao, Somme Taoiste du Vie Siecle*, p. 74).

24 Paul Andersen, "The Practise of Bugang," *Cahiers d'Extreme-Asie* 5 (1990): 15-53.

25 Cf. Mollier, *Une Apocalypse Taoiste du Ve Siecle: Le Livre des Incantations Divines des Grottes Abyssales*, p. 56.

26 *Shenzhou jing* 1. la; Mollier, *Une Apocalypse Taoiste du Ve Siecle: Le Livre des Incantations Divines Des Grottes Abyssales*, p. 94. References hereafter will be only to the Chinese text, but I wish to note here that Mollier gives an excellent translation of the entire first chapter, and I have at each turn of the way relied on her insights. The first chapter is vital because it is at once one of the clearly early chapters and because it sets the scene for all that is to follow.

27 See ibid., p. 95: a section which, in the present Taoist canon version, begins, "The people of this world here below," reads in the clearly original Dunhuang edition, "The Most High asked: Do the Chinese desire to possess the venerable scriptures, obey the masters, and search for immortality?" All references below to China and the Chinese come from Mollier's quotations of variants from the Dunhuang manuscripts.

28 The reference to the Liu-Song dynasty derives from a Dunhuang manuscript; see ibid., p. 98.

29 Ibid., p. 49.

30 Ibid., p. 68.

31 Ibid., p. 70.

32 Ibid., pp. 72-91.

33 Ibid., p. 72.

34 Ibid., p. 74, also taken from a Dunhuang version.

35 Ibid., p. 75; cf. p. 128.

36 Ibid., p. 80.

37 Ibid., p. 76.

38 Ibid., pp. 86-91.

39 Ibid., pp. 165-166.

40 Ibid., p. 173.

41 Cf. Anna Seidel, "The Image of the Perfect Ruler in Early Taoist Messianism: Lao-tzu and Li Hung," *History of Religions* vol. 9, no. 2-3 (1970): 246: "It should be mentioned that almost as many rebel leaders were named Liu as Li. ... It seems that Taoist messianism in the Six Dynasties kept alive a nostalgia for the political unity of the vanished Han empire. ... right down to the founding of the Tang Dynasty by Li Yuan, the pretender to descent from Lao-tzu."

42 Ibid., p.244.

43 Also called the "aquatic dragon," as the Mother is called the "mother of waters": I would suggest that these references to water are not to be understood as linking the Mother or the dragons to the aquatic north, but simply recall the fact that the apocalypse usually takes the form, in early Taoist messianic texts, of a flood.

44 See, for example, Daniel Overmyer, "Personal Introduction," in *The Flying Phoenix: Aspects of Chinese Sectarianism in Taiwan*, eds. Daniel Overmyer and David Jordan (Princeton: Princeton University Press, 1986), pp. xviii-ix.

6

Hope in Chinese Popular Religious Texts

Daniel L. Overmyer

Introduction

I recently completed fifteen years of work on a book about a kind of Chinese religious text called *baojuan* 寶卷 (precious volumes), books considered sacred scripture that were produced by popular religious sects in the Ming and Qing periods. My book is an introduction to the background and content of thirty-five of the earliest such texts, written in the 15th-17th centuries. This article emphasizes expressions of hope in baojuan, particularly passages that express hope for a coming savior deity in the near future to save pious believers from destruction at the end of the age. However, since "precious volumes" appeared relatively late in Chinese history, their teaching had been preceded by affirmations of hope in popular religion already for many centuries. Hence, this paper begins with a brief survey of the religious background and context of baojuan; the ways in which hope was expressed by ordinary people in the midst of their everyday activities and customs. The definition of "hope" in the paper is that of the *American Heritage Dictionary* — "To wish for something in expectation of its fulfillment."

The Religious Background of Hope in *Baojuan* Teaching

Hope in all Chinese religious traditions is based on the confidence that human beings have a vital role in the world, and can learn the knowledge and skills necessary to deal with it. This confidence is true both for the human world and for dealing with the realm of gods, spirits and demons.

These spirits can be powerful and dangerous, but humans are an integral part of the world in all its dimensions; they are made of the same *qi* 氣 stuff as the gods, and so they can learn both how to benefit from divine power and how to avoid or drive off harmful forces. There is no metaphysical reason why this cannot be done. No matter how bad things might be, there is usually something that can be done; rituals to perform, invocations to recite, spirit mediums or priests to hire or consult for their expertise. *Yiding hui you banfa* 一定會有辦法 (there must be something that can be done); this confidence is the inner core of hope in Chinese religions, the confidence that one way or another, by invoking this god or that, action can be taken, and that human beings have the right to ask, and to expect results. This is true despite the insecurity of life that was the case in China as in all other pre-modern societies, the threat of disease, natural disasters, social injustice, and ineffective or rapacious government officials.

The earliest records we have of Chinese religious activities are in the divination bones and turtle plastrons used during the Shang period (r.1500-1050 BCE), and there is already much evidence in those sources for the worship and fear of ancestors, ghosts and spirits; a sense that human efforts could not succeed without divine approval and support. Yet in the midst of this sense of dependence there is also confidence that through divination and rituals these superhuman powers can be known and dealt with. Divination could discover whether or not a certain enterprise would succeed, whether or not a problem is being caused by an angry ancestor, and why; when a sacrifice should be performed, using what. The Shang aristocracy seem to have believed that a ritual sacrifice prepared for by divination and carried out properly could constrain an ancestor or a god to respond. Through such rituals humans did not just propitiate the gods; they participated directly in the divine realm, with the expectation that their efforts could bring results. At this point Shang divination and ritual set the tone for the rest of the history of Chinese religions, with its emphasis on the vital role of humans in the cosmic process. From that role comes hope.

This sense of confidence continued in the succeeding Zhou period, as can be seen from the strongly positive descriptions of ancestor worship in the *Book of Poetry* (*Shijing* 詩經), more sophisticated methods of divination in the *Book of Changes* (*Yijing* 易經), the beginnings of a hope for immortality, and new rituals for the exorcism of harmful forces. All of these were presented as knowledge and techniques to be learned, and thus possible for humans in their own time and place.

In early Chinese philosophy too we see evidence for this confidence in human potential and ability. For example,

- Kong Qiu (Confucius), and his aspirations that he and his students could became *junzi*, superior/ideal persons, through their own efforts and learning.

- Mo Di (Mo Zi); the only theologian among the early philosophers, and yet with the sense that the love of the high god Tian is to be evaluated by the benefit it brings to humans.

- Meng Ke (Mencius) with his emphasis on our inner potential for goodness, the *siduan* 四端 (the four sprouts of goodness), that can be nourished into fully developed moral values, under our own power.

- Xun Qing (Xun Zi) and his affirmation that humans have an equal role with heaven and earth as one part of the *sancai* 三才 (three powers), and this despite Xun Qing's negative view of human moral potential.

All of the ideas served to give a sense of confidence and direction to the emerging Chinese civilization.

There is much other evidence for this sense of assurance; for example, the *Liji*'s hope that through fully expressing *li* 禮 (ritual and social obligations) we can bring about an utopia here and now, the *Datong* 大同 world of great unity and harmony.

- The rise of the new Daoist priesthood in the 4th and 5th centuries CE, with their confidence that as priests they could take their place among the gods; that with their ritual offerings, prayers, petitions and registers of gods' names they could make divine power manifest in the world to renew the vitality of the community.

- In China, even Buddhism became a more positive and confident religion with its eventual simplification in the Chan and Pure Land schools, promising direct and immediate salvation through reciting the Buddha's name or realizing the Buddha-potential of one's own inner nature. All of this provided religious foundations for hope.

This spirit of confidence can be seen as well in the beliefs and practices of ordinary people in the towns and villages. Here we see religious hope expressed through offerings to ancestors and gods and through lively assemblies and processions, all in the expectation that if carried out in the proper ways according to tradition they could renew the vitality and peace of families and community. For this we have detailed new evidence in the excellent field research of Professor John Lagerwey and his Chinese colleagues in Fujian and Guangdong.

In popular religion the central role of human beings in the ritual process is clear, for not only are the gods deified human beings, they also need people in order to fulfill their roles. Thus, in a temples festival (*miaohui* 廟會) carried out in honor of a god's birthday, worshippers must go to the temple, lift up the image of the god, place it in a sedan chair, and take it on a tour of the village, and each home in the village, with food offerings, incense, gongs, drums, horns and firecrackers at every turn. The god needs humans in order to be taken in such a procession to inspect its domain and drive away harmful forces. The god needs to be entertained with operas and puppet shows. Yes, the people depend on the gods, they need a power beyond their own, but the gods also need people. It is just at this point of need for active involvement and participation that hope appears. Dealing with written texts in village rituals, Daoist priests are hired for their expertise, but the framework of the ritual is set by village tradition and leaders. The people do their own religion. One should add that in popular traditions even one's basic fate can be changed (*gaiyun* 改運) through the proper ritual , a weak horoscope can be improved, an ancestor's grave can be moved, so ultimately fate is not entirely destined after all.

Spirit writing is also a source of hope. In traditional times it was practiced throughout society, from scholars and military officers to ordinary workers; and is still being practiced today. Devotees of spirit writing believe they can make direct contact with gods and culture heroes to recover ancient wisdom from its original sources. So this wisdom can provide guidance and hope for today. Since the 19th century spirit writing has become the basis for many different Chinese new religions, with their own organizations, rituals and sacred texts, a new source for hope.

Hope in Sectarian Scriptures: *Baojuan*

Baojuan are the scripture texts of voluntary religions associations or sects, believed to have been revealed by their gods. They are discussed in detail in my forthcoming book, *Precious Volumes: An Introduction to Chinese Sectarian Scriptures from the Sixteenth and Seventeenth Centuries*, to be published in 1998 by the Harvard Council on East Asian Studies. All of the *baojuan* published in the Ming that I have seen are printed in large characters and bound between cardboard rectangles in accordion style, in what is called "the sutra folded form" (*jingzhe zhuang* 經折狀), with pages about fourteen inches (36 cm) high and five inches (13 cm) wide. They are in one or two volumes (*juan* 卷), divided into varying numbers of chapters (*pin* 品) or divisions (*fen* 分). The title is printed on a strip of paper pasted to the cover. Many of these books open with engravings of Buddhas and deities, followed by invocations of long life for the emperor, blessings for the nation and people, and hope for the salvation of all. Next comes an inside title, which may not be the same as that on the cover, followed by verses calling on the Buddhas and deities to descend when the book is recited. This opens an introductory section that discusses the book and its message in general terms. This section is in a combination of verse and prose, and may include a table of contents listing all the chapter titles. After several pages of this material, the title and number of the first chapter appear on a separate line, followed by a prose exposition, which in turn is summarized in verse. This alternation continues through the chapter with varying verse styles. In many baojuan near the end of each chapter there is the name of an opera tune introducing a rhymed hymn to be sung. This hymn and a few lines of concluding pious verse end the chapter. Each chapter introduces some new theme, but there is much repetition; these books were clearly intended primarily for ritual recitation, not for doctrinal instruction, though that is also present. The end and beginning of each volume are clearly indicated. At the end of some *baojuan* there are notes on reprinting, and lists of donors, with the amounts contributed by each. There are variations on all of these patterns, but enough constants remain to distinguish these books from other types of writings.

In content, sectarian *baojuan* are characterized by their use of simple classical language interspersed with vernacular constructions, the alternation of prose sections with seven or ten-character lines of verse, usually in rhyme, and direct expositions of mythology, doctrinal teaching and moral exhortation. Sometimes this teaching is presented as a dialogue between the revealing Buddha or patriarch and his would be disciples.

Baojuan teaching is proclaimed to be a new revelation of primordial truth, long concealed but now available to all who believe, particularly those with the proper karmic affinity or destiny (*youyuan ren* 有緣人). This revelation appears just before the chaos and destruction at the end of the *kalpa* or *eon*; the Buddha or the Mother has taken pity on wayward, suffering humans, and in the text has provided one last chance for deliverance. Those with the proper belief and practice will survive to enjoy a transformed life in a new realm, free of all suffering. Those who miss the good news (*xiaoxi* 消息) will be lost. From this perspective, other religious traditions, including other sectarians, may be criticized or ridiculed. This sectarian self-identification is reinforced by references to special protective deities, patriarchs, members and congregational assemblies.

The foundation of religious confidence in these books is the belief that they are direct revelations from gods and patriarchs to their own devotees, promising ultimate deliverance away from purgatory and into paradise. There are specific promises and instructions in these books concerning how this hope can be realized, expressed primarily in the belief in a mother-goddess, Wusheng laomu 無生老母 (the Eternal Venerable Mother) who created the world and human beings, all of whom are her children. However, after she had sent them down to populate the earth her children became immoral and greedy, and forgot their true home in paradise with the Mother. So, for many centuries she has been sending messengers to the world to call them home. The primary messengers are three Buddhas, each descending and teaching in his own time period. The sects believe that we are now just at the end of the second time period, that ruled by the Buddha Sakyamuni; when it ends the world will be destroyed; only faithful believers in sect teachings can be saved. Then in the near future the next Buddha will appear, Maitreya. In his time the world will become a paradise.

This mythological theme is present in many of the texts that are described in detail in my book, from at least the 16th century on, but here I will illustrate it by discussing its presentation in the *Longhua jing* 龍華經 of 1654, the best known of all sectarian "precious volumes," and the culmination of their first two centuries of development.

The Dragon-flower Scripture (*Longhua jing*)

"The Dragon-flower precious scripture verified by the Ancient Buddha Tianzhen 天真 " (*Gufo Tianzhen kaozheng longhua baojing* 古佛天真 考證龍華寶經, 1654) is in twenty-four chapters in four volumes, with each volume called a "collection" (*ji* 集), named in succession after the four basic auspicious terms of the *Classic of Change, yuan, heng, li, zhen*. It was composed by a sect leader named Gong Chang 弓長, a divided form of the surname Zhang, who is understood to be a reincarnation of the Old Buddha, Tianzhen, in turn a transformation of the Venerable Patriarch Chenwu, the Buddha of Measureless Life (Wuliang shoufo 無量壽佛), and Amithaba himself. Gong Chang lived in central Hebei Province, in Gao-qiao Guan of modern Gao-yang county. Through careful investigation, Sawada Mizuho has determined that Gong Chang founded a sect called the Yuandun jiao 圓頓教 (Religion of complete and instantaneous enlightenment) in 1624, after receiving instruction from Wang Sen 王森 (d. 1619) of Shifo kou in Hebei, the leader of the Dacheng jiao 大乘教 (Mahayana sect). In the following years, Gong Chang traveled about preaching and gathering disciples, so that by the mid-1630s his sect was well established. During his travels, he collected various religious books, on the basis of which he began to write a scripture for his own sect in 1641. This task was completed by his disciples, who published the *Longhua jing* in 1654. It is a comprehensive statement of sectarian my mythology and teaching.

The End of the Age

The framework of cosmic time in the *Longhua jing* begins with the three successive periods each presided over by a Buddha that have been discussed above. In this scripture additional stages follow the reign of Maitreya, whose work is continued by sect patriarchs and members, so that here Maitreya is located in the recent past, not in the future. Within this framework the message of this scripture is set in a time of chaos and destruction that only the pious will survive. The detailed discussion of this end time continues and expands treatments of this theme in earlier "precious volumes."

The time frame is laid out in chapter thirteen, entitled "The three Buddhas continue the lamp [of the teaching]." The first is the "Ancient Lamplighter Buddha" Dipamkara, who "first apportioned and ordered the world," and arranged a Dragon-flower assembly at which all the Buddhas were gathered. His rule lasted nine kalpas and was symbolized by a green lotus with three petals. When he asks who can continue the task, Sakyamuni replies that he can, so he continues the tradition for another eighteen eons, in which a five-petalled red lotus blossoms. As celestial time moved in its cycles Maitreya responds to Sakyamuni's call, and presides over the "constellation world" for eighty-one kalpas, here described as the *mojie* 末劫 (end *kalpa*), symbolized by the opening of a golden lotus with nine petals. Maitreya is succeeded by the Venerable Patriarch Tian-zhen, who in turn is followed by the leaders of the sects and branches of the tradition. Each of the Buddhas and Tian-zhen is said to have "established the teaching to match the apex" (*dangji lijiao* 當樞立敎), to proclaim the message anew at each node of cosmic time.

The end-time during which this book was revealed is described in chapters eleven and eighteen. The setting in chapter eleven is Bian-liang (Kaifeng), with the Patriarch Gong Chang seated in meditation at a street intersection, surrounded by a brilliant light that drew the attention of passers by:

> After a long time, the Patriarch broke into song, "The mute patriarch is in perfect *samadhi*, with all his bodily gateways tightly closed. He swallows the medicine of the Prior Realm, which glistens, overturns and lets fall a lotus. With the flower of his mind mirror bright, he has begun to preach the profound and marvelous, coming from south and north to transmit the Way. This morning I am saving those with karmic affinity, and transmit to you the Way of the Prior Realm. I open the pass [out of] death and rebirth. Seek within the way out, [let your spirit] penetrate through the *niwan* 泥丸 [opening at the top of the head]. Primal ones, open

wide your eyes and quickly come to recognize Gong Chang [as patriarch]; do not worry about seeking a way out; stop the restlessness of your hands and feet. The end of the age (*mojie* 末 劫) is about to arrive; each of you must protect yourselves." When the Patriarch's song ended the men and women of the whole city came to venerate [him] as a patriarch of heaven and earth, and asked him why he had come. The Patriarch said, "I have come to transmit the faith (*chuanxin* 傳信). The end of the age will soon arrive. Where will you find peace for yourselves and establish your destiny? In your midst is a patriarch who has undertaken a celestial task; the one whom you recognize is [the Buddha] Tian-zhen descended to the mundane."

So he led many men and women to receive the dharma, take refuge, and have their salvation predicted. Then the Patriarch, taking leave of the multitude, arose, and all the people of the Way returned home weeping.

More details of the message are presented in chapter eighteen, which again opens with the Patriarch absorbed in meditation. His spirit goes to the Native Place to have an audience with Wusheng laomu:

The Mother asked Gong Chang, "Do you know about the disasters occurring in the realm below?" [He replied] "Your child does not know." The Matriarch then explained that kalpic disasters would arrive in the *jiazi* year of the lower *yuan* period, and that in the xinsi year there would be famines, droughts and floods, with no harvests. The people of Shandong would eat humans, and in that year everyone would die leaning on their walls. [In that time] husbands and wives will not look after one another, and fathers and sons will separate [= be alienated from each other]. When [these disasters] reach northern *Zhih-li* people will again die of famine.

Gong Chang asked the Venerable Mother, "When will it be possible to pass through [these sufferings]?" [She replied] "In the *renwu* year it will be better, and people will again be able to make it. But then there will be a further year of disaster, toil and illness. Mountains will waver and the earth move. The Yellow River will overflow, causing people to die [reading *si* as a transitive verb]. There will be plagues of locusts, with continuous clouds and rain. Houses will collapse, and there will be no place to find safety.

Encountering these years of disaster at the end of the age is to test people's minds. [Since these calamities are the result of] 500 years of accumulated karmic faults they have been brought on people by their own actions; there is no way of release [from them]. If this reaches the *guiwei* year there will be more epidemics.

Gong Chang then said to the Mother, "How can [people be] rescued and released from these calamities (reading bei "north"as *ci* "this")? The Mother said, "Those who study will not be harmed by these calamities, and for children of the Way who cultivate good karma [such] disasters will not cause difficulty."

This passage continues with more promises of divine aid. The Mother gives mantras to Gong Chang, telling him to transmit them to all, and adds instructions on the interior circulation of qi that will protect from epidemics. The charms she bestows are to be worn by all.

In chapter nineteen we are told that the sins of humans so angered the gods that they sent down calamities as punishment:

Because in the years at the end of the age people's minds are treacherous and crafty, extraordinarily clever, with a hundred cheating schemes, [because] the minds of men and women are not honest and steadfast, and [they] are constantly involved with opportunistic schemes and [their own] opinions, and among one hundred people there is not one with good intentions, the celestial gods were angered, and sent down all forms of calamities to test living beings. However, they still did not turn around to incline toward goodness, and still did not understand [the need for] enlightenment. So it is that now, as the end of the age draws near, it is to be feared that people will lose their lives. Because of this the Venerable Ancient Buddha of the Native Place, [the Mothers' paradise] who could not bear this, sent [the Bodhisattva] Rutong 儒童 [a rebirth form of Confucius] to descend to the mundane world to transform all humans in the world so that from that time on they would reform their evils and faults. ...

In chapter twenty-one it is the Lord Lao who is sent down by the Mother to make "dharma boats" to save all, so here the founding sages of both Confucianism and Daoism are drafted to assist with the task of salvation in the end-time crisis.

All of this leads to a great Dragon-flower assembly in which all the pious are gathered, with their names registered in paradise. As we read in chapter eleven:

> If those with karmic affinity day and night recite [this] true scripture, for all twelve [Chinese] hours of the day without ceasing, and if they are able to recite the Buddha's name, then when death approaches they will escape Lord Yama in purgatory. All the pious come to worship Tian-zhen, [who as] Gong Chang is hidden in the human world. The primal ones follow the Patriarch to the Dragon-flower [Assembly], and together reach Maitreya's court in the Native Place, where for eighty-one eons they will escape Lord Yama, [repeated] ... [and] continue long life ... and as companions of the Ancient Buddha will not descend to be reborn. ... When they reach the Native Place, little children will see the Mother's face.

Hope in sectarian scriptures was made available with the support of worshipping congregations of sect members, with their own forms of organizations, leadership and rituals. Though their teachings owe much to Buddhist and Daoist antecedents, they were organized by the people themselves as a way of taking responsibility for their own salvation. Though this sort of independent religious organization aroused much government opposition, such sects have continued to exist for 500 years, and are still active all over the Chinese-speaking world outside of the People's Republic, including Hong Kong. They are a standing witness to the persistence of religious belief and hope.

7

Maitreya:
A Locus of Hope in Buddhism

Frank E. Reynolds

I am greatly honored and very delighted to be here at the Chinese University of Hong Kong to help in the celebration of the 45th anniversary of the founding of Chung Chi College. The founding of Chung Chi was, at the time, an audacious ACT OF HOPE. From what I have been able to observe thus far, that hope is still alive and very much in the process of fulfillment.

And I am pleased by the fact that the organizers have chosen to focus this conference on the theme of HOPE. We now seem to be at the end of the modern era, or at least a major phase of it. Our times are marked by the loss of many of the hopes that were generated by the secular forces of modernity. Certainly there is a dwindling of communist hopes. Clearly there is a dwindling of capitalist hopes as the inequities that capitalism feeds, and the human and environmental destructiveness that it generates become increasingly obvious to those who have the eyes to see. And there is a dwindling of traditional liberal and neo-liberal hopes as well.

It would seem that this breakdown of modern secular hopes provides a new opening, a new space which religions might creatively enter. But if religions are to take advantage of this new situation in a positive way, they must become much more self-critical about their own hopes, and about the modes of action that are properly correlated with those hopes. It is my hope that our conference here in Hong Kong will make a serious contribution to the achievement of that goal.

I have chosen to begin my lecture this morning with a personal story — a story that I have told many times in private, but — so far as I can remember — never before in public. It is the story of how I came to be involved in the study of Buddhism. The story goes back to pre-history (actually to 1956 when Chung Chi was just five years old) — to the time when I first came to Thailand to work at the Student Christian Center and Chulalongkorn University in Bangkok.

Before I left the United States I did a good bit of preparatory reading about Buddhism, using the best books that were available in the West at the time. The picture that I got from my reading of these books was that Buddhism was a pessimistic religion — that it was a religion that claimed that all existence is suffering and that the only appropriate response to that suffering is a kind of asceticism that leads to personal annihilation.

But when I got to Thailand my experience told a different story. From all that I could see and hear, Thai Buddhism was a very up-beat religion. From all I could discern, the hopes that it offered were extremely diverse and very interesting indeed.

There was the hope for Nirvana (the cessation of suffering). And Nirvana was understood and depicted in a very positive way.

There were hopes for individual betterment in this life and in the future. The law of karma was seen not only as a fatalistic way of explaining differences in levels of happiness; it was also seen as a basis of hope for those who acted morally and engaged in proper merit making activity.

There were also hopes for social harmony and well being in the family context, in the local context, in the national context, and in the global context.

Most important and encompassing of all — there was a sense of access to a world in which a Buddha reality was present; and where, because that Buddha reality was present, all of the above mentioned hopes — and many more — were alive and well.

I don't mean to idealize Thai Buddhism, either then or now. There were, and there are, many problems — very serious problems that can very easily be identified. But lack of hope was not, and is not, among them.

The point of my story is that it was this fascinating dichotomy between what I had read about the pessimism of Buddhism and the wide array of Buddhist hopes that I had encountered, that was the central dynamic that led to my decision to become a historian of religions and to focus my studies on Buddhism. Thus my interest in the role that hope plays in Buddhism, and the distinctive character of Buddhist hope, has been simmering for almost 40 years.

When I began my study of Buddhism and what I am calling the Buddha-presence that seemed to sustain it, the immediate focus was on the Gautama Buddha, the so called "historical" Buddha. And there I discovered a figure who was himself a prime exemplar of hope. Looking at the Gautama Buddha as a prime exemplar of hope, there are three particular episodes in his story that immediately stand out. First, there is Gautama's vow to attain Buddhahood — a vow that was made many long eons ago in the time of a previous Buddha named Dipankara. And there are the correlated ACTS OF HOPE that followed, namely the series of innumerable lives extending over many eons through which the future Gautama practiced the moral and intellectual perfections that are intrinsic to Buddhahood.

Second, there is an exemplary moment of hope that occurs in the traditional narrative of the "historical" life of Gautama; an exemplary moment that occurs after he had spent his youth in the rigidly protected atmosphere of his father's royal palace. According to the well-known account, he ventured out of the palace grounds and encountered four sights: a sick man, an old and decrepit man, a corpse, and a wandering ascetic. The first three sights posed the problem of suffering in its starkest forms. But the fourth sight was clearly a vision of hope — a vision of hope that suggested that, through the way of life that the ascetic represented, desire could be quenched and suffering could be overcome. Once again displaying his character as a prime exemplar of hope, Gautama acted on the vision, left the palace life, and set out on the long search that culminated in his Enlightenment.

A third point in Gautama's story where he appears as a prime exemplar of hope comes immediately after his Enlightenment under the Bo tree at Bodh Gaya. At that time, so the story goes, he was tempted not to preach to others the truth that he had discovered — a temptation that was grounded in his fear that the people of his time were not prepared to hear and to appropriate his message. But at that point a god from the Brahma heaven — Sahampati by name — intervened, confronted Gautama, and insisted that there actually were people in the world at that time who were ready and able to hear and to respond. Once confronted with that hope, Gautama grasped hold of it; and the rest, so to speak, is history. The correlated ACTS OF HOPE were, of course, the activities of the remaining 40 years of Gautama's life — his ministry of preaching, teaching and organizing a Buddhist community.

In the Buddhist tradition the Gautama Buddha was, during the course of his ministry, not only an exemplar of hope; he was also a primary locus of hope as well.

At one level Gautama was a locus of hope by virtue of the message that he taught. Consider, for example, the Four Noble Truths which is one of the classic formulations of his teaching. The first truth is that all existence is suffering — a truth that identifies the problem that, from the Buddhist point of view, encompasses all other human problems within its ken. The second truth is that desire is the cause of suffering. The third truth is the crucial and pivotal affirmation of HOPE, namely the affirmation that suffering can, in fact, be overcome. And the fourth truth lays out the correlated ACTS OF HOPE that can enable one to achieve that goal, namely the Noble 8-fold Path that involves the practice of morality, the practice of meditation, and the cultivation of insight.

At another level — and one that is equally important — Gautama was (according to the reports of the early community) a locus of hope for his early followers because of the remarkable enabling power of his presence. In the presence of a Buddha — in this case in the presence of the Gautama Buddha — otherwise unimaginable hopes for human flourishing were both evoked and fulfilled.

In reading the early Buddhist scriptures it is abundantly clear that they convey the importance of Gautama as a Buddha-figure whose very presence was an enabling power that established a new world of religious possibilities, a new world populated by ascetics, monks and lay followers — not only by those who were spiritually advanced, but by those at the lower stages of spiritual development as well.

Given the importance of a Buddha's presence, Gautama's death inevitably generated a crisis that his followers had to engage. Not only was it necessary to preserve the Master's teachings; it was equally necessary to preserve, for the community which he had established, the absolutely crucial sense of living in his presence.

This crisis was met with a variety of different strategies. For example, Gautama's relics and the symbols of his Buddhahood became a focal point of communal and individual veneration. Here one thinks of the early Buddhist stupas (funerary monuments) and the festivals and other forms of veneration and celebration that took place around them.

Later in the development of the tradition iconic images were made in order to evoke his memory and a sense of his continuing availability. In this regard I am reminded especially of the monastic ceremonies I have witnessed in Thailand — monastic ceremonies in which the image of Gautama holds a thread that is also held by the monks as they chant the Buddhist Dharma — and also of the central images of Gautama that in all Thai Buddhist temples receive various forms of communal and individual veneration.

And there is also the process of exchange between monks and laity through which the Buddha's extended presence is continually being reconstituted. The monks, through their role as preservers and teachers of the tradition reconstitute his Dharma or Truth body. The laity, in their role as devoted patrons, reconstitute his rupa or material support body. Thus the community brings the reality and presence of the Gautama Buddha from the past into the present.

What is happening in each of these three very different situations (and many others like them) is that the Buddha world that Gautama established, and his presence within it, are being ritually remembered and recreated so that they can once again be experienced in the present.

But as successful as these efforts at ritually recreating the Gautama's Buddha world have been — and in some cases still are — the Buddhist community gradually and increasingly began to experience a sense of decline, a growing incapacity to gain access to the world that Gautama had established in a way that was complete and satisfying. It seems from the earliest Buddhist texts that Gautama himself recognized the inevitability of the decline of the religion that he was in the process of founding. According to some early texts he predicted that the decline would be complete and the religion would disappear after 500 years; according to others he predicted that the decline and disappearance of the tradition would take 1,000 years; and according to still other texts, probably composed somewhat later, the period was extended to 5,000 years.

However that may be, it is clear that — as the effects of the decline began to be seriously felt — many Buddhists began to search for other modes of access to the Buddha reality and presence. In many cases, this led to an emerging interest in Buddhas other than Gautama.

It is important to recognize that — as best we can tell from the earliest texts — Gautama and his early followers had, from the beginning, recognized the existence of a plurality of Buddhas and Bodhisattvas (Future Buddhas). As time went on, and the availability of the world and presence of Gautama began to fade, other Buddhas and Bodhisattvas began to be singled out for special recognition and attention. Among these Maitreya — the Buddha who was widely recognized as the next Buddha who would appear in this world — seems to have been the first to emerge with a significant role and an extended story.

As Maitreya came into prominence a new pattern of Buddhological access began to evolve. In this new pattern there was a dual emphasis — a mode of access to Gautama and his world of the past through remembrance, and access to Maitreya and his world of the future through expectation. This pattern, with its dual emphases on remembrance and expectation became the dominant pattern in the Theravada tradition; and it remained an important strand in virtually all other Buddhist traditions as well.

With this rather extensive but necessary background in mind, we can now turn our attention to Maitreya himself. Let me begin by looking very briefly at some of the basic similarities and differences between the stories associated with Gautama and the stories associated with Maitreya.

In the Buddhist tradition the structures that are built into the stories of the extended lives of various Buddhas are quite similar. But there are differences, and in many instances the differences are significant. This play of similarity and difference certainly is evident in the case of Gautama and Maitreya.

Like Gautama, Maitreya — according to the stories that are told about him — also made an original vow to attain Buddhahood. And, like Gautama, he spent innumerable lives spread through many eons perfecting the virtues associated with Buddhahood. But Maitreya was different from Gautama in that he was more cantankerous, and his progress along the path to Buddhahood was slower. Perhaps as a result, the process was ultimately even more successful; and thus, in many traditions, Maitreya is recognized as a Buddha whose presence will be even more efficacious than Gautama's.

Like Gautama, Maitreya, after perfecting all of the virtues, was born in the Tusita heaven where he waits, far above the earth, for the appropriate time for his final birth. In the case of Gautama, his residence in the Tusita heaven was of relatively minor importance since, at the time the story was told, he was, so to speak, no longer in residence. But in the case of Maitreya, his residence in the Tusita heaven has a crucial contemporary significance. He is residing there now, in the present; and that, as we shall see, opens up many very fascinating religious possibilities.

Finally, just as Gautama descended from the Tusita heaven and lived out his final life on earth in the past, so Maitreya will descend from the Tusita heaven and live out his final life in the future. A comparative reading of various versions of the two accounts indicates that the time of Maitreya will be an even better time than the time of Gautama. This will be true in a number of respects. But the most important is that in many traditions Maitreya, unlike Gautama, will have a glorious royal counterpart. According to these accounts, he will have, as a contemporary, a great Buddhist kin — a Chakravartin, a great Wheel-rolling monarch who will extend his benevolent rule over all the earth, and will give honor and support to Maitreya's cause.

So much for the background. The time has now come to focus in on the central topic that I wish to address — namely an examination of the basic ways in which Maitreya — as the expected Buddha of the Future — has, for many Buddhists, become a primary locus of hope. When we survey the many very diverse ways in which the stories and rituals involving Maitreya have, over the centuries, been involved in Buddhist life, four patterns stand out. For our purposes what is of particular interest is that each one of these four patterns is associated with a distinctive kind of Buddhist hope.

The first two patterns emphasize the accessibility of the Tusita heaven where the Future Buddha is believed to be presently residing. In the traditional Buddhist conception of the universe, this Tusita heaven is a relatively close-by heaven that is located within this particular cosmos in which we presently live. Because of this relative spatial closeness, and because of the relative degree of accessibility that it suggests, it is a place where the presence and the impact of the virtually perfected Future Buddha can be experienced.

Perhaps the most common form in which Buddhists have sought to exploit the accessibility of the Tusita heaven and the Future Buddha is through the development of very specific and highly developed techniques of meditative concentration and visualization. Such methods of concentration and visualization were utilized to enable the practitioner to mystically ascend into the Tusita realm. In that context the practitioner was thought to be able, because of the presence of the Future Buddha, to rapidly accelerate his progress toward enlightenment. Alan Sponberg, drawing on the writings of Wonhyo, a 7th century Korean monk, lists four very specific goals that were associated with these visualizations of the Tusita heaven, and with the mystical participation they were intended to achieve. According to Wonhyo this kind of mystical participation can ameliorate the negative karma accrued as a result of past sins. It can prevent undesirable rebirths in the future. It can assure rebirth in the Tusita heaven as a Bodhisattva (that is to say, as a Future Buddha). And it can assure that the practitioner will never suffer a relapse in his progress along the Bodhisattva path.[1]

The second pattern that I have identified within the Maitreya tradition also focuses on the on-going presence of Maitreya in the relatively accessible Tusita heaven. This second pattern highlights not so much the efficacy of Maitreya's presence in constituting a realm where personal progress along the path to enlightenment is enhanced. It highlights, instead, Maitreya's role as a locus of inspiration for the generation of new Buddhist teachings. Maitreya thus becomes an authoritative source for new Buddhist teachings that go beyond the teachings attributed to Gautama.

A classic example of this pattern is found in the stories about two figures — Maitreyanatha and Asanga — figures who are considered to be the founders of the Yogacara branch of the Mahayana teaching that developed during the early centuries of the common era. According to certain accounts Asanga (who was clearly an historical figure) often ascended to the Tusita heaven, where Maitreya taught him the basics of the new Mahayana doctrine. At a later point the Future Buddha, at

Asanga's request, temporarily (and I emphasize a temporarily) descends to earth in order to give a series of lectures that spell out the new teaching. According to the account, Asanga, who is the only person near enough to hear the lectures that Maitreya gives, then proceeds to provide a full explanation for the rest of the Buddhist community.

The other two patterns that can be discerned within the Maitreyan strand of the Buddhist tradition focus not so much on hopes that are associated with the Future Buddha's on-going presence and availability in the Tusita heaven. They focus, rather, on the time when the Future Buddha will descend from the Tusita heaven to our own earthly realm in order to fulfill his ultimate destiny.

The first of these two descent-oriented patterns presumes that the coming of Maitreya is imminent. In some versions this imminent coming is envisioned primarily in religious terms. For example, Daniel Overmyer has carefully demonstrated the role that the hope for Maitreya's imminent coming has played in a series of Chinese popular cults. These popular cults that began to appear on the Chinese scene in the 14th and 15th centuries promised salvation from this world, and the restoration of a primal unity in a world beyond. Several scholars of Japanese religions have described a variety of Japanese mountain cults in which Maitreya's imminent coming is expected and ritually celebrated.

In many other versions of this pattern, the imminent coming of Maitreya is associated with the establishment of an ideal earthly society in which both specifically religious and broader religio-political and religio-social hopes can be fulfilled. In a few cases of this type, established rulers have claimed to be the Future Buddha incarnate. Two examples immediately come to mind: the claim to Maitreyan status that was made by the Empress Wu, who ruled in China in the late 7th and early 8th century CE; and the similar claim that was made by King Bodawpaya, who ruled in Burma more than a millennium later. There are, of course, many other instances that could be cited.

But in a variety of other situations it has been the leaders or spokesmen of popular egalitarian revolts and peasant revolutions who have proclaimed the imminent arrival of Maitreya. The oldest examples that we have are to be found in rebellious Maitreya-oriented secret societies in China. More recently, particularly during the colonial period, popular, Maitreya-oriented millennial movements have emerged all across the Buddhist world.

The second of the two descent-oriented patterns of Maitreyan mythology and ritual activity is quite different from the first. This second descent-oriented pattern combines two elements — the view that the coming of Maitreya will not occur until the far-distant future, and the notion that it is possible to cultivate ways of acting in the present that will assure that one will be reborn at that most auspicious of times. For example, in Theravada societies right up to the present day, many merit-making rituals involve a highly significant Maitreyan component of this type. In the concluding segment of many very common, every-day rituals the individual who is performing them expresses the hope that the merit that he or she is in the process of gaining will facilitate his or her rebirth at the time of Maitreya's coming.

In my judgment at least, this second descent-oriented pattern has had its deepest and most profound expression in a textual and ritual tradition that has played an important role in the history of Buddhism in Thailand. It is a tradition in which two important texts have been involved. The first is the Phra Malai Sutta, a late medieval sutta that seems to have been composed in Thailand itself.[2] The second is the Vessantara Jataka, a very ancient and famous text which tells the crucially important story of the last of the previous lives of the Gautama Buddha — the life in which he perfects the preeminent virtue of selfless giving.[3]

In the Phra Malai Sutta, the protagonist for whom the text is named is a monk of great meditational prowess who has developed the mystical ability to visit various realms of the Buddhist cosmos. Like several other Buddhist figures with like abilities, he visits Buddhist hells to bring merit that has been made by the living to assuage the suffering of their ancestors who are now condemned to reside in those awful places. But the most prominent and distinctive visit that Phra Malai makes is one that takes him upward to the Tusita heaven where he seeks to question the Future Buddha concerning the time when he will descend to be reborn as Maitreya. Phra Malai does, in fact, succeed in meeting the Future Buddha; and he receives an extended response to the question that he poses.

According to the Future Buddha's response, we are presently living on the downward side of an on-going cycle of social improvement and social decline. The religion of Gautama will soon pass away, and, beyond that, the downward trajectory will continue for a very, very long period until society is in absolute chaos and the human lifespan has declined to ten years. As a result of a decision by a few persons to withdraw from society, and to meditate on the moral causes of decline and renewal, this downward trajectory will then be reversed and the upward phase of the cycle will begin. During the course of another immensely long period of time, society will gradually improve, the lifespan will increase, and finally a seemingly ideal condition will be achieved; the human lifespan will reach 84,000 years (this is obviously a very imaginative rendition!), society will be harmonious, and there will be prosperity and abundance for all. However, as soon as this zenith point has been attained, people will begin to forget the realities of suffering and death, moral standards will begin to slip, and a decline will once again begin to take place. When the appropriate point in the downward trajectory is reached (and that is the point at which a high level of well being is still being maintained, but a consciousness of suffering and death has returned), Maitreya will descend to earth to establish his religion. Those who are interested in such matters will, I am sure, note that there is, embedded in this prediction, a profound utopian ideal of the proper relationship between religion and the economic and social order. But a discussion of this utopian ideal and its significance will have to await another occasion.[4]

As the story continues, the Future Buddha goes on to tell Phra Malai that when he returns to earth he must inform the people that, if they hope to be reborn at the time of his coming, they must listen regularly to the recitation of the Vessantara Jataka. Thus when Phra Malai does return, he establishes a regular ritual tradition in which the Vessantara Jataka is recited so that those who wish to be reborn at the time of Maitreya's coming can follow the instructions that Maitreya himself has provided. Whatever we may think of the Phra Malai account of the origins of the ritual of Vessantara recitation, such a ritual recitation was, in fact, a major event in the religious life of medieval Thailand; and listening to the performance was considered to be a way of assuring that one would be reborn at the time of Maitreya's coming.

But what is the connection between listening to the Vessantara Jataka on the one hand, and the assurance of rebirth at the time of

Maitreya's coming on the other? To be sure, the Vessantara story is, along with the account of Gautama Buddha's final life, the story that Theravadins know the best and the story that they tell the most. But why should the Future Buddha single it out as the particular story that should be heard and reheard by those who hope to be reborn at the time of his coming?

The answer, I suggest, is that the Vessantara Jataka presents a story of the Gautama Buddha's penultimate life that portrays, in the most dramatic possible fashion, the inevitable and irresolvable conflicts and tensions that arise in the pursuit of Buddhist values under normal social conditions.[5] Throughout the story Vessantara — the future Gautama who is in the process of perfecting the preeminent Theravada virtue of selfless giving — acts in ways that are clearly in conflict with other more mundane Buddhist values. He gives away the beautiful white elephant which assures the prosperity of his kingdom, thereby endangering the security and well being of those for whom he is responsible; he gives up his responsibilities as a righteous ruler and retreats to the forest; and — in the most dramatic and poignant act of all — he gives away his wife and his two small children to an evil man who intends them no good.

What is more, in the text itself, and even more in the dramatic recitations that were performed by the monks, it is clear that deep sympathy is being evoked for Vessantara and for his quest for personal perfection. But at the same time, it is also vividly apparent that equal (and sometimes even greater) sympathy is being evoked for the clearly Buddhist values of social and familial responsibility that Vessantara is ignoring, and for those persons who must suffer the painful consequences of his single minded search for personal perfection.

Thus what I take to be the message of the Phra Malai/Vessantara complex can be summarized in terms of three closely correlated dimensions. First, this very profound mythic and ritual complex encourages a recognition that the coming of Maitreya cannot be expected soon, and that — in the situation that will persist until he finally arrives — people must exist in a world in which Buddhist values and virtues (particularly supramundane values and virtues on the one hand, and more worldly values and virtues on the other) are inevitably and irresolvably in tension, competition and conflict. Second, it projects a normative orientation that encourages the recognition and cultivation of the whole range of worldly and other-worldly Buddhist values and virtues, and the acceptance of the tragedy and pathos that the conflicts between these values and virtues often generate. Finally, this Phra Malai/ Vessantara complex inspires the hope that those who recognize, appreciate, and cultivate the full range of Buddhist values and virtues will ultimately be rewarded by rebirth at the time of Maitreya — a marvelous and uniquely auspicious time when the situation will be such that all of the contradictions and conflicts will be resolved and all Buddhist hopes can be fulfilled.

Much more could usefully be said about the patterns of story and ritual that have been generated in what I have chosen to call the Maitreyan strand of Buddhist history. But since time is running short, I will resist the temptation to distinguish more patterns or to add further details. But I would like to conclude by making a few more personal observations about the possible relevance of the patterns that I have identified for the situation in which we presently find ourselves.

At the beginning of my lecture I referred to the contemporary breakdown of modern, secularist hopes for the future, a breakdown that seems to be affecting the hopes that have been generated by the communist movement, by capitalist enthusiasts, and by liberal and neo-liberal secularists as well. I also suggested that this breakdown might be providing a space in which religious visions of hope could be usefully and effectively retrieved, reformulated and reinvigorated.

As I have reflected on the two sets of patterns of Maitreya-oriented Buddhist belief and practice that I have described, it has struck me that each set points toward one particular dimension of a more comprehensive, religiously sophisticated vision of hope that could be extremely relevant to the situation in which we find ourselves today. The first set (the set that includes the two patterns that crystallize around the Buddha's presence in the Tusita heaven) suggests the possibility of — and perhaps the need for, identifying an on-going contemporaneous dimension of transcendence that can facilitate two different processes, namely, the process of personal religious contemplation and progress, and the process of discovering and legitimating new levels of religious insight and understanding. The second set (the set that includes the two patterns that crystallize around the Future Buddha's descent from the Tusita heaven to earth) suggests the possibility of — and perhaps the need for — identifying a future-oriented dimension of that same mode of transcendence — a future-oriented dimension that is sufficiently imminent to motivate creative religious and social action, yet sufficiently distant to allow for the recognition and cultivation of a full range of conflicting religious values and virtues.

It is very obvious to me — and it is, I am sure, even more obvious to all of you — that in making these personal observations I have strayed far beyond the bounds of my authority and competence as a historian of religion. My only justification for taking such liberties is my hope that at least some of the more general theological and philosophical issues that the Maitreyan tradition raises will be taken up into our discussion as our conference proceeds.

Notes

1. Sponberg's discussion is contained in his contribution to an excellent collection of essays which he co-edited with Helen Hardacre. The book, entitled: *Maitreya: The Future Buddha* (Princeton: Princeton University Press, 1986) is by far the best and most accessible secondary source that deals with Maitreya, and, as such, it has been extremely useful in the preparation of the present essay.

2. Several versions are translated by Bonnie Brereton in her *Thai Tellings of Phra Malai: Texts and Rituals Concerning a Popular Buddhist Saint* (Arizona State University; Program for Southeast Asian Studies, 1995).

3. The best translation, though it is not based on a Thai version, is Margaret Cone and Richard Gombrich, *The Perfect Generosity of Prince Vessantara* (London: Oxford University Press, 1977).

4. When this paper was presented for discussion at the Fellows Seminar held at the University of Chicago's Institute for the Advanced Study of Religion, Dan Buchanen, who was the respondent who initiated the discussion, suggested that this ideal might be especially because of its relation to the present situation in Hong Kong. Buchanen noted that in Hong Kong a long period of rising prosperity is giving way to a new period in which (despite the prospect that a high level of prosperity will continue) elements of serious concern and uncertainty are entering the consciousness of the populace.

5. The interpretation of the Vessantara Jataka that I am proposing relies heavily on a draft manuscript of Chapter 7 "The Vessantara Jataka: Tragedy, Melodrama, Summa Felicitatium" in Steven Collins' manuscript that is titled *Nirvana and Other Buddhist Felicities* (Cambridge: Cambridge University Press, 1997).

8

Transformation of Hope
in Chinese Buddhism

Yün-hua Jan

Definitions of Hope

Although it is known that hope is a common phenomenon in human life and has played an important role in religious life, yet when one reviews academic studies on the subject, one would find that scholarly opinions and conclusions rather confusing. In the earlier references, hope was regarded as "the name of grace which is characteristic of the religion of the Bible."[1] It has also been pointed out by Paul Shorey that the idea of hope also exists in Greek and Roman religions.[2] In other words, the idea of hope is a Western religious notion, which has nothing to do with Asian religions. More than seventy years later, in a new encyclopedia of religion published in 1987, Peter Slater wrote a new article on the subject, in which he considered hope as a general idea that is universal in most of the major traditions including Buddhism. Slater states that "[i]f we define religion as the systematic expression of the interplay between traditional faith and transforming hope, then hope is of the essence of religion."[3] Whether his definition of religion and the idea of hope in connection with transformation is acceptable to scholars or not is not the concern of this paper. What is important here is his opinion that "each major tradition posits a future leader who focuses the hope arising from past faith." In this connection, the "Buddhists speak of Maitreya as the Buddha to come." Both the fore-mentioned references indicating that the present stage of knowledge on hope in Buddhism is, more or less, still remains without much extensive and intensive study. The underdevelopment of scholarship on this subject is partly due to the nature of Buddhist doctrine, partly due to the complexity of cultures in different regions where Buddhism spread in the course of history. Since the religion has passed through different places and stages, and underwent many transformations, what this paper plans is to discuss the following questions: The problem of hope in early Indian Buddhism, the Mahayana inspiration on China, the emergence of hope literature (*yuanwen* 願文) in Chinese Buddhism, and the hopes expressed in this literature. Through a fresh inquiry, the transformation of Buddhism may become explicator, which in turn may explain why the religion has experienced different courses and results in history.

Hope in Buddhist Literature

About thirty years ago, there was a book entitled *In the Hope of Nibbana*,[4] which is an introduction to the ethics of Theravadin Buddhism in Burma. The religious end of Theravadins is of course to attain nibbana, but nowhere is hope discussed as the title has indicated. The complexity of hope must be in Buddhism, yet no discussion on the subject fully reflects the difficult nature of the topic.

Are there notions or words of hope in Buddhist literature? As far as the early scriptures are concerned, the Pali language has some vocabulary that could be rendered as equivalent to the English word "hope." Pali words like *akankha, apekkha, abbilasa, patthana* are good examples. These words could be translated into English as "attention," "affection for desire," "longing for," "aiming at," or "hope," but none of them could be regarded as explicitly and exclusively equivalent to the word "hope."[5] What is even more significant is that none of the forementioned Pali words are regarded as the key term in the Buddhist scriptures nor in the scheme of salvation.

The main difficulty in relating hope to the early teachings of Buddhism lies in the concept of an individual. Hope must be related to a hoper and an object. However, according to the early Buddhist doctrine of the individual, every person comprises five components: *skandhas*, viz, form and matter (*rupa*), sensation (*vedana*), perceptions (*sanna*), psychic dispositions or construction (*samkhara*), and consciousness or conscious thought (*vinnana*).[6] Hope is possible when it functions within the last three components, viz, perceptions, psychic construction and consciousness.[7] Rune Johansson explains the relationship between individual components as follows:

> Sankh ara is sometimes translated by 'karma-formation,' because all activity has a moral aspect, is morally judged, has moral causes and moral consequences. There is here a close co-operation between *vinnana* and sankhara: *sankhara* is the effector of the deeds (*kamma*), vinnana is the accumulator of the effects.[8]

The Abhidhamma literature has employed two terms, *vitakka* and *vicara* in relation to hope. Narada explains them in this way: "*vitakka* may well be defined as the application of the concomitants on the object," and "*Vicara* is the continued exercise of the mind on the object."[9] These two terms describe psychological function of hope very well. However, if one goes farther, hope in early Buddhism would become questionable. This is so as a Pali scripture declares: "The wantless is in *nibbanam*." And "[b]y the destruction of desires, there is complete disinterest and cessation: *nibbana*" (SN 707, U33).[10] The Abhidhamma again confirms this point, when it states that "the second *jhana* consists of three constituents as both *vitakka* and *vicara* are eliminated at once."[11] From these scriptural authorities one may conclude that hope in Pali Buddhism occupies no significant place. It stands as a descriptive word at first, and then eliminated as a precondition to *nibbana*.

There are two other relevant points worthy of further discussion: first, it may be pointed out that Pali texts are monastic literature, thus it concentrates on the subject that priests are interested in. Henceforth, does hope exist among lay members of Buddhism? Second, what was the role for Maitreya Buddha, and who is the symbol of hope in Buddhism? As far as Pali literature is concerned, it is largely monastic in nature, the role prescribed for laymen is very limited. There are some archaeological evidences which refer to the hope of a lay donor when the donations for the construction of Buddhist monuments were made. But the hope mentioned in the inscriptions is neither clear nor outstanding. Taking the Bharhut inscriptions as examples: an inscription states that a certain object is "the gift of Sangharakshita for the sake of his parents"; or "the gift of the mother of Setaka from Purika."[12] The name in the first quoted inscription above is obviously a monk's; the second donor seems to be a lay devotee of Buddhism. Only the monk's inscription contains the word "sake," though no indication of the contents or meaning of that word is made.

Regarding to the symbol of hope in Buddhism, namely the cult of Maitreya Bodhisattva, Pali literature only mentions his name in *Cakkavattisihanada sutta*. His role was raised in commentarial texts, but it is still underdeveloped when compared to Mahayana scriptures of Buddhism. It was only after the full development of Mahayana that Maitreya was gradually transformed into a Buddha, and finally became the principal deity of the Dragon Tree Assembly, thus to save the sentient beings and guide them to enlightenment throughout future generations. After the Mahayana scriptures were translated into Chinese, a number of new development and transformations took place in East Asia; religious hope focussing on Maitreya Buddha came to a new height in history.[13]

The Understandings of Hope in Mahayana Buddhism

The development of the Mahayana movement in India brought about a new spirit to Buddhism: the attitudes of the religion was now transformed from cool to warm as far as the world is concerned. It is not only monks and nuns, but even laymen who might be all hopeful in their striving for salvation. The heavenly Buddhas and Bodhisattvas will look after the welfare of those who might be doomed and incapable of liberating themselves. It is these heavenly beings with their compassion and potent powers that attracted the Chinese masses to the religion. Being inspired by the Buddhas and the Bodhisattvas' compassionate spirit and imitating their actions and thought, the Chinese looked upon the Buddhas and the Bodhisattvas for help, which in turn further transformed Buddhism.

The Mahayana spirit of joy in all things has inevitably inspired the Chinese masses. This new spirit and attitude are found in many Mahayana scriptures. One of them, for example, has declared, "[i]ndeed nothing is difficult after practice. Simple folk, such as porters, fishermen and plowmen ... all joys of the Bodhisattvas are to be found."[14] This promise of hope, hope for ending suffering and depression is assured by Buddhas and Bodhisattvas with their respective vows and powers.

Among the heavenly Buddhas and Bodhisattvas who have had immense influence on the Chinese mind, the name of Amit abha ("Immeasurable Radiance") and his assistants, Bodhisattva Avalokiteshvara, Maitreya Buddha, Bodhisattva Samanta-bhadra and Ksitigarbha are all very significant. The religious hope in these heavenly beings, their compassion and powers, especially their vows (*Pranidhana*), have attracted immense Chinese attention, and created religious institutions, literature and liturgy that are not seen in the Indian context.

As far as religious hope is concerned, two ideas from Mahayana are particularly significant to the Chinese. The first is the Buddhist belief in the sacred text. This belief is found in Indian Mahayana as it considers that not only the words spoken by Buddhas, but even the books which embody the holy words are to be worshipped.[15] The second belief is in the vows made by the Buddhas and Bodhisattvas in the past which are found in scriptures. The vow (*pranidhana*) refers to the solemn utterance of will or the strongest hope in an extraordinary being which the Buddhist believes to be potent with real effect. These Mahayana beliefs have inspired a number of influential Chinese Buddhists to imitate the vows made by Buddhas and Bodhisattvas, and created a large number of new vows and hope that are unpe scripture contains a story which states that many aeons ago when Amitabha was born as a monk called Dharmakara (Fazang) who will be destined to become Amitabha Buddha. At that time, the monk made a series of 48 vows and declared that he himself would not attain Buddhahood unless his vows were completely fulfilled. Here we may mention a typical vow as to show this hopeful spirit: "If I attained the Buddhahood, while the sentient beings are still unable to be reborn [in my land] even though they have hoped for it for ten times, I would not achieve the omniscience of a Buddha (*sambodhi*)"(T.[16] 12, 268a). It is this generous spirit that attracted the Chinese mind, which finally developed into the massive movement of Pure Land Buddhism.

The next Mahayana inspiration came from the cult of Maitreya Buddha. As has been mentioned above, this name has a long tradition in India: by the time of Faxian's pilgrimage to India, the cult already existed.[17] Similar references are also found in the record written by other Chinese monks, yet there is no mention of an exclusive collection of scriptures on Maitreya as known in China. The scriptures exclusively devoted to Maitreya were translated into Chinese by Zhu Fahu (Dharmaraksa, ca. 265-313 CE) first, and subsequently by Kumarajiva (343-413) and I-ching (635-713) are the three great scriptures on Maitreya. Sometimes, if other translations are counted, the scriptures on the Buddha would be increased to the "six Great Scriptures on Maitreya." The Maitreya cults provided the Chinese with three kinds of hope: first, the hope for a rebirth in the land of Maitreya, the Tusita Heaven, which sometimes is also called the "Pure Land of Maitreya." Second, the promise of the participation in the forthcoming Assembly of Dragon Flower, when Maitreya comes back to the earth, to help free all the sentient beings free from suffering. And, third, the vows made by Maitreya. Each of the three hopes has created different reactions in Chinese history, ranging from cult and cultivation to peasant rebellion.

The third current from Indian Buddhism that has inspired Chinese hope is the vows and actions of Bodhisattva Samantabhadra (*Puxian pusa*). Although as early as the third century CE a translated scripture already referred to the Bodhisattva, who became more prominent only after the new translation of *Huayan jing* by Siksananda (652-710) appeared. The Sanskrit text of the translation contains a number of vows made by the Bodhisattva, the last one of which reads as follows: "By the infinite and most excellent merit acquired through perfecting the living of life of Bhadra, may those people drowned in the flood of calamities go to the most excellent city of Amitabha.[18] The vows for living the life of Samantabhadra became a popular attraction to Chinese Buddhists, from which cult and liturgy have been developed in China.

The fourth major Mahayana inspiration of hope in Chinese Buddhism is the cult of *Ti-tsang p'u-sa* (*Ksitigarbha*). Although the name of the Bodhisattva has a Sanskrit origin, which possibly indicates that he come from India, bibliographical evidences led some scholars to think that the development of the cult was probably a Chinese production. In any case, the Chinese "translation" of the scriptures related to the Bodhisattva contains some most generous statement of compassion. The popular utterances like "If I do not go to the hells, who else will do it?", or "When the hells are not empty [of suffering souls] I would certainly not to become a Buddha myself," are attributed to this Bodhisattva.

The currents of Mahayana Buddhism have had great influence on the Chinese mind, and they are responsible in many ways for the flourishing of the religion in East Asia. It is mainly under these influences and inspiration that the Chinese writers composed essays to express their hopes.

Hope in Chinese Buddhism (I)

Chinese Buddhist hopes are mostly found in a body of literature which the Chinese called "*Yuanwen*" 願文 (essays of hopes) or "shiyuan wen" (essays of vowed hopes). This form of literature became popular in China only after Buddhism flourished in the land. The literature first mentioned in the records compiled by Sengyou 僧祐 (445-518), though no sample is selected in the record. It is in the work compiled by Daoxuan 道宣 (596-667) that some "essays of hopes" were selected and preserved. Many more essays were discovered from Dunhuang manuscripts, and two of them were selected and published in the 85th volume of *Taisho shinshu Daizokyo* fifty years ago (T. 85, 1298b-c), but it did not arouse the interest of scholars. It was not until a year ago that one volume of *yuanwen* from Dunhuang manuscripts was collected, edited, annotated and published by two Chinese scholars.[19] It is a 984-page volume, which is no doubt the pioneer publication on the subject. I hope more effort on the subject will be spent as it is significant to the understanding of Chinese Buddhism. In a recent paper, Huang and his other colleagues have suggested that the style of this literature might have begun with the writings of Emperor Wu of Liang dynasty in South (i.e. Xiao Yan 蕭 衍 r. 502-549), and the essay written in connection with religious events in the Eastern Capital should be the earliest example.[20] But this suggestion seems questionable because in *Faji* 法集 compiled by the Prince of qingling (i.e. Xiao Ziliang 蕭子良, 460-494), the title of "*fayuan shu*" has already been mentioned (255, 86a). The famous writer of the period named Shen Yue 沈約 (441-513) had composed a piece of *yuan-shu* on behalf of the Crown Prince of the Ch'i kingdom of South, which should be dated before the essay of Emperor Wu of Liang dynasty (T. 52, 323a-b). As the essay written by Shen is the earliest example known so far, it is worthy of inquiry. It begins by stating that "On a certain date, the Crown Prince who is a disciple of Buddhism paid homage to the Buddhas and the holy men of the ten directions." It has also been pointed out that the possibility of the effect from the vows of hope is due to the ultimate principle (*li* 理) that could be prayed but with faith in correct wisdom [*zhang-jue* (*jiao* 角)]. Extreme wonders could be stimulated, yet it will only be ended in Suchness (*Bhutatathata*)"(152, 323a). It is only with this understanding that one may see the effects in the present moment, and thus examine whether the results are achieved. With this reason and belief, the Crown Prince called a religious assembly of one thousand monks to a palace; one hundred monks were invited to stay over to perform a ceremony of the Eight Commandments, and two bodhisattvas were ordained. The prince hoped that all the merits gained are for a peaceful and prosperous reign under his Majesty his father. He also hoped that his mother, the Empress, would live with good fortune and have whatever she longed for. He also hoped that with the merits from the occasion, all sinful creatures and spirits, the born and unborn, visible and invisible, would be purified and freed by the power of the hoped for merits. He calls "all human beings and heavenly spirits to witness the occasion and to approve the effects. So that with support from everyone we may all be saved"(T. 52, 323b).

Although the afore-mentioned essay is rather short, it is significant as it is the earliest known piece of this literature, and an inquiry thereof would not only gives us a better understanding of the literature, but also the religious hopes and reasons explained therein. The first point is the reason why hope is possible. The essay talks of "ultimate principle and extreme wonder." This illustrates the characteristic of Chinese belief in Buddhism, which is quite different from the ethical or philosophical frame of Indian Buddhism. It seems clear that the Chinese elites at that time firmly believed that Buddhism was not a faith of emptiness, but that there exists an "ultimate principle" which is formless. This belief is more congruent with Neo-Taoist philosophy than with classical Indian Buddhist thought. The second interesting aspect of the essay is its hope. Although the salvation of all living beings is mentioned, yet apart from this Buddhist terminology, good fortune, health and the peaceful reign of the ruling monarch are mentioned prominently. This is congruent with the Chinese ethics of filial piety. The third aspect of the essay is the prayer for an universal salvation of all beings, which, echoes the generous Mahayana spirit. The predominant influence of Buddhism on the Chinese mind is fully illustrated by this aspect.

The essay is referred to by Huang and his colleagues as the work by Emperor Wu of Liang dynasty in South. Though it might not be of the earliest samples of the literature, its importance should not underestimated. It is the most elaborate and important work in the history of this literature. Moreover, he was the first Buddhist king in China, his devotion and contribution to the promotion of Buddhism are unprecedented and unparalleled in Chinese history. His actions and religious zeal often recall the legends of King A'soka of India, yet the position and power of an Emperor in Chinese society was probably even more weighty and concrete than his Indian counterpart. Henceforth, the styles of writing and the hope expressed in his essay had significant influence on Chinese Buddhists.

The *yuanwen* of Emperor Wu of Liang dynasty of South was unknown to scholars for a period of 1400 years till its discovery and publication in the last year. Although the beginning part of the essay is damaged, the main parts remain in good condition. As the essay is of historical importance, it is worthy of careful attention. According to the colophon of the manuscript, the copy was made in the third year of *datong* era of Northern Wei kingdom, which was May first of 537 CE. In other words, the copy was made when the Emperor was still on the throne in the South. Apart from the date mentioned above, the essay also explains the nature and scope of hope, which is essential for understanding religious hope in Chinese Buddhism. In the first part of the damaged manuscripts, the Emperor called witnesses to be present on the solemn occasion. This is also found in the essay written by Shen Yue on behalf of the Crown Prince of Qi. From these two instances it seems safe to say that the calling of witnesses is an essential part in the making of vows of hope. The witnesses that the Emperor has called included all Buddhas, heavenly beings (*devas*), immortals (*zhuxian* 諸仙), good deities, the visible and invisible spirits. He calls upon them to witness his confession in public. He has sincerely repented whatever sins he might have committed in the past, and he hoped that he would be purified by this confession, thus to eliminate bad karma of the past. Should he unfortunately be hindered by the evil of death (*simo* 死魔), and hence lose his original mind in future, he prayed those who have witnessed the vowed hope will be compassionate to him, to help him be awake, to call the hope he had vowed to materialize. He hopes and prays that all the Buddhas, holy Dharma and holy monks of the universe will come and witness his confession. He declares that his confessions are from his own initiative and most sincere. He also hopes that all those who have witnessed the confession would approve and protect him, make him never to lose the original mind and the vows through all his future rebirths. From this statement it is clear that the Emperor wanted to become a model religious ruler, to carry the Buddhist faith into the future.

Following hope for his own personal welfare, the Emperor then turns to the benefits for his deceased relatives. He hopes the great merits acquired from his confession and vowed hopes would eliminate all the sins of his late parents and elder brothers, so that they will be freed from the four evils and the five fears, thus to have all good fortune and be reborn in the Pure Land throughout their future lives, and that his spiritual benefit might also be extended to all deceased relatives and family members. What is more interesting to note is that the Emperor also hoped that all members of his family who are still alive would also benefit from his merits. The next group of beneficiaries in the list of yuanwen includes all ministers and the people of his kingdom. Apart from these, all other beings, including his political and military enemies in the North, are all found on his list of spiritual beneficiaries. The Emperor hopes that the sins committed by these enemies will be purified by his merits. The essay concludes,

> I, Xiao Yan, a disciple of Buddha, sincerely hope that whatever I have prayed and hoped for, all will be accomplished with such great merits, such wisdom, such great powers and with such supreme result. I hope from the past till the end of the future, to the horizontal ends in the ten directions of emptiness that all beings in the three dhatus and the six realms will all able to realize their great and inconceivable hopes. I pray all the Buddhas and the holy monks in the ten directions of the endless emptiness, to come and to witness as well as to approve my vowed hopes on this solemn occasion. My vowed hopes today ultimately are not for my personal gain, but exclusively for the sake of all the sentient beings: To save them from suffering, thus to assist them to achieve Enlightenment at this moment of time.[21]

Following the essays written by Shen Yueh and Emperor Wu of Liang dynasty, this style of religious literature gradually became fashionable among Chinese elites, especially among ministers who served Buddhist Emperors. Of them, the writings of Wang Sengru 王僧孺 (465-522) are well-known works. Although Wang did not mention who was the Emperor to whom his essays were addressed, from the contents and context of the essays, we may guess that they have been written to please Emperor Wu of the Liang dynasty. There are two significant points in Wang's essays. First, in the preface of the essays, the writer offers an explanation why these religious hopes can be effective. Second, there is a list of beneficiaries. As we have seen before, Shen Yue had already provided some explanation of the subject, now Wang's essays further reinforced Shen's explanation. Wang stated: "Ultimate enlightenment is transcendent of words and letters, wonderful thinking penetrates vacuously and is beyond forms (lit. fishing traps and traces). Although it is free from all errors in terms of phenomenon, yet it always comes to respond to hope. Though it is indeterminable in the four [logical] terms, yet it never fails to react to stimuli"(T. 52, 205c). This explanation is similar to the one given by Shen Yue. These indicate the nature and the limit of the Chinese understanding of Buddhism during the period. The usage of Neo-Taoist terminology together with Buddhist terms further illustrates the development of Buddhism in China.

The second point of interest in Wang's essay is the list of beneficiaries: it lists His Majesty the Emperor first, hoping the reign will be peaceful, prosperous, happy and harmonious, and long lasting as Heaven and earth, strong and stable as gold and jade (T. 52, 206a). Then comes the benefits to His Highness the Crown Prince come next, followed by those for other princes and lords. The next group of beneficiaries includes all the palace ladies and princesses. It is particularly interesting to note that the beneficiaries mentioned in Wang's essays do not include royal ancestors or subjects, and naturally no mention is made of the enemies in North China. This omission reflects class distinctions in ancient Chinese society; only the Emperor could take the initiative to worship royal ancestors, pray for blessings for his subjects, and pardon enemies of the state. As this point the generous spirit of Mahayana falls into the social strata of China.

The essays on hope written by the Emperor and his ministers thus established examples to lay Buddhists. Thereafter a number of essays were written during the subsequent periods. Although the goal of hope might be similar, the concrete contents as well as the beneficiaries mentioned therein are subject to change according to the person who vowed hope as well as his social status. Some of these essays concentrated on the welfare of a family; this is illustrated by scroll no. 8363 of Dunhuang manuscripts preserved in the National Library of China in Beijing. This essay was written in four paragraphs. First, the hope was made with Sakyamuni Buddha as the witness. Second, the goal of the hope is the good health and security of the family. Third, that flowers, donations, food and other gifts are offered on the occasion. Fourth, the family hopes that the merits gained from the vows and gifts will secure protection from deities and holy monks, so the family will be free from disasters and calamities. The family will continue to enjoy strong bonds with officials and to have high ranks in office by themselves in all the future generations. After the family has been taken care of, the hopes returned back to Buddhist terms, namely salvation of all the sentient beings in the universe, as mentioned as the conclusion of the essays.[21]

The writing of essays on hope became very popular during the later periods as the practice spread down to people in cities and towns. Hope expressed in the essays covered a wide range of subjects: some are in memory of the dead including deceased parents, husband and wife, brothers and sisters or in-laws, lords or officials, monks and nuns. Not only the benefits of dead are the subject of essays, celebration of the birthdays of babies or elders, blessings to the newly married, congratulation for an appointment in office, ceremonies for the construction of houses etc. are all found in the essays. Some of them are clearly connected with the faith in Buddhism, some are completely unrelated to the religion. This means that the practice of writing religious vows of hope was now gradually borrowed for secular purposes.

Hope in Chinese Buddhism (II)

Historically speaking, these essays of hope were a creation of Chinese literati. Their skills in writing plus the influence of the Mahayana spirit have helped some of them to express religious hope in the form of this literature. When the practice spread widely, clergy and common folks also followed this path. Even those who have no literate skills still made an effort by copying the essays from the established patterns or invited others to write on their behalf. In the case of Buddhist clergy, some of their writings are related to their religious hope of salvation, some are written in connection with their official responsibility. The earliest extant essay written by a monk is the autobiographical account of Hui-ssu (515-577), a patriarch of the T'ien-tai school of Buddhism. Essays by other monks were collected into a book compiled by Zhisheng 智昇 (ca. 730 C.E., T. 47, 456b-474c). Many pieces are discovered at Tun-huang; a large selection of them is found in the recent book by Huang and Wu. As the aim of this paper is not to write a survey of the literature, but to study the hope expressed in it, we will select a few essays and inquire about the hope discussed therein. Attention will also be focused on the differences between hopes expressed by clergy and common folk.

As has already been noted before, the vow made by the Buddhas or Bodhisattvas is an Indian legacy; these vows have very little influence on lay folks as far as the essays are concerned. In contrast with that, the monks are more careful on scriptural authority. The vowed hopes of Hui-ssu is a good example of this difference. When the reason for making the vows is given, the monk explained it in terms of the age he belongs to: according to the Chinese Buddhist belief, the time of Hui-ssu is the Age of the deterioration of the true law of Buddhism known as *mofa* 魔法 in Chinese. Both the teaching and the scriptures that contained the true law will be destroyed completely during that age. What is worse is that not only the past Buddhas are gone, but the future Buddha is not coming down to earth. This dark age is a Buddhaless world which will last for for aeons and aeons. All sentient beings will suffer without a savior or a leader; it was indeed the age of hopelessness and helplessness. It was under these pressure and sense of urgency that Hui-ssu made his vows in a written statement: "I solemnly resolve that I shall preserve [the True Law of the Buddha] and will not let it perish. I will save all sentient beings with this teaching till the coming of Maitreya Buddha" (T. 46, 786c).[23] The monk further stated in his vows that what he hoped for is not his personal gain, but the sake of the sentient beings of that helpless and hopeless age. Hui-ssu told the story of his wish to make the vows which explained the circumstances and conditions why the vowed hope had to be taken at that particular date. He says that he has intended to vow his hopes for a long period of time, but the conditions for doing it were not complete till he traveled to the Southern Guang zhou. It was at this place was he able to make a set of golden lettered copy of *Mo-ho pan-jo p'o-lo-mi-to ching* (i.e. *Mahaprajna paramita Sutra*), and a bookcase decorated with jewels. It is only when all these were complete and available, were the hopes vowed officially. As it has been mentioned before, the Buddhist cult of scriptures was an Indian legacy that here and now we found its extension in China. Not only the cult of books was continued there, but also the value of gold was added to enforce the power and effects of the vowed hopes. The monk states, "[b]y the power from my vows and the golden lettered scripture, the world of Buddha Maitreya will be glorified. The six kinds of earthquake will occur [to signal the arrival of a Buddha]. The people of the time will be fearful and asked for the reason why the quake is taking place. After they paid homage and asked the question, the World Honoured one, Maitreya Buddha will say, "Oh this is caused by the monk who has made the copy of the scripture and solemn vows. If you wish to witness them, you must concentrate your mind on him and to call his name." The people will obey his instruction, fold their hands and call my name by saying "We pay homage to Hui-ssu." At that moment of time, the Buddha and his glorious world, the golden lettered scripture and its precious case would all manifest together at once"(T. 46, 786).

Hui-ssu further hoped that in order to realize his sacred mission to preach Mahayana Buddhism, he must attain longevity as a prerequisite to becoming an immortal and to possess the five supernatural powers enabling him to practice the path of Bodhisattvas. To attain immortality is, of course, a popular practice of religious Taoism at that time. Hui-ssu must have been aware of this practice. Probably due to this awareness, he carefully clarified his position by saying "I am not a divine nor an immortal being and I have no intention of remaining in the world forever. The reason for me to practice the methods for immortality is only for the sake of Dharma. I vow to preserve my body solely for one purpose, i.e. to meet Maitreya Buddha in Bhadrakalpa. I solemnly swear that if this is not true, I will not able to attain the wonderful enlightenment of Mahayana"(T. 46, 789b).

The Buddhist master preached to the members who were present in his assembly. They are monks and nuns, as well as wisemen, who will uphold, recite or preach this scripture of Mahaprajnaparamita-sutra at a forest or a quiet place, in a village or a town. Whenever they meet obstruction or disturbance, they should immediately fold their hands and call his name. And they will immediately be endowed with supernatural powers to deal with the situation. And, at that moment of time, he will appear in the audience as a disciple, help them to subjugate and destroy devils and heresies, thus enabling them to achieve great reputations (T. 46, 789c).

The source of Hui-ssu's hope is the cult of Maitreya Buddha, who was one of the most influential figures in Chinese Buddhism as far as hope is concerned. Besides him, there is another Buddha who even had more lasting influence than that of Maitreya Buddha, that is, Buddha Amitabha and his Pure Land (*Sukhavati*). There are many essays, poems and inscriptions that are devoted to a rebirth in the Pure Land. Of this kind of literature, the most famous and important piece should be *Yuan wang sheng li zan ji* 願往生禮讚偈 (T. 47, 472-474c). This work consists of twenty hymns, each one begins with a phrase: "With the most sincere mind I take refuge in and pay homage to Amitabha Buddha of the West. " And it ends with the words, "Along with all sentient beings I hope to be reborn in the Secure and Happy Land." This work is attributed to Shandao 善導, the famous master of Pure Land Buddhism of the seventh century. The hymns are a mixture of recitation of hymns accompanied by the worship of the Buddha, which became the standard form of expressing hope in Buddhist liturgy during the later China. In this development, confession is usually present as a preface to the hope for rebirth. On this point, Shan-tao's hymn reads as follows,

> I sincerely hope that the three jewels of the ten directions and the sentient beings of the *dharmadhatu* would accept my confession and remember my purity. I declare that along with all the living beings of the *dharmadhatu*, I will abandon evils and take refugee in the mind of wisdom (*bodhicitta*). I will think of others with a compassionate mind and see them with the sight of Buddha, thus to become a member of the bodhi family, and associated with the friends of virtue (*Kalyanamitra*). We all will be reborn at the Land of Amitabha Buddha together, eventually to become Buddhas ... (T. 47, 474a-b).

The explanation of the hymns states that this kind of hope could be expressed at the time of worshipping the Buddha, or in the process of confession. It could even be done when one is sitting or standing. In that case, a believer is only required to fold his/her hands and to pray,

> I, a disciple am a common person subject to birth and death. Because of my sinful karma I will fall into the wheel of rebirth and death in the six realms and suffer miserably. I have had the fortune of meeting a friend of virtue in this life, thus to hear the name of the Buddha and his original vows. I recite the names of the Buddha whole-heartedly and pray for a rebirth in his land. I hope the Buddha would not abandon his original vows, and I resolve to be under his control and to receive his protection. Not knowing the glory and light of the Body of Buddha, I pray him kindly to manifest his magnificent body as well as those of Bodhisattvas, *Guan-yin* (*Avalokitesvara*) and Shih-chih (*Mahasthama-prapta*). May all of them appear along with their glorious worlds. After such a prayer is made, one should keep his correct thoughts whole-heartedly, thus entering into contemplation or to sleep. Some of them may even see these while the hope is expressed, or else may see it while asleep (T. 47, 474b).

The hope for a rebirth in the Pure Land became a popular goal for many Chinese, and the hymns of Shan-tao became a standard for expressing that hope. The structure of hope in the Pure Land Buddhism is very clear: that Amitabha Buddha had made his original vows to save suffering beings. The Buddha and the Bodhisattvas are compassionate and willing to work hard to fulfill the vowed hopes. Suffering sentient beings are without hope, but if they are fortunate and meet a virtuous friend who teaches them how to arouse their minds as to discover the Buddha and his world, to recite his name and to adorn his glory, they will ultimately be saved. When they become Buddhas and acquire spiritual powers, they will work hard in the same spirit and manner, continuously saving sentient beings who still remain suffering in the realms of existence. This is the great hope, great compassion and easy path to salvation in Chinese Buddhism.

If the above mentioned essays by Hui-si and Shan-dao are seen as the classical forms of the expression of hope, these forms possessed two distinguished features. First, they are closely associated with scriptural authority and comparatively free from non-Buddhist influence. Second, both of the essays put great emphasis on the religious goal, namely the salvation of all sentient beings. These two points marks classical features of Buddhist hope. This, however, does not mean that all other essays written by monks have followed this classical forms. there were always exceptions, especially those produced at the local level. Huang and his colleagues have selected manuscripts nos. 2855 and 3332 as illustrations of variations of the subject. Both the manuscripts are under the title of "Hui-xiang ta-yuan wen;" the witnesses and the hopes expressed in them are quite different from those in the two essays discussed above.

As far as witnesses are concerned, the Dunhuang manuscripts call a number of beings. These witnesses are divided into two groups; the writer wishes one group to watch and to hear the recitation of scripture from heaven. The deities of this group include Buddhas of the ten directions, Mahabodhisattvas, holy Arhans, the eight classes of Devas, gods of the world and the hidden, Yamaraja, the great deities of the five realms, the god of Tai-shan, the registrar of the records on destiny, officers of heaven and hells, good and evil boys, and those who are with deva eyes and deva ears. The second group of witnesses all stay in the world, including the transformed body of Buddhas, precious golden lettered scriptures, the Bodhisattva of great compassion who supports religious establishments, the Sravakas who had minor achievement and uphold scriptures, and immortals; all are invited to participate in the occasion. It is hoped that with their presence the correct law will be maintained, the lamp of wisdom will shine forever, the sun and moon and the stars circulate regularly, heavenly palaces appear in the world, all good and evils are clearly distinguished, and the correct law is preached.

The second section of the essay lists the hopes of the beneficiaries. It begins with the reigning Emperor, whose long life and peaceful reign are prayed for. Other beneficiaries include Lords and Ladies, princes and ministers, provincial and district officers. After personal welfare, the essay expresses hopes for human or natural conditions. This includes peace in all directions, happiness of people and the armed forces, prosperity of education and religious activities, the abandonment of all weapons, absence of natural disasters or abnormalities; carnivorous animals and birds will hidden there will be, safety for the pregnant mothers and their babies, safe return of travelers, imperial amnesty for convicted persons, and effective medicine for those who are suffering from serious and protracted illnesses. The next group of beneficiaries in the list of hopes includes the deaf, the lame, the dumb and the persons of low intelligence. It is hoped that with the merit gained from the vowed hopes these people will be able to hear, to walk, to talk, and to gain intellect. Finally, hope is expressed for peace to every teacher and monk, admission to the Pure Land for all deceased spirits; that former karma and errors will all be eliminated; so that from this life till future rebirths the prayer will reach the Sun of Buddha forever.[24]

There are a number of significant aspects showed in this short essay on hope. First, it does not explain why and how hopes could be effective. This indicates that at the time when this essay was written, hope in Chinese Buddhism was already an accepted idea and the essays of hope seemed to be already a regular feature of religious practice. Second, the number of spirits who are invited to witness the occasion had increased; and they were divided into two groups: one group to witness from heaven, and the other invited to participate in the ceremony. The third point of significance is the list of beneficiaries, in which not only the Emperor and royal family members are mentioned, but also local officials and others. This indicates that the manner of expressing hope is no longer limited to the high classes of Chinese society. The practice has been extended from elites down to local and common people. Based on the list of beneficiaries and the official titles mentioned therein, Huang and Tseng suggest that this essay could have been written by a monastic bureaucrat. This suggestion seems sound, as there are other similar pieces which clearly mention the name and the official position of the monk bureaucrat.[25]

Conclusion

From the foregoing discussions and the evidences showed therein, it seems clear that hope in Buddhism was very limited in early history. There was a change of attitude towards hope in Mahayana doctrines, and this Indian attitude inspired the Chinese mind deeply and extensively. This new spirit and attitude were further strengthened by the belief that the age of the deterioration of Buddhism is approaching.

This belief of coming doom and desperation for salvation had a very strong impact on Chinese Buddhists; it almost transformed Buddhism from a religion of wisdom into a religion of faith. Under this impact of fear and new doctrine, many Buddhists no longer depended on their own striving to achieve enlightenment, but relied on the compassion of the Buddha and Bodhisattvas. The generous spirit and the conversion of the Chinese elites into Buddhism brought some new development to the religion; the writing of essays on hope is one of them. Apart from the continuation of scriptural references such as the welfare for the sentient beings as found in Mahayana sutras, the Chinese have given more emphasis to benefits to deceased parents and relatives, and good fortune and health for family members who are alive. Besides hope for personal benefits, political authorities from the Emperor down to local officials, from civil to military authorities, from clergy to laity, from individual to group are all mentioned very often. In this respect, Buddhism seems more closely intertwined with Chinese tradition and society when compared with its Indian background.

There is another point worthy of attention, namely the writing of essays on hope are limited to the earlier development of Buddhism in China and there is no further example of those writings from the eleventh century on. These questions could be asked: What is the significance of this lack of later documents? Does this mean a change of attitudes of hope? Or the abandonment of the practice? Recent research on Buddhist liturgy as found in the Tun-huang manuscripts is very useful for answering these questions. After an examination of the Tang manuscripts of Buddhist liturgy, Wang Chuan finds that most of the Buddhist ceremonies begin with an invocation of the names of Buddhas, and conclude with the recitation of hymns on impermanence. The whole set of the ceremonies usually comprises twelve sections. The one on hope is the ninth. It is under the heading of "shuo-jie fa-yuan" or "Discourse on the hymn and expressing hopes." Wang also finds that the inclusion of hope ceremonies continued throughout later period of Chinese history.[26]. As Buddhist ceremony remains an essential practice in China and other parts of the East Asia, it seems safe to say hope still is an important factor in Chinese Buddhism.

Notes

1. R.L. Ottley, "Hope (Christian)," in *Encyclopedia of Religion and Ethics*, vol. 6, ed. James Hastings (New York: Scribner, 1959), pp. 779ff.

2. P. Shorey, "Hope (Greek and Roman)," in *Encyclopedia of Religion and Ethics*, vol. 6, ed. James Hastings (New York: Scribner, 1959), p. 780b.

3. P. Slater, "Hope" in Mircea Eliade et.al. *The Encyclopedia of Religion* (New York: Macmillan, 1987), p. 6, 459b-497.

4. W.L.King, *In the Hope of Nibbana* (La Salle: Open Court, 1964).

5. *The Pali Text Soceity Pali-English Dictionary* (London: Luzac, 1966), pp. 5, 93, 96, 407.

6. Wm.Th.de Bary, ed. *The Buddhist Tradition in India, China and Japan* (New York: Modern Library, 1969), p. 10.

7. Maha T. Narada, *A Manual of Abhidhamma* (Kanfy: Buddhist Publications, 1968), pp. 12f.

8. Rune Johansson, *The Psychology of Nirvana* (London: George Allan & Unwin, 1969), p. 50.

9. Maha T. Narada, *A Manual of Abhidhamma*, pp. 90f.

10. Johansson, *The Psychology of Nirvana*, a969, 28.

11. Narada, *A Manual of Abhidhamma*, p. 50.

12. N.G. Majumdar, *A Guide to the Sculptures in Indian Museum*, part I, (New Delhi: 1937), p. 88.

13. Alan Sponberg, ed., *Maitreya, the Future Buddha* (Cambridge: Cambridge University Press, 1988).

14. de Bary, ed., *The Buddhist Tradition in India, China and Japan*, p. 90.

15. G. Schopen, "The phrase saprthivipradesas caityabhuto bhavet in the Vajracchedika: Notes on the cult of the book in Mahayana," *Indo-Iranian Journal* 17 (1975): 147-81.

16. Hereafter "T." refers to *Taisho shinshu daizokyo* 大正新修大藏經 (Tokyo, 1924-35).

17. Faxian, *A Record of the Buddhist Countries*, translated by Li Yongxi (Beijing: The Chinese Buddhist Association, 1957), p. 22.

18. de Bary, ed., *The Buddhist Tradition in India, China and Japan*, p. 178.

19. Huang Zheng 黃徵 & Wu Wei 吳偉 eds., *Dunhuang yuanwan ji* 敦煌願文集 (Changsha: Yuelu chubanshe, 1996); cf. Huang Zheng, Zeng Liang 曾良 & Hong Yushuang 洪玉雙, *Dunhuang yuanwan yanjiu* 敦煌願文研究, (unpublished conference paper, 1996); cf. Jas Burgess, "Report on the

Buddhist cave temples and their inscriptions," *Archaeological Survey of Western India*, vol. IV (Varanasi: Indological Sook House, 1964).

20. Huang Zeng and Wu Wei, eds., *Dunhuang yuanwan ji*.

21. Ibid., pp. 287-288.

22. Ibid.

23. Paul Magnin, *La vie et l'œuvre de huissu* (517-577) (Paris, 1979).

24. Huang Zeng & Wu Wei, eds., *Dunhuang yuan wan ji*, p. 4.

25. Wan Gengyu 萬庚育, *Zhenguide lishi ziliao — mogaoku gongyangren huaxiang tiji* 珍貴的歷史資料 — 莫高窟供養人畫像題記, ed. Dunhuang yanjiuyuan 敦煌研究院編 (Beijing: Wenwu chubanshe, 1980), pp.179-193.

26. Wang Juan 汪娟, *Dunhuang lichanwan yanjiu* 敦煌禮懺文研究 (Taibei: Zhongguo wenhua daxue boshi lunwen 中國文化大學博士論文, 1996), pp. 282, 313, esp.305.

9

Enlightenment as Hope according to the True Buddha School

Wai-lun Tam

Hope is an important religious theme especially in the Christian tradition.[1] The Christian God is a God of hope (Rom. 15:13). For the Christian, hope lies in God's promises of the return of Christ, of resurrection of the dead, and of a new creation of all things.[2] Generally speaking, no similar promise is made by any god in the Buddhist tradition.[3] There is, however, on the basis of the Buddha's experience, a promise of a path, *Marga*, which leads us to enlightenment or *Nirvana*. It is achieved not by the grace of God but through our own effort. Therefore, the Buddhist hope is enlightenment.[4]

According to Webster's dictionary, one basic meaning of the word "hope" is "to desire with expectation of obtainment," or it is "a desire accompanied by expectation of a belief in fulfilment."[5] The Chinese equivalent "*xiwang*" 希望 has a similar meaning. According to the *Hanyu dacidian* 漢語大詞典, *xiwang* means to anticipate the appearance of a certain situation or the achieving of some aims. It also means a good desire or ideal.[6] According to this usage, hope involves an ideal and a goal, and an expectation of the fulfilment of that ideal and goal. When we use the word in such a way, hope in Buddhism, again, means enlightenment. It is hope for the attainment of the same profound enlightening experience achieved by Gautama Buddha under the Bodhi tree in the six century BCE. Central to the Buddhist belief is the availability of the enlightenment experience to all living beings. This belief is well expressed in the classical doctrine of the universality of Buddha nature.[7] However, finding a modern account of the Buddhist enlightenment experience is very difficult, if not impossible. This gives us the impression that enlightenment is, after all, a remote possibility, a utopia. The Buddhist enlightenment then becomes something that we can only study as a historical phenomenon rather than a living experience.

However, a school of Chinese Buddhism has recently emerged — The True Buddha School (*Zhen fozong* 真佛宗) — which offers an opportunity to study the concept of enlightenment. This school belongs to an esoteric form of Buddhism known as the Diamond vehicle or *Vajrayana*, which was not popular in China. The True Buddha School, whose members are mostly Chinese, has developed very fast. It was started in 1973 in Taiwan but it also attracts members from Chinese communities all over the world. The school calculated the number of its members in 1984 as forty thousand but in twelve years, it has increased one hundred times and numbers four million today.[8]

In this paper, I will analyse the description of the enlightenment experience according to the founder of the True Buddha school. I will also discuss the significance of his formulation of enlightenment to our understanding of Buddhist enlightenment experience. The founder of the True Buddha school is a prolific writer. He has produced, on average, six books per year since 1975 and his writings, which his disciples publish in a series, now number one hundred and seventeen volumes. This does not include his oral commentaries on selected Buddhist scriptures that his disciples are also publishing in book form.[9] In this study, I have limited myself to his early writings, i.e. the first fifty books of his collection.[10] I will concentrate my study on the period from the school's first appearance in Taiwan to the founder's migration to Seattle in 1984.[11] It is in Seattle that the founder achieved an experience that he called enlightenment.

The founder of the True Buddha school is a Chinese named Lu Shengyan 盧勝彥, later known as the Grand Master or the living Buddha Liansheng 蓮生 (literally, born from a lotus). Lu was born in Taiwan in 1945.[12] He was known to the public first as a famous diviner, and from the year 1969 to the year 1975, he was divining people's future by means of a method involving the use of a ten-foot bamboo pole.[13] Lu claimed that every day about two hundred people came to him for divination.[14] In 1975, Lu published three books,[15] telling fascinating stories about his divination and his encounter with the world of spirits. His books were among the season's best sellers and made him even more popular and famous. Lu claimed to have received five hundred letters each month from his readers and more than a thousand requests for an appointment to see him.[16] Unwilling to spend all his time meeting his admirers, Lu limited his appointments to three nights a week.[17]

Divination was hardly Lu's primary career. He received his tertiary education in a military college in Taiwan and was trained as a surveyor. To begin with, Lu was a Christian who belonged to the Presbyterian church,[18] but he changed his faith after he had achieved the ability of divination in a series of extraordinary events. These included a vision of gods and a meeting with invisible immortals. We will first examine the series of events that transformed Lu's life and that constitutes the narrative or mythic dimension of the True Buddha school.[19]

(1) Meeting a Taoist Priest in a Dream

The turning point of Lu's life was a series of extraordinary encounters that he had when he was twenty-four. Lu told his story in his eighteenth book.[20] It began with a meeting, in a dream, with a Taoist priest who later became his teacher.[21] One morning, Lu had an unusual dream of entering a temple that looked surprisingly familiar to him. This is unusual because, being a Christian, Lu had never entered a temple before. An old Taoist priest (*Daozhang* 道長) came forward to greet him and told him that he was expecting Lu. When Lu requested a clarification, the old priest simply knocked on his head with his whisk. Lu then woke from his dream.

(2) Vision of Bodhisattvas

The same afternoon, Lu followed his mother to worship in a Taoist temple known as the Palace of the Jade Emperor.[22] Lu stayed outside the temple to watch people worshipping. An old lady who knelt before the statue of a god drew his attention. Suddenly, the old lady stood up and called his name. Lu was overwhelmed as he had never met or been introduced to the lady before. The old lady asked him to come forward and asked him whether he was a Christian who graduated from college and worked as a surveyor. Lu was astonished that lady knew so much about him. He was even more shocked when the old lady started to talk about the dream he had that morning, though he had told nobody about it. The old lady told Lu it was Bodhisattvas' intention that he should come forward and preach the Buddha's teachings. Lu objected, as he knew nothing about Buddhism, but the old lady asked him to kneel down before the statues of the gods with his palms together. When Lu did what he was told to do, with his eyes closed, miracles happened. Three bodhisattvas appeared to him, each sitting on a lotus throne. They gave him three messages: "turn your mind to the Buddha," "turn your mind to the *Dharma*," "turn your mind to kindness," respectively. Lu also saw a banner of red cloth with two Chinese characters written on it in gold: loyalty and righteousness. A voice told him that it was a message bestowed upon him from the Jade Emperor, the main deity of the temple. They should be the principles by which Lu guided his future life. Lu was absolutely stunned by what he saw and heard as he was completely unprepared for all these incredible happenings.

(3) Revealing of His Previous Incarnation

After this extraordinary vision of Bodhisattvas, Lu returned to his dormitory. That night he lay in bed but was unable to fall asleep. Pondering what had happened during the day, Lu had another vision. [23] Suddenly, he smelled fragrant sandal wood. A circle of light appeared in front of him and his body felt as if it were rising lightly. Lu felt that he flew into a circle of light under the guidance of a certain force. It seemed to him that he was in the illusory realm of the Great Void (*taixu* 太虛). He met many Buddhas and Bodhisattvas whom he did not recognize. Then, he saw large lotus blossoms, the size of automobile tires, in many different colours. In each lotus stood a child holding a small lotus of different colours. A voice spoke into his ears telling him that this was his previous incarnation — white lotus youth, *Padmakumura*, an obscure deity. [24]

(4) Visit by an Invisible Taoist Teacher

Two days later, at one o'clock in the morning, a voice wakened Lu. [25] The voice identified himself as his spiritual teacher (*lingshi* 靈師) who came to transmit to him the Taoist teachings of the School of the Three Pure Ones. [26] Lu's spiritual teacher started the lesson with a Taoist ritual dance called the Star Worshipping Footstep. [27] An invisible force simply lifted and moved Lu's feet to teach him the footstep. In the following years, the same invisible teacher continued to come after midnight to teach Lu different spells and hand gestures.

Later, the invisible teacher called himself 'Mr. Three-Peaks-Nine States,' (*Sanshan jiuhou* 三山九侯) , a little known immortal.

(5) Studying under a Taoist Recluse

Under the direction of his spiritual teacher, Lu sought out a highly accomplished Taoist master by the name of Qingzhen 清真 (d. 1971) on Mount Lientou 蓮頭山.[28] Lu told us that Qingzhen was in his eighties. He was a former Buddhist monk by the name of Liaoming, who became a recluse to practice Taoism in Mount Lientou. Qingzhen accepted Lu's request to become his disciple only after Lu had revealed his birthday and birth hour. According to Qingzhen, Lu's birthday happened to be the same as the famous Taoist Heavenly Master Zhang. [29] Suddenly Lu recognized Master Qingzhen as the Taoist whom he dreamed of on the day he first had the vision of the Bodhisattvas. Lu continued to learn from Master Qingzhen for two years on his days off from military service, until the death of his master.[30] He learnt from him different Taoist practices like the writing of magical charms, spells, alchemy, geomancy, and the divination which made him famous among the public.[31]

Lu did not make his 'transformation experience' public until six years after the encounter.[32] He did indicate, however, that he had tried to make sense of his mystical encounter by sharing and discussing it with different Buddhist monks and lay preachers.[33] They, unfortunately, all denied his experience as demonic. This, perhaps, explains why initially Lu did not want to reveal his experience to the public. Despite the denial of his experience by the Buddhists, Lu did formally become a Buddhist. He took refuge (*guiyi* 歸依) with a number of monks and received the precepts of the Bodhisattvas in 1972.[34]

As we have mentioned, Lu had offered a divination service to the public for six years after his mystical encounter. His skill in divination must have attracted a group of followers that allowed him to establish a small temple in his house in 1972.[35] Interestingly enough, Lu registered his group as a group member of the Taoist Association of China (*Zhonghua daojiao hui* 中華道教會).[36] We can recall the message revealed to him in his mystical encounter with Bodhisattvas: "turn your mind to the Buddha" and "turn your mind to *dharma*." The old lady told Lu that it was the Bodhisattvas' intention that he was to preach the Buddha's teachings. To complicate the issue further, the training Lu received from both his mortal and immortal teacher after his vision was Taoist in nature. His immortal teacher had clearly stated to him that the teaching he transmitted to Lu was that of the School of the Three Pure Ones.

Moreover, Lu's mortal teacher was a Taoist priest. Among the things Lu learnt from his teacher were Taoist practices such as the writing of magical charms, spells, alchemy, geomancy, and divination techniques. These are seldom, if ever, taught in the Buddhist schools. The training Lu received was, however, supposed to prepare him for his mission of preaching the Buddhist teaching. Lu eventually called his school Lianxian 靈仙 (School of spirits and the Immortals) which obviously has a Taoist overtone.[37] In addition, the books written by Lu in 1975 and afterwards were full of stories of Taoist activities of exorcism and divination. I, therefore, believe that, despite Lu's indication that his mission was to preach the Buddhist teaching, the True Buddha school was initially a Taoist group. In 1973, Lu established a second temple in his new home.[38] The main statues in his temple were the golden mother of the Primordial pond, a Taoist deity,[39] Sakya Buddha, and *Ksitigarbha* (Dizang wang 地藏王), a famous Buddhist Bodhisattva. This shows Lu's inclination for Buddhism. Lu explained his inclination for Buddhism by the fact that he found the Buddhist scripture, institution and ritual more structured than the Taoist ones.[40] The Buddhist school that Lu first studied was not a Tantric school (*mizong* 密宗) but a scriptural school (*xianzong* 顯宗).[41] It was in 1976 that Lu first had contact with the esoteric form of Buddhism by meeting with His Holiness the XVI Gayalwa Karmapa, the leader of the Kagyu (*bkav brgyud*) school of Tantric Buddhism.[42] It was as late as 1981 that Lu started to be formally initiated as an adept of Tantric Buddhism.[43] In 1984, Lu renamed his school as the *Lingxian zhen fo zhong* 靈仙真佛宗 (the True Buddha School of Spirits and the Immortals).[44] For simplicity, Lu later dropped the word Lingxian and called his school True Buddha School only.[45] The change of the name was occasioned by an incident in which some of Lu's disciples had usurped the School's name to publish a magazine. They also used it as an excuse to collect money from other believers without Lu's consent. Lu, therefore, renamed his school to differentiate it from the original name which had been usurped by the magazine.[46] I believe, however, that the significance of this change in a name is that it reveals a similarity between the Taoism and the Tantric Buddhism. It is the similarity that makes the transition of the school possible. We will return to this point later.

Early Teaching

Lu's reason for revealing his mystical experience six years after his encounter was to substantiate his teaching of activating the soul (*qiling* 啟靈).[47] Lu learnt the technique from his mortal teacher master Qianzhen.[48] As we have mentioned above, Lu had attracted followers since 1973 and his teaching to his early followers consisted basically of the technique of activating the soul. In order to activate one's soul, one has to practice meditation. The purpose of activating one's soul is so that one can sense, hear, or see, other souls in the spiritual world. The idea behind the concept is that a soul can be perceived only by another soul.[49] We cannot perceive the soul with our empirical sensual organs but perception is possible with our own soul. The precondition is, however, that we have to have an activated soul to possess the power of supersensory perception (*lingjue* 靈覺). According to Lu, the soul of an ordinary person is inert until his death.[50] Through practice, one can activate one's own soul in this life thus enabling one to perceive the existence of the soul. Lu's own mystical encounters, which we have described in detail above, are stories of his sudden plunge into the world of spirit. Without his asking, the ability to experience the unseen world had been bestowed on him. His mortal teacher, however, taught him that there was a way to activate one's soul to perceive other souls. This is the technique of *qiling*. Through *qiling*, Lu wanted to convince the world of the existence of souls which he believed would be the basis of all religion.[51] The essence of the practice is to experience involuntary movement of the body during one's meditation. It is not a new discovery that one may experience vibration of the body at a certain stage of one's meditation. Yin Shizi 因是子, for instance, in his famous *Yin shizi's Method of Meditation* published in 1914 also reported a similar phenomenon.[52] Lu, however, interpreted this vibration of one's body during meditation as the sign of activation of one's soul (*lingdong* 靈動). According to Lu, this involuntary movement of the body shows a generation of psychic power (*lingli* 靈力). When it is directed to one's ears and eyes, one can hear and see the spiritual world. The technique of *qiling* consists of three simple steps:[53]

(1) Sitting quietly;

(2) Chanting the Buddha's name or the name of any deity according to one's religion for about fifty minutes;

(3) Closing the palms together in prayer.

According to Lu, the vibration of the body will take place spontaneously. How soon it happens varies from individual to individual. For some it happens after a few practices. Others may take months or even years before experiencing vibration of the body during meditation. Since the vibration of the body is a concrete experience, it strengthens one's faith in both meditation and the existence of soul. Lu, therefore, claimed that he was not aiming at starting a new religion,[54] rather, he was using his teaching of *ling* to substantiate people's faith in Buddhism.[55] He later systematized his ling teaching into four steps of which qiling is only the first step:[56]

(1) *Qiling* (activation of the soul);[57]

(2) *Zhuji* 築基 (Physical exercise, literally ground works that prepare the body for advanced mystical experience of union with the ultimate);[58]

(3) *Tuna* 吐納 (Taoist Breathing exercise);[59]

(4) *Ruwo woru* 入我 我入 (Mystical experience of Dissolution of oneself).[60]

Here one sees clearly that the *qiling* teaching of Lu is only a preparation for a mystical experience of union with the ultimate. We will discuss more this further when we turn to Lu's enlightenment experience. As we discover later, even *qiling* is possible only at an advanced stage of meditation. Lu has oversimplified the process of *qiling* so as to attract followers.

Although he shows he possessed a mystical power of communicating with the spiritual world, Lu never claimed that he reached enlightenment before he migrated to Seattle. Shortly after the publication of his three books on his *ling* teaching, Lu announced that he would no longer do divination.[61] His success in divination had created the jealousy among other diviners,[62] attracted the attention of criminals,[63] and involved him in many tests from ignorant people — things which began to occupy most of his time.[64] In 1976, Lu announced that he would retreat for private religious study for three years.[65] Even after his retreat, Lu had to move from place to place to prevent people from finding him.[66] The rush of people to see him was so great that he could hardly have a moment to himself. He had received over ten thousand letters collected in twelve boxes that he could never find time to answer.[67] Eventually in 1982, he moved overseas to Seattle to find a quiet place to explore his spiritual growth. One year after his arrival in Seattle, Lu claimed that he had achieved the final goal of his practice — enlightenment.

Enlightenment Experience

In his 45th book, Lu, for the first time, claims that he has achieved enlightenment (dezheng 得證).[68] Lu describes his attainment as a process of condensing the "luminosity" of his body between the eyebrow in his meditation. This "luminosity" is conjured up by a practice of the visualization of light together with breathing exercises during his meditation. Lu explains that we first need to achieve concentration of our thoughts, spirit (shen, 神), essence (jing 精), and our breath, qi 氣.[69] Then we shall activate the return of our essence (jing) and breath (qi) to the spot between the eyebrows and arouse our "inner flame." It is this "inner flame" that produces luminosity.[70] The concentration of one's essence and spirit, and returning them to the spot between the eyebrows is likened to the process of transmitting water from the root through the trunk to the branches of a tree.[71] The returning of our essence and spirit is a spontaneous process that starts when we achieve a state of absolute tranquillity.[72] The theory that body consists of essence (jing), breath (qi) and spirit (shen) comes from the inner alchemy (neidan 內丹) tradition of Taoism.[73] According to this tradition, the three life energies that make up human beings are: (1) sexual energy or reproductive energy, (2) the breath or the vital energy of the body, and (3) the shen which is the spirit of the person. Taoist practices seek to transform the jing to the shen. There are three stages of refinement:

(1) from jing to qi (transformation of the essence of our body into breath);

(2) from qi to shen (circulation of breath in our body and refinement of our breath to spirit);

(3) from *shen* to emptiness (returning to one's original nature, the world of the numinous).[74]

By using the language of the *neidan* tradition from Taoism, Lu described his enlightenment experience as a process of activating and circulating the essences of one's body upwards and concentrating them in the spot between the eyebrows, thereby entering a state of luminosity. His enlightenment experience can also be described in three stages:

(1) A stage of no thoughts or initial tranquillity (*chujing* 初靜). This is the stage when our spirit and essence return and accumulate between our eyebrows.

(2) A stage of absolute tranquillity (*jingji* 精極). This is the stage when our soul is activated. Therefore we can see that Lu's early teaching of activation of soul, qilian, is attained only at an advanced state of meditation. According to Lu, this activation of the soul is achieved by nonaction, *wuwei* 無為, as described in the *Daode qing* 道德經 [75] or by "producing a mind which stays in no place" as stated in the *Diamond Sutra*.[76]

(3) A stage of union between Heaven and human being. It is also known as a shower of the *tianxin* 天心.[77] Lu also describes it as a merging with the consciousness of the universe.[78]

In his 51st book, Lu reiterates his enlightenment experience in the language of Tantric Buddhism. It is in this book that Lu first claims his attainment of Buddhahood.[79] He describes his attainment in four steps:

(1) Sitting in meditation according to the Great Sun *Tathagatha* (Vairocana Buddha). This consists of sitting in a full lotus posture. One has to place the right leg upon the left one. The left hand is laid upon the right one and both being placed on the legs. The body should be erect with the chest raised and the chin down. The mouth should be kept shut with the tongue touching the palate and the eyes concentrate on one object.[80]

(2) Practice of concentration on one subject (ekagra).[81]

(3) Arising of internal heat (*linger* 靈熱, literally spiritual heat) or inner flame (*neihuo* 內火). To "ignite" the inner flame, one first visualizes a flame burning at the spot where the three nadis meet.[82] The three nadis are the two imaginary paths running along two sides of the spinal column and one running within. The three nadis meet at the spot of four finger width

from the navel which is also known as the *dantian* 單田. By respiratory technique, one directs breath into the *dantian* to fan up one's imaginary inner flame until it rises up to the heart, throat, eyebrows and finally to the top of the head.[83]

(4) One will then enter a stage which is described as the heavenly nectar, or sweet dew, dropping from the head to meet the flame rising from the belly, filling the whole body with bliss.[84]

The theory of the arising and circulating of life energy upwards through the seven energy centres of our body is known as the *kundalini* in the Tantric tradition of both Hinduism and Buddhism.[85] This experience is sometimes expressed by the image of a twinbodied statue — conjunction of male and female opposites.[86] Lu explained it as a symbolic representation of ultimate happiness. According to Lu, the twin-bodied statue never indicates a practice of sex but a symbolic representation of the *yin* 陰 meeting with the *yang* 陽. The *ying* is the nectar at the top of the head and the *yang* is the inner flame at a navel. Both are present within our own body. They can be experienced only at the highest stage of one's meditation.

Later, Lu added that two practices are helpful for the process. One is the practice of reciting *mantra*.[87] The other is the practice of certain physical exercises aimed at loosening the seven nerve centres.[88] The seven nerve centres are the seven vital spots in our body where there are thick clusters of nerves. They are the anus, the genitalia, belly, heart, throat, between the eyebrows and at the top of head. The seven centres represent the elimination, reproduction, blood circulation, respiration, and ideation function of our body. These centres are known to the yoga through experience in the past.[89] The specially designed physical exercise eases the passage of the inner flame from the belly to the top of the head.

Through the mouth of the eight infant messengers of Manjusri that he met in his meditation, Lu reiterates his experience of enlightenment in four stages:

(1) A stage of warming, that is the arising of inner flame;

(2) A stage of breakthroughs, that is, when the inner flame arises to the eyebrows, light is emitted and the light breaks through the head;

(3) A stage of maintaining and testing. This is the stage during

which the meditator must resist the distraction of any illusions which present themselves;

(4) A stage of attaining, that is the union of one's luminosity with the luminosity of the ultimate consciousness of the universe[90]

Therefore, the enlightenment experience according to Lu is a reintegration of microcosms with the macrocosms.[91] The latter are represented by an immense boundless ocean of cosmic consciousness. It is unfolded to us during the highest stage of meditation. The former is represented by our own consciousness. Enlightenment experience is the state of oneness of our consciousness with the universal consciousness. A frequent description of enlightenment experience is a union of one's luminosity with the luminosity of the great sun that appears outside and approaches us in meditation. It is called the union of the luminosity of a son (*ziguang* 子光) with the luminosity of a mother (*muguang* 母光).[92] It is also known as a returning to the sea of Virocana, merging with the light of Buddha of the ten directions.[93]

Lu has used two traditions to represent his enlightenment experience. One is the *neidan* tradition of Taoism. The other is the Tantric tradition of the Indian religion. The central idea is that enlightenment has a corporeal or somatic aspect. There is a reservoir of latent cosmic energy lying in every human being. The energy is, however, in a scattered and latent state. The main idea of enlightenment is to activate and reunite all the scattered energy of our body, causing it to rise upwards along the spinal column, passing through various vital spots in the body.[94] The arousal of our life energy, causing it to dart upwards until reaching the top of our head will elevate us to a state of spiritual ecstasy which is described as the immersion of our ego with an immense boundless ocean of consciousness. It is marked by a sensation of immense light and a feeling of awe and bliss. This enlightening experience is brought about by a long persistent practice of intense mental concentration and absorption plus a cultivation of virtues.[95]

In Lu's opinion, enlightenment, however, is more than a state of spiritual ecstasy. It has to do with the obtaining of immortality. To be able to concentrate one's life energy, causing it to merge with the universal consciousness, is a technique for dying so that one is liberated from the cycle of transmigration. According to Lu, one has to be skilled and experienced in reaching the state of oneness with the universal consciousness. Entering the same state at the end of our life means emancipation from the cycle of the rebirth. It is nirvana without any remainder of the *karma*.[96]

The goal of Buddhism, the third noble truth, is often expressed in negative terms, especially in the Indian Pali scripture. It is referred to as extinction of thirst, absence of desire, and extinction of illusion and termination of the cycle of the rebirth.[97] It has to be put in negative terms because the enlightenment experience is so out of the ordinary. It belongs to a totally different category which human language cannot adequately describe. Walpola Rahula has put it nicely in a simile,

> The tortoise just returned to the lake after a walk on the land. 'Of course,' the fish said, 'you mean swimming.' The tortoise tried to explain that one could not swim on the land, that it was solid, and that one walked on it. But the fish insisted that there could be nothing like it, that it must be liquid like his lake with waves, and that one must be able to dive and swim there.[98]

This shows that the enlightenment experience is supramundane and abstract. It is bound to be out of the reach of ordinary people. The account of the enlightenment by Lu departed from the traditional account. He brought in ideas from Taoist and Tantric traditions to add a somatic dimension to the enlightenment experience, making it more tangible and down to earth. A somatic dimension means that enlightenment involves the whole complex of body and mind. It is a metaphysical concept of the union of the ego with cosmic consciousness. Yet it is realized in our physical body. Enlightenment has a somatic aspect and has a corresponding effect on our body which is a circulation of life energy within our body.[99]

Lu has also shown that the *neidan* tradition of Taoism has a parallel with the Tantric school of Buddhism — an area that calls for further research before their relationship can be stated more clearly.[100]

In his teaching, Lu reintroduces the concept of soul into Buddhism. His early teaching concerning activating our soul, or *qiling*, violates one basic teaching of Buddhism, namely the theory of no soul, but Lu has not dealt with the issue in a systematic way in his writings.[101] Given his description of his own enlightenment experience, we may state his argument as follows: the doctrine of no soul is a description of the enlightenment experience of the Buddha. Enlightenment is a dissolution of our soul and its integration into the cosmic consciousness. Therefore, an independent unchanging soul is not compatible with the concept of eternal life.

Enlightenment as an upward flowing of one's spiritual energy and as a reintegration of a microcosm with the macrocosm is seen as a lofty attainment, out of the reach of ordinary people. As Lu confesses, people come to him with day to day problems rather than with hope of enlightenment. How to make a point of contact between the lofty religious end and the mundane needs of ordinary people is a basic issue for many major religious traditions. Lu solves this paradox by teaching different expedient teachings. To people who come to him for increasing their fortunes, Lu teaches the practice of meditation on the god of wealth. He teaches them to visualize the god of wealth to bestow on the adept what he or she wants.[102] To those who are obsessed with their problems of romance, Lu teaches the practices of magnetization that draw people together and harmonize human relationships.[103] He teaches them to visualize the god of love (*Raja*).[104] For people who come to him with problems of health, Lu teaches them to meditate on the Buddha of medicine.[105] The key to enlightenment appears to be the ability to concentrate on one object, and visualization is the key to concentration.[106] The process of upward flowing of one's spiritual energy occurs spontaneously when one attains utmost concentration.

The message of the True Buddha school has to do primarily with spiritual uplift. It aims at elevating us to the state of spiritual ecstasy through which eternal life is attained. Although the True Buddha school seeks to answer the daily demands of secular life, its primary emphasis is on the sublime and the holy. The followers of the True Buddha school seek to synthesize their high ideals with the daily demands of secular life, and to transform our mundane needs and desires and redirect them step by step to the lofty goal of enlightenment.

Appendix 1

Abbreviation of Reference to the Writings of Lu Sheng Yan, the Founder of the True Buddha School.

1   Book 1 to book 17 are Lu's literary works written before his conversion to Buddhism and are outside the scope of this study.

2   I give only the English translation of the title of his works in the following list. Please refer to appendix 2 for the Chinese title of his works.

3   The edition of his works I am using is the Hong Kong reprint edition (Hong Kong: Qingshan chubanshe) in which no date of publication is given. Whenever it is possible, I give the date in accordance with his dated preface found in most of his works.

Book 18 A *Causal Discussion of Spiritual Divination* (1975)

Book 19 A *Causal Discussion of Spiritual Divination* (II) (1975)

Book 20 *Between the Spirits and Me* (1975)

Book 21 *The super-sensation of the Soul* (1976)

Book 22 *Studies on Activation of the Soul* (1976)

Book 23 *An Autobiography of the Spirits* (1976)

Book 24 *An Autobiography of the Spirits* (II) (1976)

Book 25 *The Mystery of the Spirit of Land* (1976)

Book 26 *Mysterious Power* (1976)

Book 27 *The World of Spirits* (n.d.)

Book 28 *An Inquiry into the Dark Learning of the Spirit of Land* (1977)

Book 29 *On the Sound of Spring* (1977)

Book 30 *Miscellaneous Writings in my House* (1977)

Book 31 *The Flying Carpet of the East* (1977)

Book 32 *The Wonder of Fate* (1978)

Book 33 *The Small Boat Carrying my Spiritual Thoughts* (1978)

Book 34 *The Mystery of Reincarnation* (1978)

Book 35 *The Anger of a Mud-made Bodhisattva* (1978)

Book 36 *Strange Stories and Extraordinary Tales* (1979)

Book 37 *A Collection of Mysterious Essays* (1980)

Book 38 *Lu Sheng Yan's Discourse on Spirits* (1981)

Book 39 *The Truth of Extraordinary Spirits* (1981)

Book 40 *On Writing Spiritual Charms* (1983)

Book 41 *Secret Teaching on Communication with Spirits* (1982)

Book 42 *The World Through the Third Eye* (1983)

Book 43 *Tales of Subduing Demons and Devils* (1983)

Book 44 *Record of Journey to Study the Spirit of Land* (1983)

Book 45 *The Teaching of Meditation on Luminosity* (1983)

Book 46 *The Practitioner in Seattle* (1983)

Book 47 *The Dark Teaching of the Black School* (1983)

Book 48 *The Enlightenment of the Master* (1983)

Book 49 *The Diamond Teaching of the Immortal* (1984)

Book 50 *A Reply with Anger to Slanders* (1984)

Book 51 *Mahamudra and the Highest Tantric Teaching* (1984)

Book 52 *A Small Flavour of Chan* (1984)

Book 53 *Between the Buddha and the Demon* (1984)

Book 54 *The Expedient Teaching of the Tantric School* (1984)

Book 55 *Main Tenets of Mahamudra Teaching* (1984)

Book 56 *The Perfect Teaching of the Tantric School* (n.d.)

Appendix 2

Chinese Title of Lu Sheng Yan's Publication (No. 1-17 乃早期文學作品，已售缺)

18.	靈機神算漫談	40.	靈仙飛虹法
19.	靈機神算漫談 （續）	41.	通靈秘法書
20.	靈與我之間	42.	第三眼世界
21.	靈魂的超覺	43.	伏魔平妖傳
22.	啟靈學	44.	地靈仙蹤
23.	靈的自白書	45.	坐禪通明法
24.	靈的自白書 （續）	46.	西雅圖的行者
25.	神秘的地靈	47.	黑教黑法
26.	玄秘的力量	48.	上師的證悟
27.	靈的世界	49.	靈仙金剛大法
28.	地靈探勝玄理	50.	金剛怒目集
29.	泉聲幽記	51.	無上密與大手印
30.	禪天盧什記	52.	小小禪味
31.	東方的飛甋	53.	佛與魔之間
32.	命運的驚奇	54.	密宗羯摩法
33.	載著靈思的小舟	55.	大手印指歸
34.	輪迴的秘密	56.	密教大圓滿
35.	泥菩薩的火氣	57.	道法傳奇錄
36.	傳奇與異聞	58.	皈依者的感應
37.	神奇的錦囊	59.	真佛法語
38.	盧勝彥談靈	60.	湖濱別有天
39.	異靈的真諦	61.	道林妙法音

Notes

1. In the ALTA Religion database on CD-Rom of the American Theological Library Association (August 1996), there are altogether 4, 557 entries of works on the theme of Hope.

2. See Jürgen Moltmann, *Theology of Hope: On the Ground and the Implication of a Christian Eschatology* (London: SCM Press, 1967), p. 15.

3. An exception will be the devotional form of Buddhism known as the Pure Land Buddhism which teaches the existence of a Buddhist paradise called Pure Land or Land of Bliss. For a recent discussion, see James Foard et al. ed., *The Pure Land Tradition, History and Development* (Berkeley & LA: Regents of the University of California, 1996). See also Luis O. Gomez, *Land of Bliss: the Paradise of the Buddha of Measureless Light* (Honolulu: University of Hawaii Press, 1996).

4. In contrast with the huge amount of scholarly discussion on the theme of Christian hope, there is not much work on the theme of Buddhist hope of enlightenment. As Tu Wei-ming has observed, 'despite obvious advances in textual, historical, and cultural analysis, very little has been (and perhaps can ever be) said about "enlightenment" in the scholarly community.' See his "Thinking of 'Enlightenment' Religiously," in *Sudden and Gradual Approaches to Enlightenment in Chinese Thought,* ed., Peter N. Gregory (Honolulu: University of Hawaii Press, 1987), p. 447.

5. *Merriam Webster's Collegiate Dictionary*, Tenth edition (Massachusetts: Merriam-Webster, 1996); entry on 'Hope.'

6. Luo zhufeng (ed.), *Hanyu dacidian* 漢語大字典 (Shanghai: Hanyu dacidian chubanshe, 1990) vol. 3, p. 697, entry on "xiwang 希望," the third and fourth meaning of the word.

7. On Buddha nature, see Sallie King, *Buddha Nature* (Albany: State University of New York Press, 1991) and Griffiths Paul J., *On Being Buddha: the Classical Doctrine of Buddha Nature* (New York: State University of new York Press, 1994).

8. Figures given by the True Buddha School temple in Hong Kong known as the Chen Fuh Tsung Hong Kong Lui Tsang Szu (Leizang ci). It is located at 31/F, New Treasure Centre, 10 Ng Fong Street, San Po Kong, Kowloon, Hong Kong.

9. The Buddhist scriptures that the founder of the True Buddha School has taught includes: the Heart Sutra (T8: 848-849), Kumarajiva's translation

of the shorter Sukhavativyuha sutra (T12: 346-348), the Scripture of the Original Vows of the Bodhisattva Ksitigarbha (Dizang wan) (T13: 777-790), and The Great Exposition of the Stages of the Path of Tantric Buddhism by Tsong Kha Pa (1357-1419). The preaching on these scriptures are recorded in tapes and are in the process of publishing in book form by the founder's disciples in Taiwan. This piece of information has been provided to me by the True Buddha School temple in Hong Kong.

10. See the appendix for a list of his writings. For the sake of simplicity, Lu's works will be quoted by number. Full bibliographic information are given in the appendix.

11. The True Buddha School Temple in Seattle is located at 17012 NE 40th CT Redmond, WA 98052, Seattle, United States of America.

12. Biographical information on the founder of the True Buddha School can be obtained through the home page of the school at the World Wide Website, http://www.ee.ucla.edu/~yang/truebuddha.html. See also Zheng Zhimeng, "Lu shengyan yu lianxian zhenfo zong" paper presented at the International Academic Conference on the History of Taiwan: Society, Economics and Colonization, Tamkang University, Taipei, 12-13 May 1995.

13. See Book 19, p. 23. The method of divination used by Lu consists of two kinds: (1)Yizhang qing, a possession divination which involves the use of a ten foot bamboo and a divining youth. The main idea is that Lu will empower a chosen youth so that he is possessed. By pointing with the bamboo to the appropriate characters pre-posted on a wall to form a sentence, the youth gives the answer to the question asked. (2) Huangji shu a spiritual calculation which Lu has not explained in detail. Apparently, it involves the calculation of one's eight characters and the fate of one's person can be figured out accordingly.

14. Book 46, p. 57.

15. Book 18 through 20.

16. Book 20, p. 1; cf. Book 21, p. 176.

17. Book 20, p. 39.

18. See Lu's brief autobiographical note in his preface to his book 18, p.2.

19. I have borrowed the term from Ninian Smart, *Worldviews: Crosscultural Explorations of Human Beliefs* (2nd ed.; New Jersey: Prentice Hall, 1995), pp. 74-89. Smart discusses every religious tradition in seven dimensions. Narrative or mythic dimension is one among the seven.

20. This book is translated into English by Janny Chow as *Encounters With*

the World of Spirits (California: Purple Lotus Society, 1995). The translation can be downloaded from the World Wide Web-site http://www.ee.ucla.edu/~yang/truebuddha.html.

21. Book 18, p. 4; Janny Chow, trans., *Encounters With the World of Spirits*, p. 7.

22. See Book 18, pp. 5-8; also Janny Chow, trans., *Encounters with the World of Spirits*, pp. 7-10.

23. Book 18, pp. 11-12; Janny Chow, trans., *Encounters With the World of Spirits*, pp. 13-14.

24. Lu did not reveal the exact name of his previous incarnation until he wrote his third book. See Book 20, p. 59.

25. Book 18, pp. 13-16; Janny Chow, trans., *Encounters With the World of Spirits*, pp. 15-18.

26. The three Pure Ones refer to the Taoist triad: i) the Prime Heaven God (Yuanshi tianzun 元妨天尊), the representative of the Supreme Purity Sect; ii) the Efficacious Treasure Heaven God (lingbao tianzun 靈寶天尊), the representative of the Efficacious Treasure sect; iii) the Dao de Heaven God (Daode tianzun 道德天尊), the representative of the Celestial Master sect. I believe that the school of the three Pure Ones here refers not to a specific school. It means, instead, that a teaching embraces the teachings of all the three above-mentioned Taoist schools. See Zhongguo daojiao xiehui 中國道教協會 and Suzhou daojiao xiehui, eds., *Daojiao dacidian* 道教大字典 (Beijing: Huaxia chubanshe, 1993), entry on 'Sanqing shen 三清神' (the three Pure gods), p. 87.

27. For a study on the Taoist ritual dance, see the article by Poul Andersen, "The Practice of Bugang," *Cashiers d'Extreme Asie*, 5 (1989-1990), pp. 15-53.

28. Book 18, pp. 21-24; Janny Chow, trans., *Encounters With the World of Spirits*, pp. 23-26.

29. Master Zhang or Zhang tianshi 張天師 refers to Zhang daoling 張道陵 (34-156 CE), the first heavenly master or tianshi. He was born on the fifteen day of the first month of the tenth year of Jianwu. See *Daojiao dacidian*, entry on 'Zhang tianshi 張天師,' p. 590. Lu was born on May 18, 1945, at two o'clock in the afternoon. His claim to have the same birth date and hour as Zhang tianshi must be based on a different tradition unknown to me.

30. Book 31, p. 42, and Book 18, p. 22.

31. Book 18, pp. 22-23, and Book 25, p. 1.

32. Book 18, p. 4.

33. According to Lu, the monks he had consulted includes Yinshun, Huisan, Xiandun, Jueguang, Leguo, Daoan (Book 36, p. 139). The lay preachers he had consulted include Zhufei 朱斐 and Li bingnan (Book 18, pp. 55-59). See also Book 50, p. 27.

34. Book 18, pp. 60-62, and Book 43, pp. 164-165.

35. His first temple is located at number 39 Lixing road in Taizhong, see Book 20, p. 89. I got the date for the establishing of his temple from Book 18, pp. 65-69. On the name of his temple, Leizang ci, see Book 18, p. 18.

36. Book 18, p. 69.

37. Book 18, p. 158 & Book 19, p. 87. Lu emphasizes here that his lianxian school is a Buddhist school.

38. Book 20, p. 91. His second temple was located at Number 337 Jinhua road in Taizhong.

39. The chief goddess of the Immortal in the Taoist Western paradise. Also known as Xiwangmu or jinmu. See *Daojiao dacidian*, entry on "Xiwangmu 西王母 ", p. 439.

40. Book 18, p. 69.

41. Book 43, pp. 163-165. Lu did not specify which one of the scriptural schools.

42. Book 43, p. 165. Kagyu (Literally, oral transmission lineage) is one of the four great schools of Tibetan Buddhism. This school emphasizes practice. The teachings came to Tibet around 1050 CE and were in the following century organized into the Kagyu sect. According to the tradition, it descended from Vajradhara Buddha through the Indian master Tilopa and Naropa, who passed it on to Marpa, Milarepa, and Gampopa. For a helpful discussion on the Kagyu school of Tantric Buddhism, see John Powers, *Introduction to Tibetan Buddhism* (New York: Snow Lion Publication, 1995), pp. 346-376.

43. Book 50, p. 163. Lu mentions his first meeting with Dabao fawang, XVI, that is, His Holiness the XVI Gyalwa Karmapa (1924-1981) in Book 43, p. l65. This happens in 1976 when he was 32 years old. But he did not receive the initiation from Karmapa until 1981 which is mentioned in book 50, p. 163. In book 43, p. 165, Lu also mentions that he received the empowerment from Daxi duba, XII, another leader of the Kagyu school of the Tantric Buddhism in 1976. It is not clear whether the empowerment Lu received at that time was an initiation or not. I, therefore, date his

initiation into the Tantric Buddhism in the year of 1981.

44. Book 50, a declaration was made at the back of the title page.

45. Book 99, p. 80.

46. The story is told by Lu in Book 50, pp. 96-97, 160-162. Lu also excommunicated (*kaichu*) one of his disciple as a result of this incident. See Book 50, p. 162.

47. On Lu's teaching of spirit (*ling*), see Book 18, pp. 74-76. On his teaching of activating the soul (*qiling*), see Book 18, pp. 83-90.

48. Book 20, p. 12 & p. 75.

49. Book 20, pp. 73-76.

50. Book 18, pp. 74-75.

51. Book 20, p. 110.

52. Lu K'uan Yu (Charles Luk), *The Secrets of Chinese Meditation* (New York: Samuel Weiser Inc., 1969), pp. 174, 177-178.

53. See the essay on qilian by Lu on his Book 18, pp. 89-94. The same essay also reappear in Book 19, pp. 110-113, Book 20, pp. 113-115, Book 22, pp. 13-16, Book 27, pp. 109-110, Book 41, pp. 35-38. This indicates how important is the essay on qilian in Lu's thoughts.

54. Book 20, p. 111.

55. Book 19, p. 32.

56. Book 41, p. 38.

57. On qiling as the first step of cultivating the dao, see Book 45, p. 32.

58. Book 19, pp. 137-140. Same essay also reappears in Book 20, pp. 116-118. See also Book 51, pp. 70-76. According to Lu, one has to spend three years on *zhuji* 築基.

59. Book 48, pp. 103-107, cf. Book 51, p. 68. According to Lu, one has to spend another three years on Breathing exercise.

60. Book 39, pp. 87-89.

61. In his epilogue to his book, Lu indicates that he has placed an advertisement in the newspaper that he is ceasing to divine for anyone since the rush of people is so great he has no time for his own spiritual concerns. See Book 21, p. 193. cf. Book 27, p. 114, Book 31, p. 219, and Book 32, p. 161.

62. In Book 32, pp. 97 and 143, Lu reported that he was aware of a few diviners in Taiwan who were using his name to earn a living while others criticized him badly (Book 38, p. 18).

63. Lu told us a story of a godfather who was plotting against his life. See

Book 41, p. 93.

64. Book 27, p. 114. Lu also reports that there are a lot of criticism on him in the media. See Book 39, pp. 27-28. Cf. Book 49, pp. 62-65 on his critics.

65. Book 23, p. 9. Also mentions in his epilogue to his 35th book (Book 35, p. 190).

66. Lu told us that he has moved seven times in total. See Book 41, p. 47.

67. Book 24, p. 9.

68. Book 45, p. 1 & 68. Cf. Book 49, p. 5. Lu claimed that his enlightenment is a culmination of his fourteen years of unceasing practice (1969-1983).

69. Book 45, p. 50.

70. Book 45, p. 72 & 13. C.f Book 49, pp. 56-47.

71. Book 45, p. 131.

72. Book 45, p. 132.

73. On the neidan tradition, see Isabelle Robinet, "Original Contribution of neidan to Taoism and Chinese Thought," collected in Livia Kohn (ed.), *Taoist Meditation and Longevity Techniques* (Ann Arbor: Centre for Chinese Studies, The University of Michigan, 1989), p. 317.

74. Isabelle Robinet, "Original Contribution of *neidan* to Taoism and Chinese Thought," p. 317.

75. *Daode qing*, chapter 37, 38, 48, 57.

76. T8: 749c.

77. Book 45, pp. 55-60.

78. Book 48, pp. 27-28.

79. Book 51, p. 15.

80. Book 51, pp. 19-25.

81. Book 51, pp. 57-62.

82. Book 51, p. 27.

83. Book 51, pp. 26-31.

84. Book 51, p. 28. Cf. Book 49, pp. 8-11.

85. For a brief discussion on kundalini, see Mircea Eliade (ed.), *Encyclopedia of Religion* (New York: Macmillan Publishing Company, 1987), entry on "kundalini. " See also the entry on "cakras," i.e., the seven energy centres an explanation of which is given in the following page of this paper. Lu acknowledged that he had been practicing in accordance with the method of kundalini. See Book 48, pp. 2-4 & Book 49, pp. 34-37.

86. Book 51, pp. 83-88.

87. Book 51, pp. 63-69. Cf. His discussion of the function of mantra to release

energy in our body in Book 49, pp. 57-58 & pp. 187-192.

88. Book 51, pp. 70-76. Here Lu teaches seven different kinds of exercise to loosen the seven centres of nerves.

89. For a brief discussion, see Mircea Eliade, ed., *Encyclopedia of Religion's* entry on "cakras."

90. Book 51, pp. 89-100.

91. Book 48, p. 2. The theme of dissolution of one's self with the cosmos can be traced back to the Indian Upanishads. The Upanishads teach the union of Atman with Brahman. A famous simile of salt dissolving in water is given in the Chandogya Upanishad. In the Tantric tradition, it is also known as the Laya yoga (Yoga of dissolution). See Benjamin Walker, *The Hindu World. An Encyclopedic Survey of Hinduism* (New York: Frederick A. Praeger, 1968), pp. 616-617, entry on "Yoga".

92. Book 51, pp. 116-117.

93. Book 48, pp. 2 & 119, and Book 49, p. 20.

94. Book 48, p. 47.

95. Book 19, p. 139. Lu calls the cultivation of virtue as an 'external' practice which is the ground work for an 'internal' practice of meditation.

96. Book 49, p. 47.

97. See, for instance, the discussion by Walpola Rahula, *What the Buddha Taught* (New York: Grove Press, 1983). Walpola based his study primarily on the Pali source.

98. Walpola Rahula, *What the Buddha Taught* (New York: Grove Press, 1983), p. 35.

99. It is interesting to note that Gopi Krishna (1903-?), a contemporary Indian Yogi, has made a similar point. See his Kundalini: the Evolutionary Energy in Man (Berkeley: Shambhala, 1971); and his *Higher Consciousness: the evolutionary thrust of Kundalini* (New York: the Julian Press Inc., 1974). I found many parallels in Gopi's description of his kundalini experience and Lu's enlightenment experience.

100. See Lu's own discussion in Book 55, pp. 26-32 & 84. Here Lu correlates the method of *neidan* with *kundalini*.

101. Lu explains that it is the soul or lian which is reborn in the Pure land. See Book 19, pp. 158-159. He claims that lian becomes Buddha, Book 19, p. 159, and that lian is the alaya consciousness in the Buddhist teaching, Book 19, p. 149.

102. Book 45, pp. 103-108.

103. Book 51, pp. 162-168.
104. Raja is a fierce spirit with angry appearance, three faces and six arms. He is the messenger and manifestation of Vairocana's wrath against evil spirits. See Ding Fubao, *Foxue dazidian* (Beijing: Wenwu chubanshe, 1984), entry on 'airan mingwang,' p. 1179.
105. Book 45, pp. 109-114.
106. On visualization, see Book 49, pp. 174-180.

10
Hope in Christianity:
An Interpretation

David Tracy

Manifestation and Proclamation

There are various ways to make useful distinctions among the most basic forms of religious expression. When one is attempting to highlight the reality of the participation of human beings in the cosmos and, in Jewish and Christian faith, in relationship to God, the most basic distinction is that between religion as manifestation and religion as proclamation.

Religion as manifestation signifies the sense of radical participation of any person in the cosmos and in the divine reality or ultimate reality. The sense of radical immanence in both cosmos and self is strong as, indeed, is the sense of the felt relationship of self, nature, and the divine. This sense of religion as manifestation is in sharp contrast to religion as proclamation. In the latter case (and the three great prophetic and monotheistic traditions of Judaism, Christianity and Islam are all proclamation traditions at their religious heart) a sense of God's transcendent power is also a source of the Divine disclosure as principally in history, not nature. Indeed, the proclamation traditions introduced a new sense of distance between God and human beings and a powerful sense of an interruption of the once powerful, indeed radical sense of belonging to or radical participation in the cosmos.

Of course the sense of participation in nature does not die in prophetic traditions as the Jewish liturgical year, the Christian sacraments, or Islamic ritual make clear. However, the prophetic traditions (with their strong sense of God's transcendence allied to the powerful prophetic sense of an ethical responsibility to resist evil and face historical suffering) have their own ways of relating to evil, suffering, and hope including straight forwardly ethical-political ways.

Many indigenous traditions, however, like the native American traditions in all the Americas for example, and classical Chinese traditions, have never lost the earlier religious sense of radical participation in nature and the cosmos. Those traditions (once named "pagan" by Jews, Christian and Muslims) have returned to haunt the conscience, the always ethical conscience of the prophetic, proclamation-oriented-tradition. In any mystical reading of the prophetic traditions (as in Kaballistic traditions in the ethical monotheism of Judaism) there is also a return of the repressed other, the so-called "pagan" sense of manifestation of a felt relationship uniting self, cosmos and God.

Indeed it is difficult to overemphasize how such a sense of what I will name a felt synthesis was for most ancients and medieval thinkers. I agree fully with Louis Dupre in his important and wise new book *A Passage to Modernity* that the most important and widely overlooked consequence of modernity (which he persuasively dates as beginning as early as the nominalist crisis of the 14th century and the humanist developments of the 15th century) is the breakup of both the western ancient and the medieval senses of a synthesis of God, self, and cosmos.

Clearly all Chinese and even most Jewish, Christian, and Islamic understandings of what I here call a felt synthesis of the ultimate, cosmos and self are principally expressions, religiously, of manifestation. The ancients may indeed have had a sense of cosmos that was central both to an understanding of the divine realm (the gods, even Zeus and Jupiter) and a sense of human beings as a *microcosmos* related to the *macrocosmos* and of human reason as *logos* intrinsically related to both the cosmic and the divine realms. The ancient synthesis (especially but not solely the neo-Platonic and the Stoic) were, one and all, felt syntheses of the intrinsic relationality of the cosmos, the divine, and the self. Those syntheses were grounded in various forms of religion as manifestation, i.e., in a sense of radical participation in the cosmos.

The monotheistic traditions changed but never broke this sense of felt synthesis and intrinsic relationality among God, self and cosmos and radical participation of the self in the cosmos and in God. Here it is not so much the doctrine of redemption and therefore a principal focus on evil and suffering which prevailed) as it did in the prophetic, proclamatory sense of the sinful distance from the transcendent God at work mysteriously in history and calling all to ethical-political liberating responsibility toward others, especially the oppressed and marginalized. Rather both the patristic and medieval periods (even aspects of Augustine) were dominated by reflection on the doctrine of creation. How could any radically monotheistic tradition with its doctrine of a Creator God assume the continuance, in a new transformed form, of a synthesis of God-self-cosmos? Here was the great challenge of our patristic and medieval ancestors. On the whole, they never lost a sense of radical participation and ordered relationship, the sense I called above sense of the felt synthesis of God-self-cosmos.

Clearly the fragility of the Good; they know the honest beauty of the tragic vision, and then — perhaps only then — they see what Alyosha Karamazov saw: the startling insight into the forms of all forms for the Christian, the God who is love manifested in Jesus the Christ. It is time, perhaps for all theologians to learn from an understanding of God, evil, and suffering in the feeling and thought, the new forms and content, the praxis and theories of all those who have suffered, both individually and communally, all those who perhaps act and see far more clearly than modern theologians were able to see with their carefully crafted modern theodicies.

The Search for New Forms for Christian Hope — History and the Voices of Suffering and Hope

It is a theological commonplace that the biblical God is the God who acts in history. For the Christian the decisive manifestation of the identity of this God is revealed in the person and event of Jesus the Christ. Through Jesus Christ, Christians understand anew the reality of God as the God of history: the God who acted in the Exodus history of ancient Israel is the same God who acted and thereby decisively manifested Godself in the ministry and message, the passion, death and resurrection of this unsubstitutable Jesus of Nazareth.

But how may contemporary Christians best understand this God who acts in the history of Jesus Christ? In one sense, modern progressive Christian theology has been an attempt to answer that question.

Sometimes the answer has been divorced from the actual history of the Jesus in and through whom God has decisively disclosed Godself. The emergence of historical consciousness and thereby the development and use of historical-critical methods in the Bible has proved to be, like all human achievements, ambiguous in its effects upon modern Christian understandings of God and history. On the one hand, the results of historical-critical method have freed Christians to be both more careful and more cautious in their claims for the historical character of the events (whether Exodus, Sinai or the history of Jesus) related by the Bible. On the other hand, the use of historical-critical methods sometimes removed Christians from paying sufficient attention to the details of the history of Israel and the history of Jesus as those details were narrated by the first communities — above all, for the Christian, in the passion narratives of the New Testament.

This characteristically modern loss of attention to the disclosure of the God of history in the narrative details of the passion and the resurrection narratives can be a loss of the heart of the matter. For where shall we look first for understanding the God of history? As the famous poetic rule observes, God is to be found in the details. Which details? For the Christian, above all, the details narrated by the first Christian communities on this Jesus they proclaimed as the Christ: the biblical narrative details of the ministry and message, the passion, death and resurrection of Jesus of Nazareth. Who is God? In these gospel narratives God is the one who raised this disgraced Jesus from the dead and thus vindicated his ministry and message, life and person as the Christ and, as Jesus Christ, the very manifestation of who God is and who Christians are commanded and empowered to become. Christians may now understand themselves as empowered to hope to find God above all in and through the historical struggle against evil for justice and love — the historical struggle for the living *and* the dead.

It is hardly surprising that the liberation movements and theologies of our period throughout the globe grounded in listening to and articulating the suffering and the struggle for justice of oppressed peoples are those theologies that best teach all theology to develop new forms to articulate the content of the dangerous memory of the hope released by the God of history. The form of liberation theology began with Gustavo Gutierrez's brilliant reading of the Exodus narrative and continued through what might be named the new prophetic negative theology for naming God: first name the idols of our period and then we may be able to name God more accurately.

In the liberation and political, the feminist and womanist theologians, contemporary Christian theology has found new forms to render alive its hope in the God of concrete history. This liberating God of history is not identical to the God of modern historical consciousness — a consciousness often driven by an unconscious desire to replace the biblical narratives on the God who acts in history with a modern secretly social evolutionary narrative which may comfort modern religiousness but seems incapable of rendering present any memory of the dangerous God of history.

The God of concrete history is also not identical to the God of existentialist and transcendental historicity. The God of modern Western historicity is disclosed by an analysis of the existential and transcendental conditions of possibility of the modern Western historical subject. A valuable intellectual exercise undoubtedly, but this God of historicity seems far removed from the dangerous and disruptive God of the history narrated in Exodus and in the history of Jesus.

What a curious fate modern Western Christian theologies of history have undergone. Guided by the honest belief that they were taking history with full seriousness, many theologians began to develop either theologies of historical consciousness (Troeltsch) or theologies of historicity (Bultmann). These theologies were and are serious, necessary, and honorable enterprises. And yet the questions of suffering, evil, and the God of hope recur. Where is the God of history in these modern theologies of historicity and historical consciousness? Where is the conflictual history of ancient Israel and above all where is the history of Jesus as found in the gospel narratives and remembered and rendered present anew in the Christian liturgy? Where are the conflicts, sufferings, and memories of oppression, the resistance and struggle against evil, all those concrete realities which constitute history as the struggle in hope for justice, freedom, and love? Where is resurrection as the hope for the vindication in history and beyond history of all the living and the dead? Where are the victims of history to whom the God of history narrated in the history of Jesus provides outbursts of laughter, joy and strength even in suffering as seen in the songs and tales of all struggling, oppressed peoples? Is hope only for the victors who write the histories informing modern historical consciousness?

It would be foolish to turn against the genuine, indeed permanent achievements of the great modern theologies of historical consciousness and historicity. In these theologies we can find the fruits of the great modern experiment: a defense of freedom and rights, an insistence on truthfulness, an honest rejection of the triumphalism of many theologies of history from Eusebius through Bousset and beyond in favor of the honest, critical, cautious correctives of traditional accounts achieved by the use of historical-critical methods. Surely these accomplishments are one of the permanent achievements of modern theology. At the same time, we are now at a point in our history where the underside of modernity, the dialectic of Enlightenment, must also be honestly acknowledged.

For there is an underside to all the talk about history in modern religion and theology. That underside is revealed in the shocking silence in most theologies of historical consciousness and historicity alike on the evil rampant in history, the suffering of whole peoples, the destruction of nature itself. The history of modern progressive theologies of history is too often a history without any sense of the radical interruptions of actual history, without a memory of historical suffering, especially the suffering caused by the pervasive systemic unconscious distortions in our history, sexism, racism, classicism, anti-Semitism, homophobia, Eurocentrism. Modern progressive theologies of history are always in danger of becoming religionized narratives of some other happier story than the disruptive and disturbing narrative of the message, ministry and fate of Jesus of Nazareth.

At their best modern theologies of history articulate the great continuities of history. In this relatively optimistic account of the teleological continuities of history, modern theologies of history bear certain analogies to Luke-Acts. However, many modern theologies of history, however Lukan in their emphasis on continuity and teleology, read history in a manner far different from the more careful Lukan narrative: history seems relatively free of conflict, interruption and of suffering. History seems to take the form of an unconsciously evolutionary schema that somehow always leads teleologically to the temporary victors of history, the Western moderns. Then, as was recently announced, history can be declared at an end.

History, on the modern schema, is too often a linear, continuous, teleological form with a single *telos*, Western modernity. In such a schema, God (disguised as one or another 'ism') is part of the schema, the part that provides a foundation for a theoretical theodicy and thus gives hope and consolation. God, in modern theodicies, is sometimes an important part (theism and pantheism) or sometimes a missing part (atheism and agnosticism) but almost always a part of a wider theoretical form. But what if history is not only continuity but is also deeply constituted by the detours, labyrinths and interruptions caused by historical evil and massive suffering? What if the modern social evolutionary teleological scheme underlying modern self-understanding seems to be finally and implausible? Indeed modernity's sense of continuity and confidence has been shattered by two unassimable elements: the interruption of massive global suffering in modern history and the interruption of all those others set aside, forgotten, and colonized by the grand narrative of Eurocentric modernity.

God enters post-modern history not in the form of a theoretical foundation as a consoling 'ism' but as an awesome, often terrifying, hope-beyond-hope. God enters history again not as a new speculation (even a modern Trinitarian one!) but as God. Let God be God becomes an authentic cry again. For this God reveals Godself in the form of hiddenness: in cross and negativity, above all in the suffering of all those others whom the grand narrative of modernity has set aside as non-peoples, non-events, non-memories, non-history.

God comes first as empowering hope to such peoples and theologies: a God promising to help liberate and transform all reality and promising as well to challenge and overcome the self-satisfied *logos* of modernity. God also comes to these post-modern forms of contemporary theology not only as the Hidden-Revealed God of hope witnessed in the cross, in the memory of suffering and the struggle by, for, and with the forgotten and marginal ones of history. God also comes in giving joy and strength to oppressed peoples in the struggle itself. God also sometimes comes, as the afflicted clearly know, as an ever deeper Hiddenness, the awesome power, the terror, the hope beyond hopelessness sometimes experienced in the struggle itself. Thus does the God of Job speak out of the whirlwind again in Gustavo Gutiérrez's profound later reflections on the Hidden-Revealed God of life and thereby hope. Thus does 'suffering unto God' and lamentation toward God emerge as a resistance to all modern speculation on suffering in God in the post-Auschwitz, later political theo-logia of Johann Baptist Metz. The biblical prophetic Hidden-Revealed God at its most fearsome and radical has reentered theological thought again through the reflections of whole peoples and cultures rendered into new forms of theology: New forms needed to disclose this new, uncontrollable content; new forms to render the feelings of suffering, resistance, joy and strength; new forms to allow theory to be grounded in and transformed by the demanding, cleansing, transforming praxis of the struggle whose hope is kept alive in an increasingly apathetic and technologically aenesthesticized culture. But the entry into history by contemporary theodicists is now not through the estranged and alienated self of the existentialist theologians, those admirable and deeply troubled moderns. The entry of the Hidden-Revealed God now comes through the interruptive experience and memory of suffering itself, above all through the suffering of all those ignored, marginalized and colonized by the grand narrative of modernity. In the light of that interruption, the modern 'isms' for viewing God in modern theoretical theodicies suddenly seem at best inadequate forms for understanding and rendering the content of Christian reflection on evil, suffering, hope, God.

Conclusion:

The Contemporary Search for New Forms for Hope — Back to the Future of Christian Theology

The hope of Christians is to resist evil and transform suffering. That hope is grounded in the central Christian metaphor of I John 4:16: God is love. The history of Christian reflection on hope, evil, and suffering, at its best, is the history of response to and reflection upon that reality. At times (as in easy sentimentalizations of Christian love, in refusals to face evil and suffering in order to understand what "God is love" might mean), the reality "God is love" evaporates like soft rain on a desert terrain. Some theological reflections on the God of love and hope can begin to take on the form of a mere greeting card: a clear, pleasant, harmless announcement to have a nice day.

Surely Christian theology needs to continue to study the entire history of Christian theology in order to retrieve the best reflections on what hope might mean for those who believe that, despite all appearances to the contrary, God is indeed love. Above all, as many theologians insist, we need to reflect further on the meaning of the central Christian understanding that "God is Love" is the Trinitarian understanding. Surely it is always important for any Christian response to suffering and evil to remember that God is not only source but always already word and gift. The Trinitarian God is experienced as God by Christians in prayer, liturgy, and sacrament as well as in ecclesial readings of the scriptures. We can insist on a Trinitarian understanding of God without, I hope, the kind of strange speculation on theodicy by reflections on the suffering in the inner-Trinitarian relations of Father and Son in the distinct theologies of either Balthasar or Moltmann. Rather an insight into the Trinitarian understanding of God pervading our liturgy and our prayer may best guide us to a fuller sense of the intrinsic and empowering connections between liturgy and the struggle for justice as La Cugna and Johnson insist in their distinct Trinitarian theologies.

And yet, as the logic of my paper thus far suggests, we must also turn not only to the great history of theological reflection following the Johannine insight "God is love." We must also go back to texts and traditions before John. We thus turn back driven, of course, by the realities of suffering and evil in all history and in the search for hope in responding to those realities. We are also driven back to earlier scriptural and other ancient resources by the logic of I John 4:16 itself. The first letter of John is, after all, the first commentary on John's Gospel. Thus construed, 1st John maybe read as the best metaphor which the Christian community coined by meditation in the passion narratives. And so Christian thought is drawn not merely forward into the history of theological forms from 1st John but backwards, back to the great passion narratives as the central form articulating what Christians mean by their great cry of hope, God is love.

We are drawn back first to John's Gospel that first great meditative narrative on the beauty, indeed glory, manifested in the lifting up of the Cross and its unexpected disclosure of both necessity and the Good in something like tragic beauty; we are drawn to Luke and that narrative's history-like, realistic, straight forward call to resist evil, fight for the poor, relieve suffering; we are drawn back to Matthew and his amazing narrative relating word and act beginning with its great discourse of the Sermon on the Mount (that great hymn to Christian hope) and concluding in the steady and pessimistic strains of the Great Judgment scene of the discourse of Matthew 25, the justly classical text of so much liberation theology.

Above all, we are driven today when facing the Hiddenness of God in the history of conflict and suffering to the form of Paul's relentless dialectics of God Hidden in the Cross of Jesus Christ, the Crucified One. And reflection on Paul's theological form of dialectic may yet lead us to face again the uncanny character and strangely formless form of the first of our gospels. Mark's apocalyptic tale of the eschatological prophet resisting evil demons, healing the marginal and forgotten, speaking truth to power in words which even the disciples almost never seem to understand. This self-interruptive, uncanny Markan form penetrates to the heart of human suffering in the afflicted, frightening cry of the Jesus who resisted evil and lived by hope, "My God, my God why have you forsaken me?" This cry is not the end of Mark's narrative, to be sure, but that afflicted cry from the cross is a defining moment which Christian theologians ignore at the peril of refusing to face the suffering caused by evil and, above all, by the suffering attending resistance to evil.

We may, as Christian theologians, be driven back to still earlier traditions and texts in our searches for new theological forms to respond to suffering, evil, and the God of love after the collapse of the modern forms of theoretical theologies. We should be drawn back to rethink how to read the New Testament itself anew in the light of both the Old Testament and the Greek classics. Surely it is time for Christians to read our Old, or First, Testament anew. We should also read it as the Tanakh, the book of the Jewish people whose history we presume to graft ourselves upon, the people who new post-Shoah readings of their scriptures allows us Christians to hear again and rethink how to read with the eyes of the suffering of all history the great psalms of Lament, the Exodus narrative as a tale of liberation, not conquest, the joy and the strength people find in the struggle for justice, the afflicted cries of

Jeremiah, the demands for justice of Amos, the shift in the texts we call
Isaiah from something resembling triumphalism to the startling portrait
of a liberating suffering servant. Above all we need to hear Job again
and does not join his comforters (all experts in theodicy!). Job demands
that we face the whirlwind and often formless realities of both life and
God with hope, not the false consolation of a theoretical theodicy.

Moreover, as Christian theologians attempting to think in the later
twentieth century on evil, suffering, and hope, we may also attempt to
rethink our relationship to our ancient Greek heritage as well and to
the other great traditions. Surely it is time to undo one great fault in
early Christian theology's response to the classical Greek heritage: its
seeming refusal to aid its own theological reflections on suffering, evil
and hope by attending to not only the Greek philosophers but also the
great tragedians, especially Aeschylus and Sophocles. Tragedy, as
Aeschylus saw with such clarity in all his work, is indeed frightening
but can also be an expression of hope, as in the *Oresteia* where we witness
the breaking of the cycle of violence and revenge in the founding of a
court of justice on the Areopagus. For some of the Greek writers, to be
sure, hope (*elpis*) was an entirely deceptive and destructive
phenomenon. Whenever elpis occurs in the texts of Thucydides, for
example the reader soon learns that disaster is about to occur. For
Aeschylus, however (as for Plato in his greatest vision of authentic hope,
the *Timaeus*, in contrast to his last despairing work, The *Laws*), hope is
genuine. And that Greek hope is not what Nietzsche justly called the
'easy optimism of reason' bequeathed to Western culture by the Greeks,
the first theoretical theodicists. Nietzsche's critique rings true for much
of our Greco-Roman heritage. But hope in Aeschylus and Plato partakes
of the same kind of sensibility pervading Job and Ruth, Mark and John,
the startling responses of Joan of Arc to her inquisitors and Sojourner
Truth to her inquirers, the foolish wisdom in the Christ-mysticism of
the later Tolstoy and in Simone Weil. All those figures and traditions
possessed real hope in God for they had forged new forms to express
the ancient content of that hope in facing pain by suffering and resisting
evil. The opposite of hope is never pessimism nor despair, but apathy,
and apathy is the one quality that should never be called a divine form
and should never be ascribed as a form of virtue to anyone claiming the
name Christian, as the interreligious dialogue shows so well.

11

Ethics of Hope

Choan-seng Song

What Jesus has done is to de-centralize the life and faith centralized in the temple and to re-centralize it in people. After all it is people who live their lives and practice their faith. He liberates them from what the temple has come to stand for under the religious authorities: religious legalism and political intrigue. He makes it clear that the temple itself is not the hope of the people, nor is it the hope of their nation. He remembers that the temple built by King Solomon was burned to the ground by the Babylonians. He knows that the second temple reconstructed by those who had returned from the exile in Babylon was pillaged and desecrated by that notorious Antiochus Epiphanes. What stands in front of him now is the temple rebuilt by King Herod the Great. Does he already foresee that it is also going to be destroyed? His premonition is to come true when that third temple is razed to the ground when Jerusalem falls to the Roman troops commanded by Titus, the Roman general.

But the destruction of the temple does not mean the end of people's hope. In actual fact, the temple, controlled and managed by the religious hierarchy, has been a false hope for the people. What it has offered them is an illusion of hope. It has stood in the way of what they hope and aspire: it has, ironically, stopped them from entering the kingdom of heaven;[1] it has deprived them of "the weightier matters of the law: justice and mercy and faith;"[2] it has deceived them with that beautiful appearance that conceals "greed and self-indulgence."[3] Between the hope preached by the religious establishment and the hope cherished by the people there is a great chasm. The chasm is often so great that they are diametrically opposed to each other as south from north or north from south (*nanyuan beiche* 南轅北轍 in Chinese).

What has to be done to shorten the distance between people and hope? A theology of hope that dwells on hope as future, as an "eschatological" event? How are they to be brought closer one to the other? More faith in God who has hope for us — hope that "passes all our understanding"? More faith in the all-knowing God and more theology of hope in the fulfillment of time may help us detach from ourselves and from our pressing problems of life, but are they able to help us find the "justice, mercy and faith" Jesus talked about? Do they enable us to live the reign of God not in heaven in the future but on earth in the present? These are some of the questions theologians of hope, preachers of God's kingdom, and Christians who have to live in hope in the midst of heart-breaks, conflicts and despairs, cannot avoid.

What we need to have is not more theology of hope; we have had plenty of it already. What we have to hear is not more preaching on hope; only the good God knows what it must be; we have become so used to it that it ceases to bring us excitement. But hope without excitement — is it still hope? Hope richly dressed up in a theology but meagerly related to life — is such hope still hope? The answer is of course not very encouraging. For hope to be hope, it has to be addressed to the present as well as to the future, perhaps more to the present than to the future. For hope to be hope, it has to be "contemporary" as well as "proleptic," perhaps more contemporary than proleptic.

Hope should not become outdated. Who wants an outdated hope? An outdated hope is good only for personal reminiscences, historical memories and theological nostalgia. Paul is almost right when he says that "hope that is seen is not hope."[4] But hope, not to become outdated, cannot remain perpetually hidden in the future. A hope eternally tucked away in the future may tantalize our theological curiosity but cannot fill the void in our heart and the emptiness of our spirit, created by hardships of everyday life. Hope that is unseen has to become seen to be a *real* hope. And the hope that is seen, in order not to become outdated, has to become a hope unseen that gives birth to a hope that is seen — hope that can fill the hungry stomach, lift up the down-trodden, and bring justice and freedom to those deprived of it.

Hope not seen and hope seen, have, in this way, to be in creative tension. What connects one with the other is power intrinsic to hope.

What is this power? Is it a theological power — power that emanates from our faith in God? Yes. But it also has to be an ethical power — power that enables human beings to live in this world of *wuchang*, to use a Buddhist term, that is, the ever-changing world. As a matter of fact, there is no theological power that is not at the same time an ethical power; and there is no ethical power that is not a theological power at the same time. If the ethical power of hope receives particular emphasis here, it is because it has received less attention in much of the theology of hope.

That ethical power of hope empowers us to reconstruct the lives ruined by hatred, greed and violence. That ethical power also allows us not to become cynical about the powers of evil or resigned to them. It strengthens our faith in God who, as the very source of our faith, is much closer to us than we are to ourselves. Hope is not just power. It is *ethical* power, power to change the situations that degrade individual persons and corrupt human community. Hope as an ethical power is related to God's saving power, the power that works within us, gives us courage to live, and changes our lives and the world around us. It is this ethical power that will be the focus of our continuing engagement with hope.

Incense Sticks Named "Hope"

Hope, used as a verb, besides meaning "to long for" or "to dream about," also means, among other things, "to cherish, to count on, to sweat it out, to hang in, to take heart."[5] These verbal expressions are all in the present tense. They refer to what one does to bring about what one longs for or dreams about. Hope is present already as one "hangs in there and sweats it out." To put it another way, there will be no hope if one does not hang in there and sweat it out. Hope is not a concept but an action. It does not consist merely in waiting, but in doing. It is a seed sown in the ground of the present. It is this kind of hope that we encounter in the following story. What we are about to hear is a story told in the first person. It is a testimony of someone named Kannan from India who hangs in there and sweats his hope out in a life filled with frustrations and adversities. It seems as if he is born a stranger to hope, as if he is destined not to have anything to do with hope. This is what he tells us:

> The name my parents gave me is Kannan. But it is usual for everybody to call me "Hey, cripple." I belong to a very poor family...

> My father is a coolie. I am the eldest of eight children. It was impossible for my parents to bestow any attention on us children since the battle for the belly took most of their time. I was struck by polio when I was three months old. My father, who was totally ignorant of polio preventives, tried his level best to help me. Some suggested that if my leg was washed with hot rice water it may be restored. But we ate only once a day and that, too, was the cheapest available rag (millet). Only very few times we could afford to eat rice. According to some other people's suggestion they buried me waist deep in dry sand from morning till noon for six months. My parents, who had to be away at work then used to ask other little children to watch over me. Sometimes these children used to desert me and go away. In spite of all this, my deformity remained the same.

> With someone's help I was admitted to a small school. The feeling that I was not like others was a torture to me. Other children always made fun of me, calling me "cripple." ... No one considered me as a human being. I was broken-hearted. I had to leave school to help the family and did all sorts of jobs. I gathered firewood in small bundles and started selling them door-to-door. I started selling peanuts and bananas street by street. Sometimes, knowing I am a cripple, people used to bolt away with my money and the goods. Even buses used to avoid me and pass me by.

> More than the disability in my body, society made me a cripple also inside. This was death to me. Like me, there are thousands of poor handicapped today who die inwardly like this. What else can we expect in slums, where there is great poverty and ignorance? ...

> We are not people. The pitiable condition of expecting other people's charity has killed our sense of self-respect and has brought us to a condition of less than animals. Superstitions such as "it is our fate," "it is God's curse on us," do not allow us to become people. We are poor. No good thing ever reaches us, including the International Year of the Disabled. There is little

hope for people like us.

Therefore, we, the poor slum handicapped, joined together and with the help of a group started to organize. We are now 1,200 people in eighteen slums. "Our disability is in our bodies, not in our spirit" — "we have every right to live equally with others." With these convictions we help each other. We share what we know. In a small training place those who know bag-making, book-binding, tailoring and other handicrafts share our skills and also our profits. We have named the incense sticks we make "HOPE". We go in procession to the government and demand our rights. We spread knowledge about polio prevention and employment possibilities and understanding about the causes of our poverty and degradation. We aspire to gain our dignity and our rights through our struggle. Without expecting anyone's pity or charity... .[6]

The language in which the story is told sometimes gets broken in grammar and syntax. Does it not reflect all the more how deeply the heart of the storyteller is broken and how severely his soul is injured? But this is not the whole story. There is something more in it — the power to change the conditions imposed on people such as the storyteller and to create something possible out of impossible situations. I would like to call that power "the ethical power of hope." The story, eloquent in its simplicity, is a powerful testimony to it.

"My father is a coolie"

That says it all: "My father is a coolie." The father of the young storyteller is a coolie. The term "coolie" originally comes from "*Hindi kuli*, an aboriginal tribal name," or from "*Tamil kuli*, wages," meaning "unskilled laborer or porter in or from the Far East hired for low or subsistence wages."[7] It is a pejorative term, almost as pejorative as the word "slave." As a matter of fact, the history of "coolie trade" is closely related to that of slavery. It "began in the late 1800s as a response to the labor shortage brought on by the worldwide movement to abolish slavery. The majority of those contract laborers were shipped from China to developing European colonial areas such as Hawaii, Malaya, and the Caribbean."[8] This is another "trade of human bodies" instituted by the "Christian" West for economic gains and developments.

If the coolie trade is historically related to the slave trade, the way it is carried out is not any better than that of the latter. "Conditions in the depots," it is pointed out, "where the laborers were stored awaiting shipment, and the vessels in which they sailed were cramped and inhumane, resulting in much sickness, misery, and death."[9] There must be many countless stories of suffering endured by those men on their way to the unknown destination. And there must also be as many stories of how many of them died of maltreatment and sickness without reaching their destination.

The irony is that what is started as Western colonial institution, bringing shame and indignity to laborers from Asia, became a social institution in India and China, causing the poor to suffer misery and inhumanity. Society depended on their services as much as they depended on it for their survival. The rich relied on them to maintain their lifestyle of affluence and self-importance as much as they relied on the rich for the subsistence wages to maintain their rock-bottom life. Once a coolie you are always a coolie. You are condemned to the very bottom of society. You have no rights to claim what your labor and service deserves, not to say rights as human beings. You have no rights except the charity bestowed on you by the society and by your masters.

Such coolies abounded in the China of feudal and semi-colonial days and in India that remains a caste society. Our young storyteller has the misfortune of being born to a coolie's family, condemned to a life of hardship and destitute. "The battle for the belly," as he graphically puts it, "took most of the time" of his parents and their eight children. His lot is already bad enough, but this is not all. When he was three years old he came down with polio. Medical treatment was out of the question. He was subjected to a most crude folk way of treatment, which of course proved totally futile. All his life he has to put up with insults from others and with self-pity brought about by his physical deformity. He was made a "cripple" not only in the body but more painfully in the soul and the spirit.

"We are not people"

Born to a coolie's family and made a "cripple" by polio, Kannan is treated by society as "non-human," "non-person," and of course "nobody." He was an object of ridicule at school. Innocent children can be cruel to children different from them in physical appearance and ability without knowing the hurt they are causing in others. They show contempt to those from less fortunate families not realizing they are wounding the latter's hearts. Kannan had to leave school because he could not take the ridicule and contempt from his classmates any more.

But leaving school did not leave him in peace. To help his parents with some rupees, he "went selling peanuts and bananas street by street." The sight of a crippled child selling peanuts and bananas must have excited the fancy of street urchins. He was entirely helpless when these street urchins "bolted away with his money and goods." The sight of him utterly desperate and helpless must have been as funny as pathetic. But these were not only his plights. Being a cripple from the slum seemed to have the whole society against him. He recalls sadly that "even the buses used to avoid him and pass him by." This is all he could say for himself for people like him: "We are not people." How much agony is contained in these words! Deep down in his heart is the hopelessness that saps the courage to live and debilitates the meaning of life.

"We are not people." A person forced to say this is a person without hope. A community that renders a human being to say this is no longer a fellowship built on *communion*, sharing of thoughts and emotions with one another, intimate relationships with deep mutual understanding.[10] A society that can afford hope only for the rich, the privileged and the healthy is an immoral society. It has no sympathy for those who toil and labor as "coolies." Those "coolies" may have instrumental values, providing menial services at the beck and call of their masters, but they are not supposed to be endowed with human values. A society that thrives on their hardships is a morally degraded society. And a society that allows some people to enjoy their riches at the expense of those who cannot earn enough to stave their hunger is a morally bankrupt society.

Thanks to reduction in military confrontations between East and West in recent years, the focus of world economy has shifted visibly. It has shifted from military economy to consumer economy. The target of economic development is diverted from military complexes to consumer complexes. The world has become a gigantic market where sellers and buyers are engaged in transactions of goods and money. Profit is the only thing that matters. It is the god of the market. Many nations in the world today, including some of those in what is called "the Third World," have learned to worship this god.

How serious economy is for people is not lost to politicians. Economic prosperity has almost become a single most important factor in politics. Economy has to be at the center of political campaigns. If you are aspiring to the highest elected office of a nation, you can set aside the state of national economic health only to your detriment. A presidential hopeful can get elected by asking voters one simple question: Are you better off today than you were four years ago? And the democratic presidential candidate in the United States of America won the election in 1992 with a campaign slogan that spoke to the pocket-books of its people: "It is the economy, stupid!"

The wealth of nations! Statistics of world economy shows that many nations have achieved wealth in a remarkably short time. Even some of those countries subjected to the colonial rule that exploited their human and material resources for decades and even for centuries have come up to the forefront of world economic development. But as we all know, everything has its price. Economic development has made many societies rich and prosperous. At the same time it has made them morally vulnerable. Human hope is now defined in terms of industrial outputs. It is measured in relation to the income per capita per year. It averaged is conditional to the rise and fall in stock markets. It is determined by the growth in Gross National Products. Hope in the economic life of the nations today can be bought and sold. It has become a merchandise that ebbs and flows in domestic and international trades.

In the world in which economic factors reign supreme, hope has lost its independence. It is attached to stocks. It is subsumed under commodities. It becomes relative to the volumes of transactions in goods and products, and it depends on the favorable or unfavorable trade balance. With independence gone, hope no longer commands unquestioned authority. It ceases to be an ideal to make the world a more friendly place to live. It becomes unrelated to a vision for a community in which some men, women and children do not have to say: "We are not people." Hope has become less and less human. It becomes something that can be calculated, computed. It can be found in the files of policies and strategies of economic growth and development. Hope is taken out of us human beings and relocated in the impersonal world of economic competition and survival.

The quality of hope has changed. It is no longer a human force that enables us to aspire to that which is true, good and beautiful, but a material force that sucks us into the world of things. Subjected to forces of economy, it ceases to be something that inspires the best in human beings — self sacrifice, for example, but becomes something that produces the worst in them — selfishness and greed. Hope for a large number of people in the world today is not a spiritual power any more, renewing them everyday for the arduous demands of love, justice and peace. Human beings have become "economic animals," motivated by the uncanny instinct to go after where the prey is — economic gain. The rest becomes secondary. Crippled coolies such as Kannan can be ignored or disposed of once they are regarded as hindrance to the growth of national economy and to prosperity of the few.

"Why don't you die"

Kannan is aware that he was not alone in his misfortune. There are many others in his slum area inhumanly treated and socially ostracized. "In one family alone," he remembers, "there are five or six who are deaf, blind, crippled or mentally retarded." In one family alone! Nature seems particularly cruel to that family. Fate seems to make fun of it. How can there be hope for a family with five or six of its children afflicted with one kind of deformity or another? Having to scrape a living, how could they afford any medical care?

Hope is not to be found in the vocabulary of a family such as this. It is a notion entirely foreign to them. It is a luxury as utterly inaccessible to them as medical care. Kannan calls to mind one particular case of a twenty year old woman related to his family. She was "mentally retarded and stunted in growth from birth." Her condition was congenital. Whose fault was it? Her parents? Their unhealthy diets? The polluted slum environments? The herb medicine from the quack doctor or from the medicine man she took during her mother's pregnancy? No one knows. But one thing is certain: dire poverty, below subsistence wages, poor diet, and lack of medical care, all contributed to the birth of a deformed child.

Birth of a child such as this is an end to whatever hope the parents might have had. It deprives them of the already scant resources for living. It is a burden added to the heavy burden of life they are bearing. Birth of a child brings some hope to them if the child grows up to be one additional family labor force. But when a child is born deformed, even a minimum hope such as this is gone. For twenty one years this physically and mentally disabled woman was never taken out of her house. She was left alone in her own excrement. Her parents were able to clean her only once a week. She and many others like her are reduced to "a condition less than animals." How is one to talk to such people and their families about hope? How is a religion to preach to them about hope? To speak to them about "eschatological" hope, to preach to them about hope to come, in the future, in the world to come, in life hereafter — is this not unethical, even immoral?

"It is God's curse on us"

If hope has become materialistic in the world increasingly dominated by the free market economy, what, then, about the world of religions — religions expected to equip men and women with the power of hope not only to deal with the transiency of life but to empower them to create the meaning of life in the complex world of endless struggle and competition? As the story of Kannan testifies, his own religion has failed him. His own religious community has discriminated against him and left him to struggle for mere survival. And his own people, the caste women and men, who conduct so much devotion to their gods treat him not only not as one of them but as if he is a non-person, someone who does not count in Hindu society.

Hinduism to which Kannan is born has a very long history. Hinduism, as a matter of fact, is the oldest living religion in the world with its roots dating back to prehistoric times in India.[11] It has given the world some of the finest religious writings such as the Vedas, the Ramayana, the Mahabarata, and the Bhagavad Gita. These not only represent the Indian religious mind at its deepest in search of the origin and destiny of human being, but belong to the richest heritages of the human spirit in quest of the meaning of life here and beyond. Although India, according to its constitution, is a secular state, with the majority of the population being Hindus, Hinduism plays the dominant role in the Indian way of life, from the religious to the social to the political. Perhaps it is not too off the mark to say that India is Hinduism and Hinduism is India. What one encounters in that great sub-continent of Asia is Hindu India.

With its immense diversities and differences in ethnicity, language, and religious expression, with magnificent manifestations of its fertile mind in arts, literature and philosophy, and with the gap between the great wealth of the few and the extreme poverty of many — the gap that is scandalous and even obscene, India defies description. Still, the religious literature referred to already offers us glimpses of the best and noblest in India. Take the Vedas, for example, "the oldest Hindu scriptures, older than the sacred writings of any other major religion"[12] in the world, originated "approximately between 2500 and 600 BCE."[13] In these Vedas one comes across a "Hymn of Creation":

1. Non-being then existed not nor being;
   There was no air, no sky that is beyond it.
   What was concealed? Wherein? In whose protection?
   And was there deep unfathomable water?
2. Death then existed not nor life immortal;
   Of neither night nor day was any token.
   By its inherent force the One breathed windless;
   No other thing than that beyond existed.
3. Darkness there was at first by darkness hidden;
   Without distinct marks, this all was water.
   That which, becoming, by the void was covered,
   That One by force of heat came into being.
4. Desire entered the One in the beginning:
   It was the earliest seed, of thought the product.
   The sages searching in their hearts with wisdom,
   Found out the bond of being in non-being.
5. Their ray extended light across the darkness:
   But was the One above or was it under?
   Creative force was there, and fertile power:
   Below was energy, above was impulse.
6. Who knows for certain? Who shall here declare it?
   Where was it born, and whence came this creation?
   The gods were born after this world's creation:
   Then who can know from whence it has arisen?
7. None knoweth whence creation has arisen;
   And whether he has or has not produced it;
   He who surveys it in the highest heaven,
   He only knows, or haply he may know not.[14]

These verses of creation truly astonish us. Just think that they came from that ancient world of India some millennia ago!

The hymn is dedicated to creation. There are the phenomena, natural or otherwise, one can see, even touch. To them is the hymn of praise. But how did all these things come into being? Above all, how did human beings come to be? How did the creation of all this take place? But how did creation itself happen? There must be a "desire," a "creative force," a "fertile mind," "the One in the beginning," that gave birth to the creation and all things in it. Does one not hear echoes of this Vedic hymn of creation in the creation story of Hebrew Scripture, or for that matter, in the creation stories told and creation hymns sung by many other peoples of old in different parts of the world, and vice versa? Human spirits of ancient times seem to call one to another in the depths of the creation.

But the hymn of praise to creation turns into a hymn of awe. The religious mind that responded to creation in poems of sublime beauty realizes that what one is confronted with is a mystery — a deep mystery beyond human comprehension. "Who can know from whence creation has arisen?" The gods born after the world's creation " would not know it. If the gods do not know, how could human beings, born even after the gods, know? Mystery of mysteries. The only one who knows is the One who caused creation to come into being and who "surveys it in the highest heaven." But perhaps even that One "may know not."

This is not agnosticism. Our ancient ancestors were too awed by the mystery of creation to be agnostic. Their hearts were very much in tune with the spiritual forces of the universe to give room to impiety. They were too overwhelmed by the mystery of it all that all they could do was to be silent. That even the creator who has brought all this into being may not know the origin of creation is not so much skepticism about the wisdom and power of the creator as the acknowledgment of utter ignorance on the part of human beings about God the creator.

This reminds us of the Book of Job in Hebrew Scripture, that literary master piece that explores how God is incomprehensible in face of human suffering. Towards the end of the laborious but fruitless theological harangues of his friends to force him to admit his sin for all the tragedies that struck him and his family, the author has God say to Job "out of the whirlwind":

Who is this that darkens counsel
by words without knowledge?
Gird up your loins like a man,
I will question you,
and you shall declare to me.
Where were you
when I laid the foundation of the earth?
Tell me, if you have understanding.
Who determined
its measurements — surely you know!
Or who stretched the line upon it?
On what were its bases sunk,
or who laid its cornerstone.
When the morning stars sang together
and all the heavenly beings shouted for joy?[15]

These are words from someone completely overwhelmed by the mystery of creation and awed by its infinite expanse of time and space. It is a deeply religious mind and heart speaking not out of desperation but out of a profound faith in God the creator in spite of all the travails one goes through in life.

"Where were you when I laid the foundation of the earth?" This is a final and decisive question. You may try to theorize about the order of the universe. You may try to give theological reasons for what you perceive and experience of what happens to you and to the world around you. But faced with the question of the foundation of the earth, asked about the beginning of creation, you have to admit you are utterly at a loss, that you are completely ignorant. The reason is obvious: You are simply not there! If you are not there, if you are not an eyewitness to how creation came into being, all you can do is to confess your awe and wonder. This is what the author of the Book of Job and those who composed the creation hymn of the Vedas had to do.

What we encounter here is a profound ignorance of deeply religious and spiritual nature. We human beings do not know what takes place behind what we can see, smell, hear and touch. Things we see may not reflect the reality in the innermost part of the divine being. What we hear may be distortion of the voice of truth in the mind of God. What we touch may keep us from perceiving the compassionate heart of the all loving Mother-Father God. And what we comprehend may be we ourselves and not that Being beyond our comprehension. But religion, especially organized and established religion, has always directed our spiritual aspiration and religious sensibility, not to that creating, all loving, yet incomprehensible God, but to what we can see, hear, touch or comprehend with our senses and minds — rituals, doctrines, canons, even taboos.

A religion, when substituting its rituals, doctrines, canons and taboos for the creating, loving and incomprehensible God, becomes a crisis to itself and a danger to its believers and adherents. It makes a clear distinction between what is acceptable and what is not acceptable, whereas for God what is acceptable to it may be unacceptable and what is unacceptable to it may be acceptable. It draws a line between what is true and what is not true, but for God what is true for it may be untrue and what is untrue to it may be true. In many instances it allows no doubt as to what is sacred and what is profane, what is holy and what is secular. It even divides people between us and them, between us who are favored and saved and them who are not. But the chances are that for God what it considers sacred and holy may be profane and secular, what it rejects as profane and secular may be sacred and holy. It is also most likely to be the case that God does not separate us from them and them from us, or those who are saved and those who are not saved as a religion often does.

How could God the creator function with such dichotomies as a religion does without ceasing to be God the creator? Is God still the all loving God when God discriminates one group of men, women and children against other groups as a religion tends to do on grounds of one's religious affiliation, racial origin, gender, sexual orientation, class or caste? Does God have a preference for certain religious communities and believers over against others? Is God prejudiced against those who are economically deprived and physically disabled such as Kannan, our storyteller? In short, is God the God of hope for the privileged only? And people like Kannan are left without hope — hope not only from his society but also from God of his own religion?

As Christians we read in our Bible that the God of Jesus has nothing to do with the God just described. His God is not a dichotomous God — a God who divides what God has created in nature and in human community into hostile camps and warring factions. Did not Jesus exhort his followers and say: "Love your enemies and pray for those who persecute you, so that you may be children of your God in heaven"?[16] His God does not judge according to your religious affiliation or sectarian loyalty; his God is solely concerned whether your heart is in the right place.

Jesus is reported to have made a statement that shows his deep insight into human nature and by inference his most penetrating critique of what goes on in the name of religion: "It is not what goes into the mouth that defiles a person, but what comes out of the mouth that defiles."[17] How true! Are not divisions within a religion and conflicts between religions often results of inflammatory words that come out of the mouth of the religious authorities and fanatical believers? This can be applied to all religions, including Christianity.

From the creator God to the God related to the world, from the powerful but remote God to the loving God close to human life and community — this is a long spiritual quest of humankind. Religion is an effort on the part of human beings to translate this spiritual quest to images, symbols, forms and teachings that are more accessible to human devotion and graspable to the human mind. But when these images, symbols, forms and teachings get detached from the faith in God in us but beyond us, and become ends in themselves and objects of human faith and devotion, religion begins to be beset by corruption of power and greed. This is what happened to Jesus' own religion. He took upon himself the task to reshape it so that it could once again serve God and people in need.

The spiritual quest and the philosophical search we encounter in the Vedas are no exception to this almost universal course traveled by religion — from adoration of the creator God to formulation of rituals and teachings in the service of that adoration finally to the replacement of the devotion to God with loyalty to human religious constructions. In the Vedas we do come across efforts to put religious devotion to work in daily life, to wrestle with ethical expectations of that devotion. This, for example, is what we read in the Vedas:

> 1   The gods inflict no hunger as a means to kill:
>   Death frequently befalls even satiated men.
>   The charitable giver's wealth melts not away;
>   The niggard never finds a man to pity him.

2   Who, of abundant food possessed, makes hard his heart
Towards a needy and decrepit suppliant
Whom once he courted, come to pray to him for bread:
A man like this as well finds none to pity him.

3.   He is the liberal man who helps the beggar
That, craving food, emaciated wanders,
And coming to his aid, when asked to succor,
Immediately makes him a friend hereafter.

4.   He is no friend who gives not of his substance
To his devoted, intimate companion:
This friend should turn from him —
here is no haven —
And seek a stranger elsewhere as a helper.

5.   The wealthier man should give unto the needy,
Considering the course of life hereafter;
For riches are like chariot wheels revolving:
Now to one man they come, now to another.

6.   The foolish man from food has no advantage;
In truth I say: it is but his undoing;
No friend he ever fosters, no companion:
He eats alone, and he alone is guilty.

7.   The ploughs that cleaves the soil produces nurture;
He that bestirs his feet completes his journey.
The speaking brahmin earns more than the silent;
A friend who gives is better than the niggard.[18]

There words speak to our hearts as well as to our minds. They enrich the treasury of wisdom human beings are inspired to utter throughout the ages.

In tone, words, even in ethos these verses of the *Rig Veda* from ancient India do not sound foreign to the Christian ear accustomed to the wisdom taught by the sage who composed "the Proverbs" in Hebrew Scripture. One is told, for example:

Do not withhold good from those to whom it is due,
when it is in your power to do it.
Do not say to your neighbor,
"Go, and come again, tomorrow I will give it" —
when you have it with you.
Do not plan harm against your neighbor
who lives trustingly beside you.

> Do not quarrel with anyone without cause,
> when no harm has been done to you.
> Do not envy the violent
> and do no choose any of their ways.[19]

Proverbs such as these are moral maxims developed out of a long experience of life. They are words of wisdom containing profound religious truth. This is what one hears further:

> Do not rob the poor
> because they are poor,
> or crush the afflicted at the gate;
> for the Lord pleads their cause
> and despoils of life those
> who despoils them.[20]

For the sage of "the Proverbs" moral concerns are not a matter of expediency; they are "divine imperatives" because they belong to God's nature, the God who stands with the poor and defends them. God, however one may describe God, is a moral God.

What we have in "the Proverbs" is *theo-logical ethics*, ethics developed from theology and theology translated into ethics. Essentially, this is what constituted the heart of the message of the prophets. It is this prophetic tradition that Jesus inherited and pressed hard the religious authorities of his day to face the ethical implications of what they believed and taught. In what he said and did, whether in his controversy with Jewish religious leaders or in his teaching and preaching before the men and women who followed him, he called them to grapple with the ethical consequences of their faith.

In this matter Jesus is very serious. He sounds urgent. He is not dealing with something that can be postponed or deferred. Take the story of Zacchaeus, for instance.[21] Noticing the anxious Zacchaeus in the tree, Jesus offered to stay with him, a chief tax-collector hated and shunned by his own people. This was Jesus' acceptance of him without condition. It set his life in motion in a completely different direction right away. He offered to make amend of the wrongs he had done against people. This was a dramatic turn of events. But Jesus' proclamation was even more dramatic. "Today," he declared, "salvation has come to this house!" Today, and not tomorrow. On the spot and not somewhere else in the synagogue or at the temple. This very moment and not the end of time. The present time and not some future time. What made Zacchaeus' hope of salvation real was his decision to practice his faith at once in response to Jesus' message. What he practiced was an ethics of hope, hope realized not only for himself but for those whose life had been exploited before.

But has Christian theology grasped the urgency of hope Jesus' presence generated? The answer cannot be that certain. Theology and ethics have gotten divorced one from the other. They have gone their separate ways. The result is disastrous: little ethics in theology and little theology in ethics. This leads to the poverty of both theology and ethics. When it comes to the theme of hope, there has been in recent years too much theology of hope and too little ethics of hope. Hope, as has been said earlier, gets separated from the present and eternally postponed. Does not the sage of "the Proverbs" also tell us at one point, "hope deferred makes the heart sick?"[22] Surely it does. Does it not also make the heart of Kannan and the hearts of those women and men like him sick? Surely it does. Hope deferred also makes God' heart sick because "God pleads the cause of the poor."

For the *Rig Veda* from which we have been quoting ethics is also grounded in theology. Although the Vedic hymns "were composed for an audience primarily occupied with earthly goods: health, long life, many sons, abundant cattle, wealth,"[23] they do not extol earthly goods at the expense of God or gods. Does not the hymn just quoted begin by saying, "the gods inflict not hunger as a means to kill"? God is not vindictive. God does not terrorize helpless men, women and children with disasters. God is a Being that can be trusted, relied upon, rain or shine. Longing for such God is the heart of human religious activity, ancient or modern, East or West. This is the unsophisticated and unindoctrinated part of faith. It is an innate part of the human being as *homo religiosus*. It is something that predates established religions. This is certainly the case for Christians. And it is no less true for people of other faiths such as Hindus.

But in the development of organized religions, this loving God becomes less and less loving. This God of compassion grows less and less compassionate. What emerges is a God or Gods grown more and more remote from worshipers, more and more unapproachable by believers. All the while religion is busy at work to extend the distance between the loving God and the longing people. It takes upon itself the role of a match-maker between God and people. On the one hand it has made itself indispensable in this role with structures of religious hierarchy and bureaucracy of priesthood. It, on the other, packages and repackages God, makes God and remakes God, to resemble more its own likes and dislikes than God in God's own self.

How this God, created by religion has frightened many believers and alienated others! "The Roman Catholicism of my children," recalls a former Roman Catholic nun, "was a rather frightening creed. James Joyce got it right in *Portrait of the Artist as a Young Man*: I listened to my share of hellfire sermons. In fact Hell seemed a more potent reality than God, because it was something I could grasp imaginatively."[24] Are not Christians in the Protestant churches also brought up on sermons on eternal damnation of "infidels" in Hell and everlasting bliss in Paradise for those who have accepted Jesus as their personal savior? Buddhism too has a large share of fear of Hell with its vivid and lurid — almost too vivid and too lurid — descriptions of how those who have committed evil suffer unspeakable torment and pain in Hell. For that matter, is there a religion that is free from the religious terror committed against unsuspecting believers?

Kannan in his story tells us that he too is a victim of a religion turned into terror. In his case that religion is Hinduism. Crippled and living in the slum, he and people like him are made to say, what they suffer is not only "our fate," but "God's curse on us." To attribute one's misfortune to fate is bad enough, but to believe it to be God's curse is even worse. "Curse" is a heavy word. It is a vindictive word. It is a hate word. And it is an angry word. You curse someone when you are angry, when you are hateful, when you are vindictive. When your personal misfortune, your physical deformity, your poverty-stricken life, is believed to be the results of God's curse, the God you worship is an angry and vindictive God filled with hates.

Is this God the God who "inflicts not hunger as a means to kill" in the Vedic hymn to which we referred? It cannot be. God who curses is not God. God who has to be vindicated does not deserve to be God. And the God who hates — how can that God be the God who gave birth to all things? Such God does not exist in reality. It only exists in human imagination. It is a religious fiction created by those who hold power over people's spiritual well-being. The real God has no taboos. There is nothing in the real God to repulse us human beings. Between the real God and us human beings there are no taboos. The God surrounded by taboos and protected by them from human approach may be the God of a religion, but cannot be God in God's own self.

"There is no hope for people like us"

Cursed by God, you become totally hopeless. This is your last resort as human beings. You may be able to endure your physical pain. You may get used to the derision of society. But how can you endure the pain in your heart caused by the belief that you are cursed by God? How can you resign to the idea that you are abandoned by God? And how can you grow accustomed to a God who "drops stones on you who have fallen into a well" (*luojing xiashi*), to use a Chinese idiom, meaning "beating you when you are already down, when you are already suffering so much in body and in spirit"?

For innocent members of a religion God is their last hope. They are not versed in erudite teachings and doctrines. They are not educated about the meanings many religious images and symbols are supposed to tell them. Even though they may dutifully perform rituals and pay their dues, they are ignorant of what is going on behind worship services and religious ceremonies. But what they do is to recite prayers, to worship at temples and churches, to carry out religious duties, to placate and please their God, to obtain favor from their God, to be protected by their God from illness, misery, perversity, or calamity.

Religion for ordinary believers is something that takes place in earnest between worshipers and God, between human beings and the divine being, between the frail, finite, mortal women and men and the powerful, infinite, immortal God. The physical parts of a religion — temple, church, sanctuary, images, icons, organizations such as orders, bureaucracy, priesthood, spiritual exercises such as worship, prayer, meditation — these and many others prescribed or proscribed for them are aids, paths, ways, or approaches to what is fundamentally related to them, to what concerns them in a decisive way, namely, God.

God is the heart of their faith. God is the center of their life. And God is the sum total of their hope. To be alienated by God causes anxiety in them. To be left alone by God makes them feel uneasy and empty. To be abandoned by God drives them desperate. And to be cursed by God is to become outcasts both socially and religiously in a culture shaped by a religion and dominated by it. Listen to this prayer from Africa offered to Imana, the great creator of Ruanda-Urundi:

> O Imana of Urundi (Rwanda), if only you would help me! O Imana of pity, Imana of my father's house (or country), if only you would help me! O Imana of the country of the Hutu and the Tutsi, if only you would help me just this once! O Imana, if only you would give me a rugo and children! I prostrate myself before you, Imana of Urundi (Ruanda). I cry to you: give me offspring, give me as you give to others! Imana, what shall I do, where shall I go? I am in distress, is there room for me? O Merciful, O Imana of mercy, help this once![25]

"O Imana, help me just this once!" This prayer out of extreme distress must have been in the hearts of tens of thousands of Ruwandan victims of the fierce tribal war between the Hutu and the Tusi triggered by the assassination of Juvenal Habyarimana, President of Rwanda. How many of them died with this prayer on their lips!

Imana, the creator God, "is honored but not feared, as the creator God has no power to harm."[26] The God who is not feared and the God who has no power to harm. Is this not the most "primitive" and thus most authentic belief in God in the depths of human religious consciousness? Is this not something almost universal, East or West, ancient or modern, established religion or popular religion? But somewhere along the way this God who is not feared, becomes a fearful God and this God who has no power to harm obtains enormous power to harm. This must have happened even before human religious activities became organized into religious institutions. But the transformation of God who is not feared and has no power to harm into the God who is feared and has the power to harm especially came to be part of organized religion. Religion as it gets structured and organized loses innocence. It becomes a buffer state, so to speak, between God and believers. It claims to be more than it actually is. It alleges to be able to, do things beyond its limits. This is when a religion becomes an idolatry, taking the place of God, making itself the object of people's devotion and loyalty.

God is affected by a religion that trespasses its boundary, breaching its human boundaries and infringing upon divine precincts. It begins to do many things in the name of God — instituting religious laws, setting up hierarchy of power and authority, developing doctrines and canons, instituting heresy hunting, waging wars, and even renaming God in God's name. A religion, instead of alleviating guilt and bringing peace, causes anguish and fear. How else is one to explain a prayer to God as desperate and hopeless as this "Sumero-Akkadian Prayer?"

> In ignorance I have eaten that forbidden by my god;
> In ignorance I have set foot on that prohibited by my goddess.
> O Lord, my transgressions are many; great are my sins.
> O my god, (my) transgressions are many; great are (my) sins.
> O goddess, (my) transgressions are many; great are (my) sins.
> O god whom I know or do not know, (my)
> transgressions are many; great are (my) sins.
> O goddess whom I know or do not know, (my)
> transgressions are many; great are (my) sins;
> The transgression which I have committed, indeed I do not know;
> The sin which I have done, indeed I do not know.
> The forbidden thing I have eaten, indeed I do not know;
> The prohibited (place) on which I have set foot, indeed I
> do not know;
> The lord in the anger of his heart looked at me;
> The god in the rage of his heart confronted me;
> When the goddess was angry with me, she made me become ill.
> The god whom, I know or do not know has oppressed me;
> The goddess whom I know or do not know has placed
> suffering upon me.
> Although I am constantly looking for help, no one takes
> me by the hand;
> When I weep they do not come to my side.
> I utter laments, but no one hears me;
> O my god, merciful one, I address to thee the prayer,
> "Ever incline to hear me;"
> I kiss the feet of my goddess; I crawl before thee.[27]

This is a prayer of laments. The soul who utters it is utterly confused. The spirit that pours it out is in fear. The believer who mutters it is confronted with the God who refuses to listen. The God addressed in the prayer is an oppressive God. That God is the God of despair and not the God of hope. A prayer such as this reveals the dark side of a religion that threatens, people with God's anger and punishment.

No religion is free from representing of God in this way, not even the religion of ancient Israel. There are psalms in Hebrew Scripture that extol the glory of God, celebrate God's majesty, give thanks to God for God's saving love. But there are also psalms that give vents to distress, frustration, uncertainty and fear. We hear, for example, a psalmist pleading with God, saying:

> O Lord, do not rebuke me in your anger
> or discipline me in your wrath.
> For your arrows have sunk into me,
> and your hand has come down on me.
> There is no soundness in my flesh
> because of your indignation;
> there is no health in my bones
> because of my sin.
> For my iniquities have gone over my head;
> they weigh like a burden too heavy for me.
> My wounds grow foul and fester
> because of my foolishness;
> I am utterly bowed down and prostrate;
> all day long I go around mourning.[28]

We do not know what troubles the psalmist. It may be a sudden tragedy. It may be a grave illness. Whether tragedy or illness, the suffering of the psalmist is the indication of God's anger and punishment.

But does God cause human beings to suffer? And having caused suffering, does Go let it be known that the suffering caused by God is also God's punishment? But in the Sumero-Akkadian prayer there is confusion as to what wrongs have been made and what transgressions have been committed. In the Hebrew psalm, although the psalmist confesses saying: "I confess my iniquity; I am sorry for my sin,"[29] one is not quite sure who has really committed iniquity and sin. For immediately after the confession one hears the psalmist saying: "Those who are my foes without cause are mighty, and many are those who hate me wrongfully."[30] Is it not quite evident that the iniquity and sin for which the psalmist prays for God's forgiveness are in fact not committed by the psalmist but by the enemies?

The psalmist of Hebrew Scripture and the suppliant of the Sumero-Akkadian prayer both have got things wrong. If common belief leads them to think that illness or misfortune is the divine punishment for sin, they must reject it as not true. They must have faith enough to say their God who is love does not punish them in this way. On the contrary, God is standing by their side, in pain and in love embracing their sick body or their frightened spirit. If it is their religion that has taught them to believe that they justly deserve God's displeasure and punishment for what they have done, they must be able to muster enough courage to say their God is not a vindictive God. And if they are accused of the iniquity and sin they have not committed or do not remember having committed, they have to raise their voice and protest. They must be able to say a religion that compounds their suffering with God's anger and identifies it with God's punishment is a wrong religion, a morbid religion, an oppressive religion.

It is religion and not God that is against worshipers. It is a religious institution and not the divine order that commits believers to suffering. For us to be free for one another and particularly for God, we may have to be free ourselves from religion, from the religious institution that makes us fearful of God, humiliates us in front of God, from a religion that compels our psalmist to implore God at the end of his prayer: "Do not forsake me, O Lord; O my God, be not far from me."[31] The reason is simple: the God of your religion may forsake you, but God who created you will never forsake you; the God of your religion may be far from you, the God who gave birth to you is never far from you. This God who never forsakes you and who is never far from you is your hope, and not the religion that teaches you to be religious lest God forsake you and stay far away from you.

By the same token, that Sumero-Akkadian prayer does not have to end with these words: "I kiss the feet of my goddess; I crawl before thee." Kissing the feet of someone is an expression of servitude. This is what religious authorities demand, not God. Crawling before someone is an act of humiliation. Again this is what those who hold power over you expect from you, and not God. The true God, the God who created you, nurtures you, and protects you from harm's way will not treat you like a servant, a minion, a slave, a criminal. That God will not ask you to crawl before God to humiliate you, to shame you, to degrade you. It is the religion that has taken the place of God, that has control over you, that demands you to perform such acts of humiliation.

No wonder Kannan and many men, women and children like him, suffer under oppressive religious establishments and traditions. They bear "God's curse" on their bodies. Cursed by God, they are also cursed by their fellow human beings. Kannan recalls that "this was death to him," that "there are thousands of poor handicapped today who die inwardly." Dying inwardly can mean only one thing: spiritual death. Physical death does not have to bring about spiritual death. The body dies, but the spirit lives on. But when the spirit dies, even though the body is still alive, the person dies with it. The person who is physically alive but spiritually dead is said to be *xingshi zourou* 行屍走肉 in Chinese, namely, "a walking corpse." The religion that makes people, particularly the poor and the disabled, feel they are as well as dead not only does injustice to human beings but to God, not merely betrays people but God.

For a religion not to be of despair to people but hope to them, inner transformation is necessary — transformation from a religion of injustice to that of justice, from a religion of fear to that of assurance, from a religion of despair to that of hope. It has to go back to its roots, recover what is true and good there, and reconstruct itself in response to the call from the past and to the demands of the present. In Christianity this is called "re-formation" that took place in Europe in the sixteenth century. But for a religion to have future, re-formation has to take place not merely once, but twice, three times, any number of times from time to time. Religion is such an incorrigible thing very much like politics. It quickly succumbs to the temptation of power. It easily becomes a prey to greed. Before it knows, it allows itself to serve the rich and the powerful, and does disservice to the poor and the powerless. It readily yields itself to authoritarianism, dictating believers' life with rigid teachings and doctrines, antiquated ideas and beliefs.

Judaism of Jesus' time badly needed a reform. Jesus took upon himself the task of bringing about inner changes in his own religious tradition. The cost, we all know, was high. He paid for it with death on the cross. Christianity founded on this Jesus also needed reforms. Mention has already made about the re-formation of Christianity in Europe in the sixteenth century. Buddhism is no exception. In China and in Japan it had to be rescued from time to time from compromises with political powers and from indulgence in avarice to remain true to the spirit of its founder and to practice the self-sacrifice exemplified by the Bodhisattvas.

There should, in short, be no room for a God who curses human beings in religions. Hinduism, to which Kannan, our poor and disabled story-teller belongs, is no exception. One has to be reminded that

> the Vedic gods have an intimate relation of love with human beings. Every individual has the right to be loved by the gods and also to love the gods in return. ... The gods love human beings, and human beings are referred to as desirous of loving gods (Deva Kama). The god Agni has been referred to as one of the most affectionate gods who loves human beings as a father loves his son or as an elder brother loves his younger brother. Agni has been called a father, brother, and even a son. Even the battle-god Indra is regarded as an affectionate god. These very tendencies are responsible for the path of devotion (Bhakti Marga) which appears in its full bloom in the Bhagavad Gita.[32]

How does the god of love turn into the god who discriminates, who takes the side of the privileged against the disinherited? Is not religion — the religion that comes to represent the interest of the ruling class — responsible for it?

The fact is that the religion with which Kannan is familiar leaves him to cope with his own misery. The society to which he belongs does not treat him as a human being. And the strangers he meets outside the slum where he lives only take advantage of him, a poor cripple who cannot defend himself from their ridicules and exploitation. Where can he turn for help? Not to his parents; they themselves are helpless. Where do they seek relief from their hardships? Not society. Society is either indifferent to him or turns against him because of the centuries-old religious prejudice against people like him. Where can he have his hope rekindled — hope to live as a human being, hope to be free from anxiety, and hope to overcome death of the spirit? Not his religion. It is the very religion of his that created discrimination against the poor, the crippled, the outcasts. Kannan seems to have exhausted all his resources, material and spiritual. He seems to be trapped in the fate decreed for him from eternity. He seems destined to endure the curse of God until the end of his life.

Ethics of Hope

But fortunately for him, Kannan was able to turn around before he had reached the end of his rope. Luckily for him, he did not have to give up in despair but was able to have his hope rekindled. It was not his society that enabled him to be human again. Nor was it his religion that empowered him not to give in to the death of his inner self. He realized that he could not expect his society to give him back his humanity. He also became aware that he could not depend on his religion to rejuvenate his hope to live as a respectable and useful human being. Like freedom, hope has to be earned, and not to be received as charity. Like justice, hope has to be won, and not to be picked up ready made. Also like love, hope has to be nurtured, and not to be taken for granted. For hope to be hope, it has to be a motivating power that changes what you are supposed to be to what you have to be. Hope is something closely related to all aspects of our life, both external and internal. It is an energy to turn what cannot be seen into what can be seen, what is in the future to what is present, what is envisioned to what is real. In other words, for hope to be hope, it has to be an ethical power to change things.

Hope is an Ethical Power

Hope as an ethical power is a self-transforming power. It makes us aware of the power working in us to change us. It awakens in us the desire to overcome obstacles that inhibit our growth to be a full-fledged human being. It empowers us to break the chains that bind us — chains of self-pity, resignation and submission. For Kannan, our storyteller, that ethical power of hope makes him realize "the pitiable condition of expecting other people's charity" that "killed our sense of self-respect and brought us to a condition less than animals."

Charity can be shown without love and it often does just that. This kind of charity may enhance the self-respect of the charity giver, but it diminishes the self-respect of the charity receiver. Charity can be administered impersonally, and it is often done just in that fashion. In our society, East or West, charity organizations proliferate. It grows into machines that dispense charity as if it is a commodity. Charity often contributes to the false sense of spiritual well being on the part of the charity giver, but it often suppresses the spirit of the charity receiver to strive for self-improvement. This is what Kannan and many people like him in slums came to realize. Hope as an ethical power made them realize the unethical nature of small charities thrown at them, to humiliate them, to perpetuate their pitiful condition, to keep them subservient to them as coolies and slaves forever, or even to be rid of them. We are reminded of Jesus' parable of "the rich man and Lazarus."[33] Poor and covered with sores, Lazarus had to fight with the dogs for the scraps of food discarded by the rich man and his guests. He literally lived like animals, if not less than animals. He died without self-respect, perhaps just as many of Kannan's contemporaries in India, believing it was his fate to be cursed by God. But Jesus goes on to repudiate this popular belief. At this point his parable moves from realism to symbolism, from depicting what is often the case in human community to what the latter must be. What Jesus shows us the scene of bliss in Paradise with Lazarus in Abraham's arms and the rich man in hell suffering extreme torments. In the parable all this happened after their death. But what Jesus tries to emphasize must be the ethical power of hope that turns human community from suffering to joy, adversity to happiness, hell to paradise. If hope does not have such ethical power, it is not hope. This must be one of the things Jesus tries to bring home to his listeners.

The ethical power of hope inspires us, motivates us, and compels us to take actions. In Kannan and his friends that ethical power of hope began to stir them up and make them restless. Hope has to be *ethical* precisely for this reason. Ethics is concerned about, among other things, "normative inquiries about the principles, standards, or methods for determining what is morally right or wrong, good or bad."[34] But is this all there is to it about ethics? Ethics, just as other disciplines, has to be engaged in inquiries about "principles, standards or methods," to determine what is morally right or wrong, good or bad." But ethics, like philosophy and theology, deals with too many principles and standards and too little what these principles and standards can do to enable us to practice right instead of wrong, good instead of bad. History tells us and our experience confirms that more wrong than right has been done and more bad than good has been committed in the human community.

We do not have to bring up those horrendous tragedies such as the Holocaust, the tribal massacres in Rowanda, or the ethnic cleansing in Bosnia. Just take the case of Kannan our storyteller. The moral standards prevailing in India teach people not to treat other human beings like animals just because they are poor and disabled, but Kannan and people like him are treated just as such. The religious principles advocate that God is all loving and good, but they are shunned as if this loving and good God can also cast curse on them. In the society of India as in any other society people are taught, from early in their lives, ways not to wrong others and to do good to others, but they can still despise, ridicule, even exploit, unfortunate women and men such as Kannan.

What is the problem? How is one to resolve the obvious contradiction here between what "the law" demands and what is actually practiced? Here is an insight partially addressed to our concern here:

> A normative basis is not sufficient unto itself, since the tradition does not address all aspects of reality. Scientific theories which attempt to interpret empirical facts must be added. Both theories and facts are essential in ethics because they give understanding and empirical grounding to those in situations in which ethical decisions must be made. Without theories and facts, norms wander around in confusion, unable to inform the situation.[35]

Norms, theories and facts are closely related. The importance of this interrelationship cannot be emphasized enough. To illustrate it, we are invited to

> consider poverty in the Third World. Approximately five hundred million people are seriously malnourished in a world with more than enough food to go around. This is a fact. The numbers, however, only indicate magnitude. Economic and political theories are necessary to give meaning to the numbers and suggest alternative courses of action. Norms, such as Christianity's concern for the poor, make these numbers a scandal and are the basis for selecting among competing economic theories an alternative course of action.[36]

This is an effort in the right direction. Theology and even ethics have been too much preoccupied with basic norms and assumptions. These latter has shaped theories that explain realities. In the world today, such high-handed methods do not work any longer. Theology and ethics have to face the facts of how people live and suffer, letting these facts develop theories and shape norms and principles.

But this is still not enough. Even theories and norms constructed on the basis of facts and realities, that is, informed by what is really happening to men, women and children in their struggle to live, are often powerless to change the status quo. "A just world economic order" is one example. It is based on the recognition that the prevailing world economic order is an unjust order that makes a rich nation richer and a poor nation poorer. Lack of moral integrity on the part of those who profit from the unjust economic order has to be exposed. But an economic order that can do justice to the poor is not likely to be put into place any time soon. Norms and theories derived from facts do not have the power to change the status quo. We must ask again: what is the problem, then?

The situation just described is very much like that of what took place between Jesus and a rich young man.[37] It so happens that a rich young man approached Jesus with a question of "what I must do to inherit eternal life." He confessed to Jesus that he had done all that he was expected to do as a responsible member of society and religious establishment. He must have struck Jesus as a sincere person, for Jesus "looked at him and loved him." He did not come to test Jesus. He was not there to grind a theological axe with Jesus. He was not instigated by Jesus' opponents to make life difficult for Jesus. To this honest, earnest and devoted young man this is what Jesus said: "You lack one thing; go, sell what you own, and give the money to the poor, and you will have treasure in heaven; then, come, follow me." This was too much for him. "He was shocked," Mark, the author of the Gospel that bears his name tells us, "and went away grieving, for he had many possessions."[38] The rich young man had mastered all the right principles of his religion. He was at home with all the correct religious norms he learnt from his tradition. Still, he was shocked when Jesus told him to put into practice those moral principles and religious norms.

If norms and principles developed independently from facts will not change the world, nor will the norms and principles reconstructed on the basis of facts and realities. Those norms and principles possess no ethical power to change the world. The hope they offer to people is an empty hope. It has no moral conviction. It possesses no ethical power. Political hope offered by ambitious politicians tends to be this kind of hope. And most of the hope preached from the religious pulpit — hope in the future, hope in the promise of God, hope to come at the end of time — is this kind of hope. This kind of hope cannot redress the suffering of Kannan and people like him. It cannot make them live as human beings. It only allows them to live at the mercy of gods and other human beings.

For hope to be ethical, it has to create a new meaning in a life that has been devastated by physical disability and human abuse. An ethical hope is a creative hope, a hope that gives birth to a new human being and creates a new community. This is exactly what happened to Kannan and the people like him. This is the turning point in his story. He tells us how "the poor slum handicapped joined together and with the help of a group started to organize. We are now 1,200 people in eighteen slums." Their hope is no longer the charity society gives and withholds at will. It does not depend on the religious institution that preaches hope but dispenses despair. Their hope, the real hope, the hope that brings change to their lives and to their community, is their joining together as a community. Isolated, they are helpless victims, but joined together, they are a community with a purpose. Scattered, they are objects of taunt and abuse, but bound together they gain power to be subjects of their own life and destiny.

A City of Hope

They are, Kannan is proud to tell us, "1,200 people in eighteen slums." You may laugh at one individual with impunity, but you cannot do so with 1,200 people. You may mistreat one pitiful person, but you cannot mistreat 1,200 persons organized to defy you. As a lonely individual, he or she is disabled and handicapped, bound to be defeated and disposed of. But as 1,200 persons, they are no longer disabled or handicapped. United in the body, heart, mind and soul, they — each and every one of them — become whole persons not to be made fun of, not to be slighted, not to be abused. This is what Kannan means when he says: "Our disability is in our bodies, not in our spirit." This is a declaration that they are fully human, even more human than those who are able in their bodies but disabled in their spirit. This is also the statement of their hope. What offers more hope than the spirit revitalized to reconstruct the life that was crushed and the community that had lost its moral integrity?

"Our disability is in our bodies, not in our spirit," says Kannan. This is a profound" statement to come from a man who, though simple and unlearned, has gone through so much in his life. It is a penetrating insight that makes clear what it is that makes a human being human, not the appearance but the soul, not the external beauty but the inner beauty, not outward pretensions but the strength that reflects the freedom of the spirit. These words of Kannan's remind us of what Jesus once said to his disciples as he was sending them out on a preaching mission: "Do not fear those who kill the body but cannot kill the soul; but fear those who can destroy both soul and body."[39] The spirit that is not disabled can empower the body to overcome its physical limitation to serve the purpose of life. And the soul that survives the violence done to the body can be reunited with the body to give birth to a new life. The spirit and the soul together can recreate the body ravaged by illness and unite women and men in building a new community.

In this community of twelve hundred people from eighteen slums hope becomes a present reality. Hope is not somewhere in the temple but in the midst of them when they help each other. Hope is not an abstract concept but a present reality when they help each other. Hope is manifested, becomes visible, touchable and graspable when they share the skills of bag-making, book-binding, tailoring and making handicrafts, including profits from their labor. If hope is not an abstract idea, it is not a religious jargon either. The hope grasped by twelve hundred disabled men, women and children from eighteen slums is a "material" hope — hope that can be handled with their hands, that can be tasted in the food they have earned with their living and working together as a community.

This community of twelve hundred people also makes incense sticks they call "HOPE" — hope in capital letters, hope in bold letters. As the incense stick of hope burns, "smoke of hope" fills their workplace. Hope here is not an abstraction; they can smell it. It is not in a distant future; they inhale it and let it fill their whole being. They become people of hope — hope on their persons, hope inside them and outside them.

They themselves become hope, to themselves, to one another, and even to the future generations. Their hope is as vivid as the pulse they feel in their veins. It is as real as the bags they make. It is as solid as the book they bind. It is as beautiful as the handicrafts they make. No wonder they name their incense sticks "HOPE."

And they are determined that their hope has to be extended to others. A hope is genuine when it inspires hope in others, when it kindles hope in others, when it becomes contagious to others. A hope that does not inspire others is a selfish hope, and a selfish hope is a false hope, a hope gained at the expense of others. A hope that does not kindle hope in others is a barren hope. A barren hope only yields despair, resignation and death of the spirit. And a hope that is not contagious does not grow, multiply and spread. It becomes less and less vigorous, grows dimmer and dimmer. At last its fire is extinguished, reduced to a heap of ashes with no sign of life.

This is not the kind of hope with which Kannan and his friends lighted their incense sticks. Theirs is a hope that grows, expands and reproduces. They "go in procession to the government and demand their rights." They "spread knowledge about polio prevention and employment possibilities and understanding of the causes of their poverty and degradation." The actions such as these they have taken and continue to take manifest the ethical power of their hope. They are not contented with the hope they have found for themselves. They do not light the incense sticks of hope in their workplace and forget what is happening to other unfortunate souls out there in the streets.

The hope they have found is the hope that not only changes them but also others, even the society around them. In their hope is this ethical power to change. They may be ignorant about principles of hope. They have no idea what norms of hope mean. They are not able to develop theories of hope. They are totally unfamiliar with theology of hope. But they can practice ethics of hope. Their ethics of hope consists in the realization that they have rights to live as human beings just as anybody else, especially just as those who treat them less than human. It comes from the awareness that their physical disability is something that can be prevented, that they have the responsibility to make as many people aware of this as possible. It teaches them that their misfortune and their poverty have the causes deeply rooted in society, politics and religion, and have nothing to do with their God.

Above all, their ethics of hope enables them to reach this resolution: "We aspire to gain our dignity and our rights through our struggle without expecting anyone's pity or charity." This in essence is the ethics of hope. Hope is something to be striven for. Hope disguised as pity or charity is not hope. Hope, they have realized, is the resolve to stand on their own feet. It is the determination not to rely on the whims of others for their survival. It is a decision to struggle against social, political and religious powers to gain what is their due as human beings. Ethics of hope is ethics of resolve, determination and decision. It is an active ethic. It is an ethic of actions gained from the practice of it.

It is this ethics of hope that Father Kovalski, a Polish Roman Catholic priest who had gone to live in the slums of Calcutta that came to be known as "the City of Joy" learned from slum dwellers. Celebrating Christmas with Hindus and Muslims in "the City of Joy" he was moved to share with them these thoughts from the depths of his heart:

> It is easy for anyone to recognize and glorify the riches of the world. But only a poor person can know the riches of poverty. Only a poor person can know the riches of suffering ... And it is because the poor are the only ones to be able to know such riches that they are able to stand up against the wretchedness of the world, against injustice, against the suffering of the innocent. If Christ came to be born among the poor, it is because he wanted the poor to teach the world the good news of his message, the good news of his love for humankind.

> Brothers and sisters of the City of Joy, it is you who today are the bearers of that flame of hope. Your Big Brother [people address him this way to show their respect and affection for him] can promise you that the day will come when the tiger shall lie down with the young child, and the cobra will sleep with the dove, an all the peoples of all the nations will be as brothers and sisters.[40]

Father Kovalski went to the city of misery only to find a city of joy. He went there to teach the slum dwellers love and compassion only to learn that they are loving and compassionate people. Above all, he went there expecting to deal with men, women and children in despair, but what he encountered were people of hope. That city of joy was a city of hope.

True, there is plenty of misery and suffering in that "City of Joy." People steal, quarrel and hurt one another. The sanitary conditions are appalling. But in the heart of the slums and in the souls of slum dwellers Father Kovalski has found human beings helping one another in times of crises, sacrificing even their lives for the good of others, and striving to regain their dignity as human beings. This is the reason why, he is to realize, that people can still smile, even burst out into laughter sometimes, transforming the city of misery into a city of joy. After a few years he has become thoroughly convinced that redemption is a reality among the people he came to live with, perhaps more real than the world he had left behind him.

Apparently Father Kovalski gets carried away at times by what he has experienced. This is reflected in the thoughts he shared with his slum friends at Christmas. As he looks at the faces of women, men and children who have adopted him as their brother — faces ardent, innocent, peaceful, bearing no signs of malice or ill will toward one another even for a few moments gripped by the mysterious spirit of that baby born in a far away country to suffer and die, that paradisic vision seen by Isaiah, that indomitable prophetic soul of ancient Israel, came to his mind, the image of "the wolf living with the lamb, the leopard lying down with the kid, the calf and the lion and the fatling together, and a little child shall lead them.

Notes

1   Mt 23:13.

2   Mt 23:23.

3   Mt 23:25.

4   Rom 8:24.

5   *Roger's 21 st Century Thesaurus*, ed. The Princeton Language Institute (New York: Bantam Doubleday Dell Publishing Group, Inc., 1993), p. 378.

6   M. Kannan, "Testimony to an Unshakable Belief," in *Witnessing Together amidst Asian Plurality*, preparatory materials for Asian Mission Conference 1994 (Seoul-Korea, 25 April - 2 May 1994) (Hong Kong: Christian Conference of Asia, 1994), pp. 18-19.

7   *The New Encyclopedia Britannica* (Chicago: Encyclopedia Britannica Inc., 1987), vol. 3, p. 601, vol. 1.

8   Ibid.

9   Ibid.

10 See *Webster's New World Dictionary* (New York: The World Publishing Company, 1970), p. 247.

11 *The World Book Encyclopedia* (Chicago: World Book, Inc., 1983), vol. 9, p. 224.

12 Ibid., p. 224.

13 *A Source Book in Indian Philosophy*, eds., Sarvepalli Radhakrishnan & Charles A. Moore (Princeton: Princeton University Press, 1957), p. xvii. There are "four Vedas (Rig Veda, Yajur Veda, Sama Veda, and Atharva Veda), each of which has four parts, known as Mantras, Brahmanas, Aranyakas, and Upanishads. The Mantras (hymns), especially the later ones in the Rig Veda, constitute the actual beginning of Indian philosophy." (Ibid., p. xviii.

14 Ibid., pp. 23-24.

15 Job 38:1-7.

16 Mt 5:44-45; par. Lk 6:27.

17 Mt 15:10; par. Mk 7:15.

18 The *Rig Veda*, ibid., pp. 29-30.

19 Prov 3:27-31.

20 Prov 22:22-23.

21 Lk 19:10.

22 Prov 13:12.

23 Mircea Eliade, *A History of Religious Ideas*, vol. 1: *From the Stone Age to the Eleusinian Mystics*, trans. Wilard R. Trask (Chicago: The University of Chicago Press, 1978), p. 198.

24 Karen Armstrong, *A History of God, the 4,000 Year Quest of Judaism, Christianity and Islam* (New York: Ballantine Books, 1994), p. xvii.

25 See Mircea Eliade, *From Primitives to Zen, A Thematic Sourcebook of the History of Religions* (London: William Collins Sons & Co. Ltd./Fount Paperbacks, 1977), pp. 268-269. The rugo "is the fence surrounding the homestead and, by metonymy, the homestead itself" (ibid., p. 269).

26 Ibid., p. 268.

27 Ibid., p. 273.

28 Ps 39:1-6.

29 Ps 38:18

30 Ps 38:19.

31 Ps 38:21

32 I. C. Sharma, *Ethical Philosophies of India*, ed. & rev. Stanley M. Daugert
    (Lincoln/Nebraska: Johnson Publishing Company, 1965), p. 73.

33 Lk 16:19-31.

34 See William K. Frankena & John T. Granrose, eds., *Introductory Readings
    in Ethics* (Englewood Cliffs/New Jersey: Prentice-Hall, Inc., 1974), p. 1.

35 Robert L. Stivers, Christine E. Gudorf, Alice Frazer Evans & Robert A.
    Evans, *Christian Ethics, a Case Method Approach* (Maryknoll: Orbis Books,
    1989), p. 4.

36 Ibid., pp. 4-5.

37 Mk 10:17-22; pars. Mt 19:16-22; Lk 18:18-23.

38 Mk 10:22.

39 Mt 10:28; par. Lk 12:4-5.

40 Dominique Lapierre, *The City of Joy* (New York: Warner Books, Inc., 1985),
    p. 489.

41 Isa 11:6.

42 Isa 40:4.

12

Interpretation of Hope in
the Context of Hong Kong:
A Tillichian Perspective[1]

Pan-chiu Lai

Introduction

This paper aims at exploring the significance of the theology of Paul Tillich (1886-1965) for a contextual Christian interpretation of hope in Hong Kong, a religiously pluralistic society undergoing dramatic political change. There are several reasons for choosing Tillich's theology as the subject matter of this study:

1. "Paul Tillich," according to Carl Braaten, "made the greatest contribution to the interpretation of the Kingdom of God among the theological leaders of the last generation."[2]

2. Interpretation of hope is regarded by Tillich as an essential task of theology. Tillich holds that "all images of eternal life are symbols and not statements about empirical objects or happenings."[3] It is therefore necessary for theology to interpret, analyze and conceptualize the meanings of these symbols. These symbols of hope, according to Tillich, can be religious or secular.[4]

3. Tillich is deeply interested in inter-religious dialogue, not only the dialogue with non-Christian religions, e.g. Buddhism, but also the dialogue with secular ideologies, e.g. communism and nationalism, which he calls quasi-religions.

4. Tillich's interpretation of hope is profoundly contextual in the sense that it was formulated in response to the challenge derived from the contemporary socio-political context.

It is therefore very interesting to investigate how Tillich's own interpretation of hope and his "interpretation" of other interpretations of hope can provide valuable insights for a contextual interpretation of hope in Hong Kong.

The Development of Tillich's Contextual Interpretation of Hope

Hope became a dominant theme in Tillich's late thought.[5] In his sermon "The Right to Hope," written only a few months before his death in 1965, Tillich begins with the Biblical text of Romans 4:18, "In hope he believed against hope."[6] This short phrase succinctly summarizes Tillich's endeavor of interpreting hope which is carried out in a despairing situation and in a struggle with alternative interpretations of hope.

According to Tillich's own account, he began to employ the symbol "Kingdom of God" to formulate his eschatology or his interpretation of hope in the 1920's. His decision to adopt the symbol "Kingdom of God" as the cornerstone of his interpretation of hope was influenced by his experience of the First World War, which is regarded as the turning point of his life and thought.[7] Tillich participated in the religious socialist movement in Germany after the First World War and became dissatisfied with many other existing interpretations of hope. In his own words,

> It was the dissatisfaction with the progressivistic, utopian, and transcendental interpretations of history (and the rejection of the non-historical types) that induced the Religious Socialists of the early 1920's to try a solution which avoids their inadequacies and is based on biblical prophetism. This attempt was made in terms of a reinterpretation of the symbol of the Kingdom of God.[8]

Since Tillich's interpretation of the symbol of the Kingdom of God originated in such a profoundly political context, particular emphasis has been placed on the political aspect of the symbol.

In contrast with the traditional understanding of eschatology that its proper subject matter is the "last things," Tillich suggests that eschatology should deal with the *relation* of the temporal to the eternal.[9] The core issue in eschatology, as Tillich understands it, is always the *present* relation of the temporal to the eternal, however future-sounding the symbolism might be.[10] Tillich also suggests that all eschatological symbolism must be rooted in "immediate existential experiences."[11] The symbol "Kingdom of God" is to be understood as the answer to the existential question about the meaning of History.[12] Since groups rather than individuals are the direct bearers of history, the answer to the question of the meaning of history has to be predominantly political.[13] As Tillich remarks, "[i]t is significant that the symbol in which the Bible expresses the meaning of history is political: 'Kingdom of God,' and not 'Life of Spirit' or 'economic abundance'." [14]

It is rather important to note that in some of Tillich's writings in the late 20's, he tends to identify Christ rather than the Kingdom of God as the answer to the question of the meaning of history.[15] Tillich even does not discuss the Kingdom of God in his *Die sozialistische Entscheidung* (1933).[16] As a whole, the concept of the "Kingdom of God" is less central than the concept of "Kairos" in Tillich's exposition of the theological basis of religious socialism.[17] With the concept of "Kairos," Tillich expresses the hope that Europe would enter very soon into a new epoch of Theonomy after an epoch of Heteronomy (Middle Age) and an epoch of Autonomy (Enlightenment). Tillich stresses, "We are convinced that today a kairos, an epochal moment of history is visible."[18] Although Tillich's interpretation of hope formulated in his *The Socialist Decision* might sound rather utopian,[19] this is no longer the case in the formulation in his later writings. As John Clayton notes,

> In Tillich's early writings, the *Kairos* in *now* and *theonomy* is an
> empirical possibility in the present; in his later writings, Kairos is
> increasingly identified with some past time, most notably with
> the appearance of Jesus as the Christ, and *theonomy* is
> transformed into an eschatological hope of which there are in
> time only anticipations.[20]

This shift of emphasis in Tillich's interpretation of hope was largely caused by the political development in Europe after the First World War. At the Oxford Conference on Life and Work in 1937, Tillich delivered a paper re-interpreting the kingdom of God as a criterion to judge the three contemporary "demonic" phenomena: nationalism, dictatorship and capitalism.[21] At that time Tillich still upheld his religious socialism, but later on Tillich was forced to further revise his interpretation of hope, especially the expectation of Kairos. The political development in Europe made him realize that the Kairos would not appear as immediate as he had expected. He admits in a lecture delivered in Berlin 1951,

> But my own personal feeling is that today we live in a period in which the Kairos, the right time of realization, lies far ahead of us in the invisible future, and a void, an unfulfilled space, a vacuum surrounds us.[22]

In "The Right to Hope," Tillich re-interprets the kingdom of God in a rather realistic tone. He says,

> The goal of mankind [humankind] is not progress towards a final stage of perfection; but it is the creation of what is possible for the human being in each particular state of history. ... For the Kingdom of God does not come in one dramatic event sometime in the future. It is coming here and now in every act of love, in every manifestation of truth, in every moment of joy, in every experience of the holy.[23]

We can see that Tillich's interpretation of hope was contextually shaped. He developed and formulated his interpretation of hope in response to the changing political, social and historical situations. In addition to these, Tillich's encounter with Buddhism also contributed to the development of his interpretation of hope.

In the essay "Historical and Non-Historical Interpretations of History: A Comparison" (1939), Tillich suggests that there are two types of interpretation of history, i.e. history is interpreted through nature and history is interpreted through itself. These two types of interpretation are ultimately exclusive and one must choose either one of them.[24] But in *Systematic Theology* Vol. 3 (1963), Tillich recognizes one particular strength of the non-historical interpretation, though he still finds the mystical interpretation of hope fundamentally inadequate. He says,

> There is no symbol analogous to that of the Kingdom of God. But there is often a profound compassion for the universality of suffering under all dimensions of life — an element often lacking under the influence of historical interpretations of history in the Western world.[25]

Tillich further suggests that the encounter of Christianity with the Asian religions, especially Buddhism, which affirms a compassionate attitude towards the suffering of other living beings, may give an opportunity to reinstate the "Kingdom of God" as a living symbol.[26] Tillich's interpretation of the Kingdom of God in his *Systematic Theology* Vol. 3 represents his own attempt at reinstating the "Kingdom of God" as a living symbol.

Tillich's Interpretation of the Interpretations of Hope

Before exploring Tillich's own interpretation of the symbol of the Kingdom of God, it is necessary to investigate the reasons for his rejection of other interpretations of hope or what he calls interpretations of the meaning of history. According to Tillich, there are three different non-historical interpretations of history giving negative answers to the question of the meaning of history: the tragic, the mystical, and the mechanistic. Other than these, there are also three historical interpretations offering positive but inadequate answers to the question of the meaning of history: progressivistic, utopian and transcendental.[27]

The tragic interpretation of the meaning of history can be found in the ancient Greek thought. In this view, history does not run towards any historical or trans-historical aim but in a circle back to its beginning. There is nothing beyond or above this stretch of time which itself is determined by fate. The glory of life in nature, nations and persons is praised, but there is no hope and no expectation of an immanent or transcendent fulfillment of history.[28]

With regard to the mystical interpretation, Tillich suggests that this can be found in Taoism and some Indian religions, including Buddhism. In the view of this type of interpretation, historical existence has no meaning in itself. History itself can neither create the new nor be truly real. The emphasis of this interpretation is on the individuals and particularly on the comparatively few religious elites who are aware of the human predicament. Tillich finds the mystical interpretation dissatisfactory because it contains no impulse to transform history in the direction of universal humanity and justice. What it offers is only one way to cope with the ambiguities of life and that is to live with them.[29]

The mechanistic interpretation of hope, according to Tillich, is based on the modern mechanistic worldview, which may be associated with reductionistic naturalism. Unlike the classical Greek thought, this mechanistic interpretation does not emphasize the tragic element in history or the greatness of human existence. Since it is related to the technical control of nature by science and technology, it has in some cases a progressivistic character. However, it is also possible to derive an attitude of cynical devaluation of existence in general and of history in particular.[30] Tillich thinks that these non-historical interpretations offer no hope in the proper sense of the word, for they expect nothing new to take place.

According to Tillich, progressivism is the belief that there is a universal law determining the dynamics of history and that history is running ahead toward an aim. Human society is necessarily progressing through human endeavor, especially science and technology. Although this aim is inner-historical, progressivism remains a quasi-religious symbol because it gives impetus to historical actions, passion to revolutions, and a meaning of life for many.[31] However, progressivism is not adequate because depression is also a fact of history and in some aspects, such as the moral act in freedom, there is no progression at all. Tillich admits that there is progress in science, technology, and education, but not in moral act as an act of freedom. Even the justice of democracy which represents progress above other forms of justice is a progress only in quantitative sense and not in qualitative sense. Each political system points to the justice of the Kingdom of God and there is no progress from the one to the other in this respect.[32]

Unlike progressivism which takes progress as an infinite process without an end, utopianism believes in a final state of fulfillment.[33] Utopianism is the belief that the utopia, which literally means "no place," will be established on earth and that history will arrive at the perfect stage in which the ambiguities of life are conquered.[34] Tillich regards utopianism as a form of idolatry because it gives the quality of ultimacy to something preliminary. Furthermore, it disregards the always present existential estrangement and the ambiguities of life and history. This kind of interpretation of history or hope, in Tillich's view, is both inadequate and dangerous.[35]

Tillich also finds the "transcendental" interpretation unsatisfactory.

This transcendental interpretation can be found in some forms of the Christian tradition, particularly orthodox Lutheranism. This interpretation suggests that Christ appeared to save individuals within the church from bondage to sin and guilt and to enable them to be received into Heaven after death.[36] Tillich finds that there are three shortcomings in the transcendental interpretation:

1. It contrasts the salvation of the individual with the transformation of the historical group and the universe, thus separating the one from the other.
2. It contrasts the realm of salvation with the realm of creation and therefore may have the Manichean danger.
3. This view interprets the symbol of the Kingdom of God as a static supernatural order into which individuals enter after their lives and, as a result, excludes culture as well as nature from the saving processes in history.[37]

Tillich's Own Interpretation of Hope

As there are so many interpretations of hope (six have been mentioned above), one has to ask the question: how can we distinguish genuine or true hope from false or foolish hope? Tillich attempts to answer this question concerning how to distinguish genuine from foolish hope. He suggests,

> Where there is genuine hope, there that for which we hope, has already some presence. In some way, the hoped for is at the same time here and not here. It is not yet fulfilled and it may remain fulfilled. But it is here, in the situation and in ourselves as a power which drives those who hope into the future. There is a beginning here and now. ... Where such a beginning of what is hoped for is lacking, hope is foolishness.[38]

Tillich's suggestion here can be said to be a further development of his view concerning religious symbol in general expressed in his book *Dynamics of Faith*. In that book Tillich proposes two criteria, based on the nature of religion as ultimate concern, to evaluate religious symbols. The first criterion is whether the ultimate symbol expressed is really ultimate. The second criterion is whether the symbol is alive. In other words, "whether it can adequately express an ultimate concern and in such a way that it creates reply, action, and communication."[39] An adequate interpretation of hope, accordingly, should point to the ultimate reality which is trans-historical or eternal, and be related to the immediate experience and present reality. As we are going to see, Tillich's interpretation of the symbol "Kingdom of God" aims at providing an interpretation of hope which affirms not only the "ultimate" but also the "immediate" character of the Kingdom of God.

Tillich regards the symbol "Kingdom of God" as the most embracing eschatological symbol. He notices that alongside with the symbol of the Kingdom of God, there are also symbols of "Spiritual Presence" and "Eternal Life" in the Christian tradition. However, Tillich argues, the connotations of the symbol "Kingdom of God" are more embracing than those of the two others, although each of these symbols includes the other two. Tillich suggests that while the Spiritual Presence emphasizes the inner-historical character and the Eternal Life the trans-historical,[40] the kingdom of God covers both the inner-historical and the trans-historical side. With regard to the symbol "Kingdom of God," Tillich suggests,

> As inner-historical, it participates in the dynamics of history; as trans-historical, it answers the questions implied in the ambiguities of the dynamics of history. In the former quality it is manifest through the Spiritual Presence; in the latter quality it is identical with Eternal Life.[41]

With regard to the Kingdom of God within history, Tillich holds that "where there is manifestation of the kingdom of God, there is revelation and salvation."[42] While Christ is the central manifestation of the Kingdom of God in history, the churches are the representatives of the Kingdom of God in history.[43] However, Tillich further points out that the Kingdom of God is not restricted to the religious realm or the daily life of individuals.[44] The Kingdom of God is a dynamic power struggling with the demonic forces in churches as well as empires. Tillich believes that the Kingdom of God is not only in the world history, but also comprises the whole of reality.[45] The other forms of life and the inorganic world are included not only in the Kingdom of God in history, but also in the Kingdom of God as the end of history.[46]

Tillich insists that the trans-historical side of the Kingdom of God which is also expressed in the symbol "Eternal Life" embraces not only human beings but also all other beings. Tillich holds that eternal blessedness is attributed to those who participated in the Divine life, not only to human beings, but also to everything that is.[47] Tillich further clarifies that instead of being a future state of things, the eternal is always present, not only in human beings who are aware of it, but also in everything that has being within the whole of being.[48] As Raymond Bulman aptly comments, Tillich's eschatology contains a grand unitary vision which is political as well as transcendent, social as well as individual and cosmic as well as historical.[49]

Based on its affirmation of both the inner-historical and trans-historical characters of the Kingdom of God, Tillich particularly reminds the churches that as representatives of the Kingdom of God in history it is their task to keep alive the tension between the consciousness of presence and the expectation of the coming.[50] Tillich's view of democracy reflects his two-character theory of the Kingdom of God. Tillich affirms that "[i]n so far as democratization of political attitudes and institutions serves to resist the destructive implications of power, it is a manifestation of the Kingdom of God in history."[51] However, he also reminds that the democratic system is the best so far, but it is not absolute and should not be identified with the Kingdom of God.[52] Tillich believes that historical sacrifice of individuals in every political system is inevitable.[53] But he insists that if one is demanded to sacrifice for something bearing no relation to him or her, it is enforced self-annihilation and not genuine sacrifice. Genuine sacrifice fulfills rather than annihilates the one who makes the sacrifice.[54] Tillich suggests that the kingdom of God is manifest wherever historical sacrifice and the certainty of personal fulfillment are united.[55]

Towards a Contextual Christian Interpretation of Hope

Hong Kong is a religiously pluralistic society. Besides the traditional religions, including Christianity and the traditional Chinese religions, there are several secular ideologies in Hong Kong, including nationalism, humanism, materialism and secularism. At the moment the people of Hong Kong live in the shadow of the June Fourth event in 1989 and on the threshold of 1997 when Hong Kong changes from a British colony to a special administrative region of China. The capitalist economic system of Hong Kong will be preserved for at least 50 years after 1997, according to the Sino-British Joint Declaration. For some years, the people of Hong Kong have been attempting to fight for greater degree of political freedom and democracy without success. The Hong Kong people's feelings of frustration and anxiety are understandable. Besides these, Hong Kong is also a polarized society situated in a seriously polluted environment. The gap between the poor and the rich has become wider and wider in recent years. What this context calls for is an interpretation of hope which can inspire people's imagination and action for a just society, a more democratic political system and a better environment.

But what are the interpretations of hope available at the moment? From the political circle, we can hear the promise that both the political stability and the economic prosperity of Hong Kong will be maintained. Many people hope that the future of Hong Kong will be even more glorious after its returning to its motherland. There seems to be no upper limit for the economic progress of Hong Kong. Unfortunately, social justice is not included in this progressivistic hope. From the religious circle, the predominant interpretation of hope refers to a "spiritual" and non-political future for individuals in another world. The theological tradition of the mainstream of the Christian churches in Hong Kong may give the most illustrative example of the transcendental interpretation of hope. Many other religions in Hong Kong, especially the Chinese popular religion, may give similar non-political interpretations of hope.[56]

From the discussion above, one may find that the context of Hong Kong is quite similar to that of Tillich in the 1920's — hoping for a better social and political system on the one hand and dissatisfied with the existing interpretations of hope on the other. What then is the significance of Tillich's interpretation of hope for Hong Kong? In the perspective of Tillich's theology, a contextual Christian interpretation of hope needs to be done in response to the challenge derived from the socio-political situation and also in dialogue with other interpretations of hope. In the Hong Kong context, it has to be carried out not only in response to the secular interpretations of hope and also in dialogue with Chinese religions as well as the mainstream of Christian theology in Hong Kong.

Secular Interpretation of Hope in Hong Kong

In response to the challenge of the secular interpretations of hope in Hong Kong, a theological interpretation of hope should perform a twofold task — apologetic and polemic. On the one hand, it needs to defend the Christian hope in face of the criticism coming from secularism, materialism, progressivism, humanism, etc. As the Bible says, "Always be prepared to make a defense to any one who calls you to account for the hope that is in you, yet do it with gentleness and reverence" (1 Peter 3:15, RSV). On the other hand, it is necessary to take on some of the secular ideologies and point out their inadequacies, especially that of progressivism and secularism.

Tillich was concerned particularly in the question of historical sacrifice of individuals. He insists that the assumed well-being of a "last generation" does not justify the evil and tragedy of all previous generations; no future true justice and happiness can annihilate the injustice and suffering of the past.[57] This is the same concern underlying Peter Berger's proposal of "demythologizing" the myths of development. According to Berger, there are two types of mythology of development: myth of growth and myth of revolution. Both types of mythology promise a glorious future in which all people will be well to do. The common underlying message of these myths is: in order to achieve this aim some sort of sacrifice is necessary and justifiable. The myth of growth (usually being employed to justify the capitalist way of development) suggests that we can have economic growth first (i.e. letting some of us get rich first) and then the wealth will be fairly distributed. During this process, the well-being of the poor cannot be safeguarded and the polarization of the rich and the poor should be tolerated. The myth of revolution (usually being employed to justify the Communist way of development) suggests the opposite that we should have equality first and then getting rich all together. During this process, the interest of those who are rich and the political freedom and human rights of individuals will not be guaranteed. Both types of mythology can be used by any governments to justify their particular programs of development. They also give people reasons for their suffering and the ground for hope. What Peter Berger suggests to be done is "demythologization," which means to face the fact and to calculate the cost. In concrete terms, we have to ask: Who will pay the price and who determines whom to pay? Is this decision democratically made? Is it fair? How to falsify the promise made?[58] From the perspective of Tillich's theology, one has to add: Do the people of Hong Kong, especially those who have made sacrifice for the prosperity of Hong Kong, share the benefits of economic development? A theological interpretation of hope may involve a demythologization of the myth of development in Hong Kong.

With regard to the democratic movement in Hong Kong, a Christian interpretation of hope should affirm that it is right to hope for democracy in spite of its non-ultimacy, and that the democratic movement itself demonstrates that this hope is not a foolish one, but a genuine hope which has its root in present reality. As Tillich says,

World history is a cemetery of broken hopes, of utopias which had no foundation in reality. But there is also fulfillment of historical hopes, however fragmentary it may be. The democratic form of life which has become reality is a fulfillment of old ideas about the equal dignity of men [and women] before God and under the law; and it could become reality because there were social groups in which the idea was already effective, so that it could grow into reality.[59]

In Dialogue with the Chinese Religions in Hong Kong

Although Tillich had no direct experience of dialogue with the Chinese religions, his experience of encountering Japanese Buddhism made him reflect on the interpretation of the kingdom of God. Tillich admits that compared with the Buddhist idea of nirvana, the Christian symbol of the Kingdom of God seems to be an anthropocentric symbol in which animals and plants are insignificant. However, he suggests that the kingdom of God is not only a social symbol; it is also a symbol which comprises the whole of reality.[60] According to Tillich's analysis, the Kingdom of God has four connotations: political, social, personalistic, and universal.[61] The personal, social and political connotations are essential and never missing elements of the Christian experience because the symbol of the Kingdom of God takes its symbolic material from these spheres.[62] The fourth connotation affirms that the symbol of the Kingdom of God is not exclusively for human beings; it involves the fulfillment of life under all dimensions.[63]

Tillich thinks that while Christianity is able to learn from Buddhism and to develop a profound compassion towards the suffering of other forms of life, it seems impossible for the Asian religions to accept the symbol of the Kingdom of God in anything like its original meaning. Tillich suggests that it is because the personal, social and political spheres are radically transcended in the basic experience of Buddhism which is expressed in the symbol of "Nirvana."[64] Tillich may have underestimated the potential of Buddhism in this aspect and may have overlooked the Pure Land tradition and the messianic movements in Buddhism. However, he is quite right in pointing out that Buddhist-Christian dialogue may benefit the construction of ecological theology and the Christian interpretation of hope in the context of ecological concern.

With regard to the traditional Chinese religions, Tillich suggests that the Chinese doctrine of Tao represents the mystical form of non-historical interpretation of history. In this tradition, while the Tao is the eternal law of the world, it is both the norm and the power of human life. The present is a consequence of the past, but not at all an anticipation of the future.[65] Tillich boldly asserts, "[i]n Chinese literature there are fine records of the past but no expectations of the future."[66] Tillich's identifying Taoism as a form of the mystical interpretation of the meaning of history is misleading and possibly wrong.[67] Tillich is definitely wrong in his remark concerning Chinese literature. It is quite right to say that classical Confucianism and philosophical Taoism had not developed an eschatology comparable to that of Christianity and that in pre-Buddhist China, the interpretation of hope in Chinese religions was basically this-worldly oriented.[68] However, there are too many counter-examples to Tillich's bold assertion. There were many messianic movements and forms of eschatological literature in China.[69] It is undeniable that Tillich's knowledge about the Chinese religions is far from adequate. Of course we should not expect Tillich, a Western Christian theologian who died in the middle of the 1960's, to have any extensive and in-depth knowledge of Chinese religions. The important point to be made is: a contextual and indigenized theological interpretation of hope may need to have dialogue with the interpretations of hope in the Chinese religions, including Confucianism, Chinese Buddhism, religious and philosophical Taoism, and popular religion in Hong Kong. It is also noteworthy that although there were messianic movements and eschatological literature in the Taoist and Buddhist traditions, compared with the Christian churches and organizations in Hong Kong, the traditional Chinese religions in Hong Kong as a whole are even less outspoken with regard to political issues. Christianity may need to raise the matter together with the ecological issues in its dialogue with the other religions in Hong Kong.

In Dialogue with the Mainstream of the Christian Tradition in Hong Kong

A contextual Christian interpretation of hope may need to point out the inadequacy of the "transcendental" interpretation of hope dominant in the theological tradition of the Christian churches of Hong Kong. In terms of soteriology, this tradition emphasizes the salvation of individual's soul at the expense of any consideration for the salvation of nature. In terms of eschatology, it is individualistic, other-worldly, futuristic, and revolutionary in the sense that the Kingdom of God is to be established by God alone and will come suddenly and dramatically.[70] For Tillich, this interpretation of hope is inadequate because no individual destiny is separated from the destiny of the universe.[71] It is not only selfish but also foolish to hope for oneself alone. At the end of the sermon "The Right to Hope," Tillich makes this final remark:

> Participation in the eternal is not given to the separated individual. It is given to him in unity with all others, with mankind [humankind], with everything living, with everything that has being and is rooted in the divine ground of being. All powers of creation are in us and we are in them. We do not hope for us alone or for those alone who share our hope; we hope also for those who had and have no hope, for those whose hopes for this life remain unfulfilled, for those who are disappointed and indifferent, for those who despair of life and even for those who have hurt or destroyed life. Certainly, if we could only hope each for himself [or herself], it would be a poor and foolish hope. Eternity is the ground and aim of every being for God shall be all in all. Amen.[72]

Conclusion

Although Tillich's interpretation of hope is not free from shortcomings,[73] his theology gives valuable insights for an interpretation of hope adequate for the context of Hong Kong. His interpretation of the interpretations of hope may provide a useful heuristic device to interpret the various interpretations of hope available in Hong Kong. His own interpretation of hope, which is centered at the symbol of the Kingdom of God, may be particularly capable of addressing to some of the important issues raised in the context of Hong Kong. His approach to interpreting hope in response to the socio-political context and in dialogue with other interpretations of hope demonstrates a viable way of interpreting the Christian hope in the context of Hong Kong.

Notes

1. This is a revised version of my paper presented first at the conference and then published under the title: "A Contextual Reflection on Tillich's Interpretation of Hope," in *Ching Feng*, Vol. 39 No. 4 (December 1996), pp. 287-306.

2. Carl Braaten, "The Kingdom of God and Life Everlasting," in *Christian Theology* eds. Peter Hodgson and Robert King, (London: SCM, 1983), p. 291.

3. Tillich, "Symbols of Eternal Life," *Harvard Divinity Bulletin*, 26 (April 1962), pp. 3-4, & 9. See also: Raymond F. Bulman, "History, Symbolism, and Eternal Life," in eds. *Paul Tillich: A New Catholic Assessment* Raymond Bulman and Frederick Parrella , (Collegeville: The Liturgical Press, 1994), p. 122.

4. Tillich, *Systematic Theology*, vol. 3 (London: SCM, 1978), p. 348.

5. See Ronald H. Stone, "Introduction," in Paul Tillich, *Theology of Peace*, edited by Ronald H. Stone (Louisville: Westminster/John Knox Press, 1990), p. 23.

6. The sermon was first published in *Neue Zeitschrift fur systematische Theologie und Religionsphilosophie*, vol. 7 no. 3 (1965), pp. 371-377. It is reprinted in: (1) Mark Kline Taylor, ed., *Paul Tillich: Theologian of the Boundaries* (London: Collins, 1987), pp. 324-331; (2) *Christian Century*, 107 (N 14, 1990), pp. 1064-1067; and (3) Paul Tillich, *Theology of Peace*, pp. 182-190.

7. See Wilhelm and Marion Pauck, *Paul Tillich: His Life and Thought*, Vol. 1: *Life* (London: Collins, 1977), pp. 40-56.

8. Tillich, *Systematic Theology*, vol. 3, p. 356.

9. Ibid., p. 298, emphasis added.

10. Ibid., pp. 298-299.

11. Tillich, "Symbols of Eternal Life," *Harvard Divinity Bulletin*, 26 (April 1962), p. 3; see also: Raymond Bulman, op. cit., p. 122.

12. Tillich, *Systematic Theology*, vol. 3, p. 356.

13. Ibid., p. 308, & 312.

14. Ibid., p. 311.

15. See Pan-Chiu Lai, *Towards a Trinitarian Theology of Religions: A Study of Paul Tillich's Thought* (Kampen: Kok Pharos, 1994), pp. 62-65.

16. See Tillich, *The Socialist Decision*, trans. by Franklin Sherman (New York: Harper & Row, 1977).

17. Concerning the concept of "Kairos," see Tillich, "Kairos," in *The Protestant Era*, tr. by James Luther Adams (Chicago: The University of Chicago Press, abridged edition 1957), pp. 32-51.

18. Ibid., p. 48.

19. For a critique of the utopian character of Tillich's interpretation of hope, see George H. Tavard, "The Kingdom of God as Utopia," in *Paul Tillich: A New Catholic Assessment*, Raymond Bulman and Frederick Parrella eds., p. 141.

20. John Clayton, "Tillich and the Art of Theology," in James Luther Adams *et al.* (eds.), *The Thought of Paul Tillich* (San Francisco: Harper & Row, 1985), p. 279.

21. See Tillich, "The Kingdom of God in History," in *Theology of Peace*, pp. 25-56.

22. Tillich, *Political Expectation* (New York: Harper & Row, 1971), p. 180.

23. Cf. Tillich, "The Right to Hope," *in Theology of Peace*, pp. 188-189.

24. See Tillich, "Historical and Nonhistorical Interpretations of History: A Comparison," in *The Protestant Era*, pp. 16-17.

25. Tillich, *Systematic Theology*, vol. 3, p. 352.

26. Ibid., p. 356.

27. Ibid., pp. 350-356. See also Tillich, "Historical and Nonhistorical Interpretations of History: A Comparison," in *The Protestant Era*, pp. 16-31.

28. Tillich, *Systematic Theology*, vol. 3, p. 351.

29. Ibid., pp. 351-352.

30. Ibid., p. 352.

31. Ibid., pp. 352-353.

32. Ibid., pp. 333-339.

33. Progressivism, according to Tillich, may appear in two forms (1) progress as an infinite process without an end; or (2) belief in a final state of fulfillment. While the former is progressivism, the latter may be called utopianism. See ibid., p. 353.

34. Ibid., p. 354.

35. Ibid., p. 355.

36. Ibid.

37. Ibid., pp. 355-356.

38. Cf. Tillich, "The Right to Hope," in *Theology of Peace*, p. 185.

39. Tillich, *Dynamics of Faith* (New York: Harper & Row, 1958), pp. 96-97.

40. Tillich, *Systematic Theology*, vol. 3, p. 357.

41. Ibid.

42. Ibid., p 364

43. Ibid., p. 364,& 374.

44. Ibid., p. 381.

45. Ibid., p. 377.

46. Tillich explains this with his doctrine of the participation of nature in the process of fall and salvation. For details, see Pan-Chiu Lai, "Paul Tillich on Humanity and Nature: A Chinese Perspective," *Logos and Pneuma: Chinese Journal of Theology*, vol. 7 (Fall 1997), pp. 149-173 (in Chinese, with an English abstract on pp. 293-294).

47. Tillich, *Systematic Theology*, vol. 3, p. 405, 409, 432,& 436.

48. Ibid., p. 400.

49. Raymond F. Bulman, op. cit., p. 116.

50. Tillich, *Systematic Theology*, vol. 3, p. 391.

51. Ibid., p. 385

52. Ibid., p. 347,& 385.

53. Ibid., pp. 347-348.

54. Ibid., p. 392.

55. Ibid., pp. 392-393.

56. See Li Zhu Fan and Jie Hou, "Hope in Chinese Popular Religious Consciousness," paper at the Conference.

57. Tillich, *Systematic Theology*, vol. 3, p. 373.

58. For details, see Peter Berger, *Pyramids of Sacrifice: Political Ethics and Social Change* (Harmondsworth: Pelican Books, 1977), pp. 23-47. It is interesting to note that the case of China has been changed from the myth of revolution to the myth of growth after the economic reform underlying which is the message of letting some of the people get rich first.

59. Cf. Tillich, "The Right to Hope," in *Theology of Peace*, p. 187.

60. Tillich, *Systematic Theology*, vol. 3, p. 377.

61. Ibid., p. 358.

62. Ibid., p. 357.

63. Ibid., p. 359.

64. Ibid., p. 357.

65. Tillich, "Historical and Nonhistorical Interpretations of History: A Comparison," in *The Protestant Era*, p. 17

66. Ibid.

67. Tillich makes no distinction between philosophical Taoism and religious Taoism. Some of the schools or sects of the Taoist religion are messianic and/or eschatological.

68. See Judith Berling's paper: "Threads of 'Hope' in Traditional Chinese Religions" and Mu-Chou Poo's paper: "The Nature of Hope in Pre-Buddhist Chinese Religion" presented at the Conference.

69. See the following papers presented at the Conference for details: Feng Mou Li, "The Hope of Salvation in the Taoist Belief of 'Eschatological Calamity' by the Sect of Ling-Pao in the Six Dynasties;" Frank Reynolds, "Maitreya: A Locus of Hope in Buddhism;" John Lagerway, "Taoist Messianism in Medieval China;" and Daniel Overmyer, "Hope in Chinese Popular Religious Texts."

70. John Macquarrie gives a typology of Christian interpretations of hope by listing four pairs of contrast: (1) individual vs. social, cosmic; (2) this-worldly vs. other-worldly; (3) evolutionary vs. revolutionary; and (4) realized vs. future. There can be totally sixteen types of hope. For details, see John Macquarrie, *Christian Hope* (London: Mowbray, 1978), pp. 86-88.

71. Tillich, *Systematic Theology*, vol. 3, p. 418.

72. Cf. Tillich, "The Right to Hope," in *Theology of Peace*, p. 190.

73. With regard to Tillich's interpretation of the interpretations of hope, the Buddhists and the Taoists may complain that Tillich's typology or comparison is not fair because they are not trying to offer an interpretation of history at all. With regard to Tillich's own interpretation of hope, his

explanation on how the eternity appears in history or how the temporal is to be elevated into eternity is not very satisfactory. His use of the expression such as "invasion" (of the Eternal into the temporary) sounds too supernaturalistic. See Tillich, *The Religious Situation*, trans. H. Richard Niebuhr (Cleveland: The World Publishing Company, 1956), p. 176.

13

Hope and Its Interpretation in the Returning Community of Isaiah 56-66

Archie C. C. Lee

Introduction

Hope as expressed in the Bible is definitely context-specific and historically-culturally conditioned. The presentations of it in different portions of the Bible and its interpretations in subsequent periods in various Jewish as well as Christian communities inevitably exhibit some socio-political dimensions. The social location of the original audience has shaped the way hope was perceived and the socio-political context of the interpreter provides a perspective through which hope is understood. In any concrete crisis situation where hope, or the lack of it, plays a significant function in determining the proper communal response to the pressing issue of uncertainty for the future, it is natural that conflict of interpretations of hope is bound to prevail.

The aim of this paper is to look into the exilic community in Isaiah 56-66 to see how hope is being interpreted by social groups in Babylon and in Palestine. The socio-political situation of Hong Kong, in the face of the return to the "motherland," will be introduced to enable a meaningful engagement and creative dialogue between the chosen biblical text and the living social text of the present writer. This paper does not intend to present general views of after-life or messianism in the Bible but focuses on tracing the articulation of hope by the returnees from the Exile in the face of growing conflicts and agonies experienced at the community level as a whole.

The sociological study of and contextual approach to Isaiah 56-66 has been rightly emphasized and focused in recent scholarship, setting the text in the context of the post-exilic communities. Robert Carroll, Paul Hanson and Daniel Smith, to name just a few, have made use of knowledge of social science to enlighten the socio-political matrices of the post-exilic community.[1] In view of the current discussion, I submit, the experience and the aspiration of the Hong Kong people in the run-up to the return of sovereignty to China will provide a concrete context for, and an existential testimony to, the understanding of the struggles and conflicts in the returning community of Isaiah 56-66. A longing for an open, inclusive, as well as righteous community that embraces the diversity of experience and plurality of identity is expressed in the text.

As the 155 years of British colonial rule of Hong Kong ends on June 30, 1997 and Hong Kong is to return to China on July 1, 1997, the issue of hope in the midst of uncertainty and change is naturally raised among citizens of the Hong Kong community. A re-reading of the Book of Isaiah, especially the so-called Trito-Isaiah (Isaiah 56-66) may shed light on the Hong Kong situation which, being a "social text" itself, may contribute to our interpretation of the text through the cross-textual hermeneutical process I have proposed previously in other writings.[2] In brief, the process involves reading at least two texts in parallel with the aim to creatively integrate them in a meaningful way that relevant theologies may evolve, which will address the issue of Christian identity in a non-Christian world. In the case of Hong Kong, it is the Hong Kong Chinese Christian identity that becomes the focal concern of cross-textual reading.

Reading Between the Exile and the Crown Colony

For the people of the Exile, the one appropriate question to ask, other than the ones whether Yahweh cares or not, whether God has the power to save or not, is: "How did they perceive their hope in the face of uncertainties and hopelessness, and how did they articulate it in the event of the return promised by Deutero-Isaiah?" The people taken to Babylon in 597 and 586 BCE were deeply concerned with their future. If there is hope, it is no doubt being shaped by their shattering experience of political defeat, social displacement and the destruction of the temple of Yahweh. Should there be hope, it is inevitably sustained by their die-hard faith and aspiration, or formulated in terms of the uncertainty of the forthcoming unknown home-ward journey through the vast geographically extended wilderness, not to mention the danger of this repatriation journey. Though theologically understood as transformative restoration to the holy mountain of Yahweh, the return is a difficult decision to make for the settlers in a foreign land.

Fifty years had gone by since the exilic community was exiled to Babylon (586-538). They certainly settled down quite well, according to the admonition in Jeremiah's letter (Jeremiah 29), they were to build houses, plant gardens, and provide marriage for their children.[3] Of the original exiled generation, those that survive are now old. If ever their hope of returning home can be sustained, will these aged men and women actually go back? The younger generation may have been taught of the homeland, to whom a vision of Jerusalem was nurtures and a sense of belonging — in short — an identity of being a people from Palestine; but, will they leave their "home" in Babylon and take their whole families to return to an unfamiliar new "home"?[4]

The long period of separation and individual development of the two communities, the exiled in Babylon and the majority left behind in Palestine, have created differences in life styles, cultural orientations, socio-political identities and even religious practices and forms. A watershed has set in that further divides the Diaspora from the Palestinian community. Any interpretation of hope which does not take into account of this socio-political and religio-cultural settings of the period of return and restoration will be misleading if not naively distorting.

The social experience and political context of Hong Kong in face of 1997 can enhance our reading of the interpretation of hope in the text of Isaiah 40-66. There are, of course, important differences between the two situations. In the case of Hong Kong, the "return" does not involve physical migration of the people back to the homeland, as the exilic community in Babylon had to do. The people of Hong Kong are not taking a journey to an old place, but metaphorically "returning" to the Chinese sovereignty. The people themselves are not given a choice; whether they like it or not, both the land and its people are to be handed over to China. A new political regime is taking over. For those who do not wish to be part of it and have the means, the only option available is to embark on a second exile to foreign countries. This is exactly what some of the wealthy people: capitalists, the business community and professionals have tried to do. However, the majority of the people of Hong Kong have to stay behind to cope with the reality of the return in 1997.[5]

The fact that more than half of the people in Hong Kong were refugees from China during the political upheavals in the mainland, especially after the communist takeover of power since 1949, bespeaks the close traditional cultural links, family ties and emotional attachment of Hong Kong to China on the one hand, and the break and alienation from China on the other, which is particularly so for those who experienced political turmoils in the last fifty years.

That we have to recognize and detect the continuity and discontinuity of the culture and structures in the two societies is of paramount importance which can never be over-emphasized. The hope of return proclaimed in Deutero-Isaiah, and the kind of hope implied in the Sino-British Joint Declaration 1984 and the Basic Law of the future SAR (Hong Kong Special Administrative Region of China) will have to be worked out to accommodate the socio-political reality. Taking into account the anthropological dimension of these promises, hope is not an easy task to achieve.

The Socio-political Dynamics of the Return

It is generally agreed that Trito-Isaiah (Isaiah 56-66) dates from after the year 538 BCE when Cyrus, King of Persia, issued the edict that allowed the exiled to return to Jerusalem to rebuild the temple, and ends before 515 BCE when the rebuilt temple was consecrated.[6]

The proclamation of Second Isaiah did not come to pass: "not only did the nation's not stream to Jerusalem — the descendants of the Israelites deported by the Assyrians failed to reappear. The majority even of the deportees in Babylon elected to remain there." [7]

Trito-Isaiah has depicted a situation totally different from that of the excitement and jubilation as expressed by the salvation oracles of Deutero-Isaiah. What is reflected in these chapters is a situation of conflicts, quarrels and disputes among the returnees from the Babylonian Exile, whose hope has turned into bitter disappointments.[8] Joseph Blenkinsopp explains the historical occasion and the cause of conflict in terms of the emergence of dissenting movements and intra-group conflicts. He describes the situation in this way:

> The consequent return to the homeland of some of the deportees or their descendants though probably not in the form of an immediate and enthusiastic *aliyah* [immigration] as the Chronicles would have us believe, must have created a situation in which conflict was practically inevitable. Now, for the first time, we have two distinct groups, whom for convenience we may call the Palestinians and the Babylonians, both claiming to be the genuine heirs of the old Israel destroyed in the massive disasters of the sixth century.[9]

Setting Isaiah 40-66 in the time of the Exile and return, Peter D. Miscall sees the style and scenes depicted in these chapters as "more consistently visionary and metaphorical than in chapters 1-39." He further advocates a view that these chapters are "a dream set in a nightmare time, and they are a dream troubled by reality."[10] Surely, Deutero-Isaiah's promise of release and return has to be worked out in the terms of the socio-political realities.

Social conflict is inevitable when two communities that have developed along different lines and in different cultural settings rejoin after being separated for over half a century.[11]

Exactly what the conflicts are, as reflected in post-exilic texts: Trito-Isaiah, Haggai and Ezekiel etc., is not easy to pin-point. The evidence is not unambiguous. Morton Smith and Bernard Lang trace the conflict to the pre-exilic "Yahweh alone movement" and the syncretists left behind in the land.[12] It may be true that the majority of the people were left behind in the land, and syncretistic religion was practiced, as Ezekiel's vision of the ruined temple testified (Ezekiel 8:1-18): no conclusive evidence can be provided to substantiate that the division of the exilic people and the community left-behind in Palestine community is to be drawn along the lines of "Yahweh alone"/ "syncretist."[13]

But, it is beyond dispute that conflict between opposing factions and rival groups did exist in the post-exilic community. The evidence of dissension and confrontation is detectable in the present form of the text of Isaiah 56-66.

As to the identity of the different factions and the nature of the division, scholars are divided and, at present, are far from reaching any agreement. Basically, a sociological analysis of the post-exilic situation is being adopted. Paul Hanson has proposed an important study using what he terms as a "contextual-typological approach." He traces the origin of the conflict to the struggle of two parties, the hierocratic group and the visionaries. The former was associated with the control of the official cult and the temple while by the latter, Hanson refers to the disenfranchised Levites who, in rejecting the position of the status quo, were denied participation in the temple services at Zion.

Seen from the complexity of the text and the polarity of voices in the community of Hong Kong in the face of 1997, the theory put forward by Paul Hanson appears to be too simple and, at the same time, over-rigid in creating a sharp dichotomy between the oppressed, powerless visionaries and the priestly, powerful oppressors of hierocratics. Any analysis must take into account the Palestinian group, the returned minority and the disapora community (Ezra 8:35). The issue of re-distribution of power either to the people as a whole or to the leaders, as well as the question of redefinition of identity, are the two major concerns that occupied the attention of the people and shaped their theological positions.

Re-interpretations of Hope

The inner community conflicts and the bitter accusations in Trito-Isaiah do not render the high expectation of the promise and hope for the proclaimed salvation of Deutero-Isaiah meaningless. On the contrary, these eleven chapters of the last part of the Book of Isaiah highlight a significant theological challenge, a challenge that raises our theological discourse on God's promise and prophetic word of hope to a higher level. Paul Hanson has summed up this challenge that in these chapters "we will find the word of God entering the harsh realities of human struggle and suffering. The vision of God's purpose is not lost, but its applicability in a situation that seems hostile to God's peace becomes problematic."[14] Though the community wants to return, restore and rebuild a full and happy future, the obstacles are so many that hope seems to be obscured and frustrated:

> Therefore justice is a far from us, and righteousness does not reach us; we wait for light, and lo! there is darkness; and for brightness,

but we walk in gloom.
We wait for justice, but there is none; for salvation, but it is far
from us." (Isaiah 59:9, 11b).[15]

Compared with Deutero-Isaiah, the great prophetic voice for God's
salvation during the exilic time, Trito-Isaiah's utterance presents a
different perspective. Israel is now admonished to act righteously in
response to the announced, but somehow a delayed or failed salvation.
Isaiah 46:12-13, assumed by some scholars to be in the mind of the author
of the first verse of Trito-Isaiah, illustrates the difference in
understanding:[16]

> Harken to me, you stubborn of heart, you who are far from
> deliverance: I bring near my deliverance, it is not far off, and my
> salvation will not tarry; I will put salvation in Zion, for Israel my
> glory (Isaiah 46: 12-13).

Isaiah 56:1-2 links the hope of the community in terms of the coming of
God's salvation and righteousness, closely with the community's
"keeping of justice" and the "doing of righteousness." Thus understood,
hope is interpreted as being grounded on the ethical dimension of human
response in the present (Isaiah 60:21; 61:1-3; 62:12). This is a way to
reduce the dissonance created by the failure of expectation of salvation
and the frustration of hope in the returned community.[17]

> Maintain justice, and do what is right,
> for soon my salvation will come and
> my deliverance be revealed.
> Happy is the mortal who does this,
> the one who holds it fast,
> who keeps the Sabbath, not profaning it,
> and refrains from doing any evil (Isaiah 56:1-2).

Dissonance is to be reduced by employing the explanatory schemes of
firstly, by locating the failure in the community's cultic and dietary
offenses as well as their immoral behavior (56:2-7; 57:3-10; 58:1-13; 59:
1-15; 65:1-7),[18] and secondly, by reiterating the same fulfillment of hope
by adding the time element, "soon" (Isaiah 56:1).[19]

The seeming failure of prophecy or its delayed realization is
explained with the note that the hope of salvation is certainly "coming

but it has not quite arrived yet so everybody behaves properly until it does arrive."[20] Keeping justice and maintaining righteousness are not exactly means for salvation, but appropriate preparation. This admonition means to challenge the community to put into practice in a specific situation the commitment of God to justice and righteousness.

Another way through which hope is formulated and articulated accords with the so-called "democratization" of power and privilege. The religious monopoly of priesthood has excluded others from participating in it, gaining access to the religious power and sharing the cultic responsibility of the community. Bitterness of division, accusation against opponents and rupture within the community (Isaiah 66:5) prompted an affirmation of God's attitude to the temple and the official cult (Isaiah 66:1-4).

The servant passage in Isa 61:1-6 explicitly "shows signs of a profound generalization of the priesthood."[21] Addressing the whole people, Isa 61:6 says:

> You shall be called priests of the Lord, You shall be named ministers of our God.

Holiness and righteousness are bestowed on the people (60:21; 62:12) and not restricted to any group as in Ezek 44:19, 23. The nations, too, will get to the holy mountain of Jerusalem, and God will also take some people from the nations as priests and Levites (Isaiah 66:21).

In its present form, Trito-Isaiah includes texts that present inconsistencies that betray its complexities and multiplicities. On the one hand, there are passages that clearly take an open liberal position and widen the cultic boundary to include foreign elements, eunuchs and aliens (Isaiah 56:3-8) which is in direct contradiction to Deuteronomy 23:1-8. Membership in the cultic community is clearly no longer defined by birth, race and social positions. On the other hand, there are also texts that express anti-syncretistic religious forms and practices (Isaiah 57:5-13; 65:3-5, 7, 11; 66:34), which are usual expressions of faith of the common people. If the so-called "universalization" (Isaiah 66:18-23) and "democratization" of Israel's sacral institutions evidenced in Trito-Isaiah (contrary to the restrictive attitude in Numbers 18:1-7; Ezekiel 44:7-9; Nehemiah 9:2) are a genuine attempt to extend the royal (Isaiah 55:3-5; 62:3), the priestly (Isaiah 61:6; 66:21) and the prophetic

(Isaiah 61:1-3) offices to the common people in order to foster an open and inclusive community, it is inevitable that allowance has to be made to accommodate syncretistic processes, especially when even the controversial liberal position on the status of eunuchs and aliens is sanctified.

One further means to assure the hope of the community is to uphold the power of the word of God. In the exilic writings, there is a shift of emphasis on the gift of prophecy from an individual to the people/ community as a whole (cf. Joel 2:28-29). The word and spirit of Yahweh have taken up an important role in the future of the community.[22] The sureness of the word of God, in contrast to the lying words of humans (Isaiah 59:3-4, 13), is affirmed in the prologue as well as the epilogue of Deutero-Isaiah (Isaiah 40:8; 55:10-11). Trito-Isaiah further uses the standard prophetic formula "thus says the Lord" to convey the notion that the message contained in the book is divine oracle. The formula occurs in the beginning and concluding chapters (56:1, 4; 65:8, 13; 66:1, 12, 23) and a variation of it, "oracle of the Lord" (n^{e}'um YHWH) is also used (56:8; 66:2, 17, 22). This evidence prompts Grace Emmerson to raise the question of the role of prophet portrayed in Isaiah 56-66.[23]

Interpretations of hope for the returned community can also take an eschatological turn. As the experience of being excluded from the power structure and the reality of growing bitterness and hostility within the divided community deepened, the bright and fascinating vision of restoration embodied in Deutero-Isaiah had to be re-interpreted in the face of disillusionment brought about by the rupture and rift within the community. Hanson asserts that "disintegrating historical circumstances prompted new modes of conceptualizing that restoration of hope."[24] The result was the emergence of an interpretation perspective which attributes to the increasing detachment from the historical reality of politics and social involvement.

There is a great emphasis on the hope for the eventual separation of the righteous from the wicked (Isaiah 57:19-21; 66:24). This is expressed in apocalyptic or eschatological terms which add a transcendental dimension to the prophetic word.[25] The community now believes that only a divine act can bring about changes and sustained hope. God's initiative will be expected:

> Because the former troubles are forgotten and are hidden from
> my sight. For I am about to create new heavens and a new earth:
> the former things shall not be remembered or come to mind. (Isa
> 65:16-17)

> For as the new heavens and the new earth, which I will make,
> shall remain before me, says the Lord; so shall your descendants
> and your name remain. (Isaiah 66:22)[26]

One last re-interpretation of hope in Isaiah is concerned with the "servant" metaphor of Deutero-Isaiah. The single "servant" referring to the nation Israel has been re-interpreted by the plural "servants" highlighting the present reality of suffering and humiliation, which is expected to be alleviated and transformed into blessed existence by the faithfulness of God (Isaiah 65: 8-16a).[27]

With these re-interpretations of the prophetic word, the Isaiah circle, as rightly observed by Carroll, "created a very rich hermeneutic that enabled the prophetic vision to survive long after its day and to influence subsequent events in the community's life in Jerusalem. The flexibility created by the interpretative processes gave prophecy a good defense against dissonance arousal and kept alive hope and vision for the community."[28]

Conclusion

Hope is engendered and nurtured in times of deep crisis in which the meaning of existence and identity of the community are called into question.

The exilic disaster no doubt provides such a situation with great urgency. What surprisingly flourishes in the face of a shattered world order, threatening chaos, and an intensifying disruption is the profound conception of a future and contextual re-interpretation of hope that sustains the faith of the community.

To the believer in God, an appeal to divine intervention is the most powerful and effective means of all re-conceptions. The Exile of the people of Israel with the destruction of the temple, the collapse of the monarchy, and the capture of the city of Jerusalem, represent the victory of chaotic powers over the created order of the cosmos. Norman Cohn observes: "Only a god who in the beginning had converted primordial chaos into the ordered world could re-establish such a world."[29] This represents the biblical articulation of the unarticulable, the human hope that is derived from beyond the human reality.

If our reading of the returned community is correct, it is not difficult to see the returned minority as having a peripheral existence at the margin of society. Their return will present a challenge to the present order and status quo defended by those who remained in Palestine. The latter may also conceive the returnees as a threat to social stability, as the returned community certainly would seek for wider participation in the social structure and sharing of political power. They may even seek for legitimization and affirmation of their exilic experience of being exposed to foreign influence and plurality of culture. How this new identity contributes to the restoration of Israel in the post-exilic period is an area worthy of further vigorous research by scholars.

The Hong Kong 1997 experience has enlightened my reading of Isa 56-66. The two-fold hope for ensuring "stability and prosperity" and "Hong Kong People Ruling Hong Kong" as promised again and again by our political leaders, as well as the preservation of social and economic structures as indicated in the Sino-British Joint Declaration, represent our quest for the continuity of social matrices on one hand, and our earnest longing for the dismantling of colonial rule on the other. Wider participation in and sharing of the power structure by Hong Kong people are much desired in the post-1997 era. Democratization is seen as the way to express this wish of the people, affirmation of the significance of our peripheral position vis-a-vis the central, and our hybrid identity is yet another. The latter may have been perceived by some to be more far-reaching in the long run than the former. An open, inclusive community that can embrace plurality and facilitate the integrity of humanity is definitely part of the hope that can sustain the new Hong Kong community. Space has yet to be created to accommodate the past experience of the community in a creative way that helps to nurture great hope for the future.

Notes

1   Robert Carroll, *When Prophecy Failed* (New York: The Seabury Press, 1979). Paul Hansen, *The Dawn of Apocalyptic: The Historical and Sociological*

Roots of Jewish Apocalyptic Eschatology (Revised Edition; Philadelphia: Fortress Press, 1979). Idem, Isaiah 40-66 (Louisville: John Knox Press, 1989). Daniel Smith, The Religion of the Landless: The Social context of the Babylonian Exile (Bloomington, Indiana: Meyer Stone Books, 1989).

2   Archie Lee, Biblical Interpretation in Asian Perspective, *Asia Journal of Theology*; idem, Genesis 1 from the perspective of a Chinese Creation Myth, *Understanding Poets and Prophets*, ed. Graeme Auld (Sheffield: Sheffield Academic Press, 1993), pp. 186-98; idem, The Chinese Creation Myth of Nu Kua and the Biblical Narrative in Genesis 1-11, *Biblical Interpretation*, 2,1994, pp. 312-24.

3   Archie Lee, Exile and Return in the Perspective of 1997, *Reading from this Place, vol. 2, Social Location and Biblical Interpretation in Global Perspective*, ed. F. Segovia and Mary Tolbert (Minneapolis: Fortress Press, 1995), pp. 97-108.

4   Some of the ideas and a few paragraphs in this paper appear in another paper entitled "Biblical Interpretation of the Return in the Postcolonial Hong Kong" presented in the Annual Meeting of the American Academy of Religion, 1997.

5   A more detailed analysis of the Hong Kong situation is given in an article by Archie Lee, ibid.

6   Claus Westermann, *Isaiah* 40-66 (London: SCM Press, 1969), pp. 259-96. There are passages that show that the temple was still in ruin: 44:26, 28; 45: 13; 49:16,19; 51:3; 52:9; 54:3; 60:10; 61:4; 63:18-19; 64:10-11.

7   Norman Cohn, *Cosmos, Chaos and the World to Come* (New Haven: Yale University Press; 1993), p. 157.

8   Elizabeth Achtemeier, *The Community and message of Isaiah 56-66. A Theological Commentary* (Minneapolis: Augsburg Publishing Home, 1982), pp. 12-13.

9   Joseph Blenkinsopp, "The 'Servants of the Lord' in Third Isaiah: Profile of a Pietistic Group in Persian Epoch," *The Place is Too Small For Us: The Israelite Prophets in Recent Scholarship*, ed. Robert P. Gordon (Winona Lake, Indiana: Eisenbrauns, 1995), p. 394.

10 Peter D. Miscall, *Isaiah* (Sheffield: JSOT Press, 1993), p. 19.

11 Daniel Smith, *The Religion of the Landless* (Bloomington, Indiana: Meyer-Stone Books, 1989), p. 179.

12 Bernard Lang, *Monotheism and the Prophetic Minority: An Essay in Biblical History and Sociology* (Sheffield, 1983), p. 55.

13 The Majority of the people of Israel was left behind in Palestine, cf. Ezekiel 33:24. There were dissenting understandings on the status of the two communities. Both Jeremiah (ch. 24) and Ezekiel (11:14-16) favour the exiles. John Bright, *A History of Israel* (Revised ed.; London: SCM Press, 1972), pp. 349-51, undermines the faith and fate of those remained behind in Palestine and sees continuity of the people in the exiles while Martin Noth points to Palestine as the centre of Israelite history and religion, see *The History of Israel* (London: Adam & Charles Black, 1960), p. 291. Recently Keith W. Whitelam calls our attention to the bias of scholarship towards the Palestinian community, see *The Invention of Ancient Israel: The Silencing of Palestinian History* (London and New York: Routledge, 1996).

14 Paul Hanson, *Isaiah 40-66* (Louisville: John Knox Press, 1995), p. 192.

15 Note the Hebrew word for wait meaning hope and expect.

16 Claus Westermaun, op cit., p. 309. Grace I. Emmerson, Isaiah 56-66 (Sheffield: Sheffield Academic Press, 1992), p. 101.

17 Robert Carroll, *When Prophecy Failed*, pp. 152-54

18 Restoration of the will includes action of the people in caring for the poor, the hungry and the homeless (Isaiah 58).

19 Robert Carroll refers also to Isaiah 10:25, pp. 146-47.

20 Robert Carroll, ibid., p. 153. The play on words is clearly discerned in the Hebrew text: keep justice...keeps Sabbath... (Isaiah 56:1-2).

21 Daniel Smith, op. cit., p. 191.

22 Grace I. Emmerson, *Isaiah 56-66* (Sheffield: Sheffield Academic Press, 1992), pp. 74-75

23 Ibid., p. 71

24 Paul Hansen, *The Dawn of Apocalyptic* (Philadelphia: Fortress Press, 1979). A good summary of Paul Hansons argument with fair criticism is found in Grace Emmersen, op cit., pp. 85-94. On the poor social and economic situation of Palestinian community, see Haqqai 1:6.8-11; 2:16-17; Zechariah. 8:10; Isaiah 58:3-4; 59:9-15; and Nehemiah 5:1-5.

25 Peter Blenkinsopp attributes to the prophetic-eschatological minority of Trito-Isaiah (ibid., p. 394) while Paul Hanson (*When Prophecy Failed*, p. 154) refers to as the beginning of apocalyptic vision. Recently, Stephen Cook has published his view on millennial groups in power, which counteracts the deprivation theory which sees the origin of apocalyptic groups in the marginalized of society. See *Prophecy and Apocalypticism, The Postexilic*

Social Setting (Minneapolis: Fortress Press, 1995), pp. 1-19.

26 There are scholars who read Isaiah as a unity by noting the similarities in linguistics, thrones and structure between the opening and closing chapters of Isaiah. See Anthony J. Jomasino, Isaiah 1.1-2.4 and 63-66, and the composition of the Isaianic Corpus, *JSOT*, 57 (1993), pp. 81-98

27 Robert Carroll, *When Prophecy Failed*, p. 155.

28 Ibid., pp. 155-56.

29 Norman Cohn, *Cosmos, Chaos and the World to Come: The Ancient Roots of Apocalyptic Faith* (New Haven: Yale University Press, 1993), p. 153.

14

Biblical Hope for the Redemption of the Creation as a Basis for Ecological Concerns

Chee-Pang Choong

"In the beginning God created the heavens and the earth" (Genesis 1: 1, RSV). This is how the Bible starts. This statement of faith is shared by at least three religious traditions-Jewish, Christian and Islamic. It is reiterated in the Apostles' as well as the Nicene creeds of Christianity. The Hebrew word *bara'* in Genesis 1:1, translated "created" in the RSV is used predominantly of God's creative activity in the Old Testament. It is used here in Genesis 1:1 to affirm the absolute sovereignty of the Creator in bringing the ordered universe out of primeval chaos. The idea of "chaos" is expressed by the Hebrew phrase *tohu wa bohu* ("without form or void" in Genesis 1:2a). The word *bara'* occurs quite frequently in Deutero-Isaiah when referring to God's creation of the material world (e.g. Isaiah 40:26, 28; 45:12), to the calling into being a new people of God's own choice (Isaiah 43:1, 7, 15).

The creative power of God is in His "spirit" (Genesis 1:3). The Hebrew word *ruah*, which could also be rendered "wind," is also thought to be the source of human life:

> The spirit of God has made me, and the breath of the Almighty gives me life," says Job (Job 33:40; see also Ezekiel 37:9-14).

In the Bible, both the Hebrew word *ruah* in the Old Testament and its Greek counterpart *pneuma* are often used theologically to refer to God's divine presence as well as dynamic activity.

The creation of human beings in the sixth day, the last day, in Genesis

1:26, 27 has been regarded as the "apex of the creation pyramid."[1]

As Gerhard von Rad has rightly observed, "The creation of man is introduced more impressively than any preceding work by the announcement of a divine resolution: 'Let us make man.' God participates more intimately and intensively in this than in the earlier works of creation."[2]

Gerhard von Rad thinks that the use of the verb *bara'* (*create*) three times in Genesis 1:27 alone is of "fullest significance for that divine creativity which is absolutely without analogy": [3]

> So God created man in his own image, in the image of God he created him, male and female he created them (Genesis 1:27).

It is obviously designed "to make clear that here the high point and goal has been reached toward which all God's creativity from v. 1 on was directed."[4] Most scholars take the Hebrew word *'adam* ("man") to mean "mankind" collectively in this context.

The Hebrew words selem ("image") in 1:26, 27 and demut ("likeness") in 1:26 are often interpreted and understood differently because of their shades of meaning. Von Rad is critical of those interpretations which "one-sidedly limit God's image of man's spiritual nature, relating it to man's 'dignity,' his 'personality' or 'ability for moral decision,' et cetera.[5] Citing Ezekiel 28:12 where man is described as "the signet of perfection, full of wisdom and perfect in beauty (*kelil yopi*) and Psalm 8 where man is thought to have been made just "little less than God" and crowned "with glory and honor" (Psalm 8:5), von Rad opines that "the marvel of man's bodily appearance is not at all to be excepted from the realm of God's image."[6]

Martin Luther, who believes that since much of this "image" of God in man has been lost through sin, said "we cannot understand it to any extent" except to say that it is "something far different, namely, a unique work of God... something far more distinguished and excellent...."[7] Perhaps the vital concern for man is really not in what *particular* areas that he bears God's image or is like God, but rather as von Rad has rightly stated, "man is like God in the way in which he is called into existence, in the totality of his being."[8]

This point is particularly important when one considers the so-called "cultural mandate" that the Creator-God is often thought to have given to man in Genesis 1:26-28, because in the matter of human dominion over the rest of non-human creatures, the text is evidently far more interested in *the purpose* of humans being the image-bearers of God than the *nature* of God's *image per se*. The domination of man over the sub-human creation "is not considered as belonging to the definition of God's image; but it is its consequence, i.e. that for which man is capable because of it."[9] *Selem* ("image") in the context of man's cultural mandate means that man alone is God's representative, commissioned to maintain and enforce God's rule over the earth. The Hebrew verbs employed to express man's exercise of this dominion are notably strong: *kabas* ("subdue") and *rada* ("have dominion over") in Genesis 1:26-28. Rightly perceiving the great significance of man's dominion over the non-human creatures, Luther says:

> Here the rule is assigned to the most beautiful creature, who knows God and is the image of God, in whom, the similitude of the divine nature shines forth through his enlightened reason, through his justice and his wisdom. Adam and Eve become the rulers of the earth, the sea, and the air. But this dominion is given to them not only by way of advice but also by express command. Here we should first carefully ponder the exclusiveness in this: no beast is told to exercise dominion; but without ceremony all the animals and even the earth, with everything brought forth by the earth, are put under the rule of Adam, whom God by an express verbal command placed over the entire animal creation. Adam and Eve heard the words with their ears when God said: "Have dominion." Therefore the naked human being — without weapons and walls, even without any clothing, solely in his bare flesh — was given the rule over all birds, wild beasts, and fish.[10]

The divine mandate given to man to exercise dominion over the non-human creation leads to a vital tripartite relations between the Creator-God, man and the non-human creation: man as God's image-bearer now rules over the non-human creation as God's representative and he is ultimately accountable to God in terms of responsible stewardship; and the non-human creation also has the responsibility to fulfill God's purpose for it. "Precisely because man's sovereignty is a delegated sovereignty, he stands in a position of responsibility before God."[11] Although the word "care" — care for the non-human creation — is absent, its basic idea is already inherent in God's mandate to man, since dominion necessarily assumes the continuous existence and well being of those creatures under man's rule. The tripartite relations between the Creator-God, man and the non-human creation is vital in understanding the true meaning of the human "fall" and its effect, not only on man, the sinner, but also on the non-human creation.

The biblical narrative about the fall of man in Genesis 3 is subject to all sorts of interpretations. But there seems to be a general consensus of opinion with regards to the basic nature of man's disobedience to the Creator-God, i.e., man's evil desire "to be like God," to be self-autonomous, and to want to manage one's own life without reference to God. The immediate result of that attempt is one of alienation, an estranged relation that has developed between man and his Creator-God, a relation that causes man to want to hide himself from God's presence (Genesis 3:8-10). This estranged bilateral relation also has a profound effect on the nonhuman creation which comes under man's dominion: "cursed is the ground because of you [Adam]; in toil you shall eat of it all the days of your life ... in the sweat of your face you shall eat bread till you return to the ground, for out of it you were taken; you are dust, and to dust you shall return" (Genesis 3:17b-19). The message is clear and powerful. What man, the ruler of the earth, does, for good and for ill, necessarily affects his physical environment. There is an unbreakable solidarity between man and the ground, including "the fish of the sea ... the birds of the air ... and ... every living thing that moves upon the earth" (Genesis 1:28). While critical biblical scholars and theologians might have great reservation taking this vital bond between man and the created order literally, modern environmentalists would have little difficulty doing so. In evidently "pre-scientific" language, Luther makes this comment on the cursing of the ground on account of man's sin:

> Moreover, it appears here what a great misfortune followed sin, because the earth, which is innocent and committed no sin, is nevertheless compelled to endure a curse ... it does not brings forth the good things it would have produced if man had not fallen ... I have no doubt that before sin the air was purer and more healthful and the water more prolific; yes, even the sun's light was more beautiful and clearer.[12]

Even granted that Luther is here using the language of "myth," one would have to acknowledge the fact that the air in Luther's time would most probably be "purer and more healthful" than today's. This would be equally true with reference to the water and the sun light, although the sixteenth century Reformer probably knew nothing about "acid rain," the "greenhouse effect" or the "ozone layer"!

In biblical thinking, man and his environment always interact with one another, and since the Creator-God is also involves in the interaction, the relations become a tripartite one. As such, a society obedient to God receives blessings from the creation:

> And all these blessings shall come upon you and overtake you, if you obey the voice of the Lord your God. Blessed shall you be in the city, and blessed shall you be in the field. Blessed shall be the fruit of your body, and the fruit of your ground, and the fruit of your beasts, the increase of your cattle, and the young of your flock. Blessed shall be your basket and your kneading-trough. Blessed shall you be when you come in, and blessed shall you be when you go out (Deuteronomy 28:2-6).

The reverse is also true:

> But if you will not obey the voice of the Lord your God or be careful to do all his commandments and his statutes which I command you this day, then all these curses shall come upon you and overtake you. Cursed shall you be in the city, and cursed shall you be in the field ... and cursed shall you be when you go out (Deuteronomy 28:15-19).

When man is finally cast out of the Garden of Eden, his work — all the activities that the "cultural mandate" entail — now becomes a painful struggle for survival instead of enjoyment and celebration of God's bountiful gifts. Just as man has revolted against his Creator-God and hence frustrates the express purpose which God had for him, the physical environment is now doing the same to man, its ruler, thereby foiling its original purpose of existence. Thus, instead of yielding its natural fruit for man's need and enjoyment in due seasons "thorns and thistles" from the ground shall be brought forth to him (Genesis 3:18a).

The eighth century prophet Isaiah of the Old Testament also sees a direct link between human behaviour in the world and the desolation

of the earth and understands the latter as a divine judgment because of
the sinfulness of the earth's inhabitants:

> Behold, the Lord will lay waste the earth and make it desolate,
>> and he will twist its surface and scatter its inhabitants.
>> ...
> The earth shall be utterly laid waste and utterly despoiled;
>> for the Lord has spoken this word.
> The earth mourns and withers,
>> the world languishes and withers;
>> the heavens languish together with the earth.
> The earth lies polluted
>> under its inhabitants;
> for they have transgressed the laws,
>> violated the statutes,
>> broken the everlasting covenant.
> Therefore a curse devours the earth,
>> and its inhabitants suffer for their guilt;
> therefore the inhabitants of the earth are scorched,
>> and few men are left.
> The wine mourns,
>> the vine languishes,
>> all the merry-hearted sigh
> (Isaiah 24:1,3-7).

A strikingly similar idea is found in other prophetic utterances:

> Hear the word of the Lord, O people of Israel;
>> for the Lord has a controversy with the inhabitants of the
>> land.
> There is no faithfulness or kindness,
>> and no knowledge of God in the land;
> there is swearing, lying, killing, stealing, and committing adultery;
>> they break all bounds and murder follows murder.
> Therefore the land mourns,
>> and all who dwell in it languish,
> and also the beasts of the field,
>> and the birds of the air;
> and even the fish of the sea are taken away
> (Hosea 4:1-3).

How long will the land mourn,

> and the grass of every field wither?
> For the wickedness of those who dwell in it
>> the beasts and the birds are swept away,
>> because men said, "He will not see our latter end."
>
> ...
>
> They have made it a desolation;
>> desolate, it mourns to me.
> The whole land is made desolate,
>> but no man lays it to heart
> (Jeremiah 12:4,11).

Subsequent history continues to witness to the mourning and desolation of the land. Human beings continue to exercise their rule over creation in terms of dominion almost to the total neglect of care. This has been particularly true in the history of Western culture since the Enlightenment. Some modern scholars even try to make the Protestant theology of Luther and Calvin responsible for this sad state of affairs. In the words of H. Paul Santmire:

> As the earth groans in travail, it appears that those who stand in the traditions of Luther and Calvin are ill-equipped to respond to the global environmental crisis theologically. It appears, indeed, that in this critical instance the Protestant mind is suffering from a severe case of hardening of the categories. The Protestant mind has become fixed, not to say fixated, on what Karl Barth called "the-anthropology," the doctrine of God and humanity. This has meant, in turn, that Protestants generally have approached the earth almost exclusively via the theology of a divinely mandated human dominion over nature.
>
> What is required, therefore, is a certain kind of theological healing, inspired by one of the great principles of the Reformation; *sola scriptura*. The Bible begins with the creation narratives of Genesis and ends with the Book of Revelation's vision of a new Jerusalem established in the midst of a new heavens and a new earth. The Protestant mind needs to be made whole, so that the voice of the Reformation tradition in our day can claim the entire creation for God once again, rather than focusing almost exclusively on God's history with humanity, while the natural world is interpreted as a kind of staging area for that divine-human drama. [13]

Santmire thinks that the Christo-centric theology of Karl Barth has not quite departed from the Reformation tradition:

> By the time of Karl Barth, the Reformers' the-anthropocentric focus had been systematized, especially by theologians who wrote in the tradition of Immanuel Kant and Albrecht Ritschl. Such thinkers taught that God cannot be known in nature, and they often implied that God cannot even be encountered in nature. Both Kant and Ritschl maintained, systematically, that the divinely posited purpose of nature was to provide a place in which God could create, educate, or redeem "a kingdom of spirits." Kant and Ritschl also accented the theme that the proper relationship of the human creature to nature is dominion — concept that often was taken by their followers to mean domination.
>
> Theirs was a pristine logic. If the raison d'etre of nature is essentially instrumental, why not use nature like the instrument it is for the greater glory of the underlying divine purpose, which is the creation and exaltation of the human creature? That nineteenth- and twentieth-century theologians like Ritschl, who stood in the Kantian tradition, also were serving scientific, technological, and economic interests is also noteworthy in this context.
>
> Karl Barth's theology exploded in the midst of this scenario with a resounding no. In the name of his famous christological concentration, he took issue with what he considered to be the all-too-easy nineteenth-century identification of bourgeois progress with the coming of the kingdom of God. But he did so, as one of his most important essays states, in the name of *The Humanity of God*. He was chiefly concerned with God and humanity, in Christ Jesus ...
>
> Nature only comes into view in Barth's thought in two respects: first, as the stage for God's covenant history with humanity; second, as the field in which the human creature exercises a limited but undeniable lordship, akin to the divine lordship over the creation ...
>
> The problems of this kind of Protestant the-anthropology of nature are many.[14]

Max Weber, who perceives great strength in the Protestant theology of dominion over the created order, argues strongly that it was the concept of the "calling" inherent in this theology that is the essence of the spirit (*Geist*) of modern capitalism which became vigorously developed following the Lutheran Reformation in the various puritan sects: Calvinism, Methodism, Pietism and Baptism.[15]

Weber finds this spirit altogether lacking in oriental religio-ethical traditions such as Confucianism. This is what he sees as the basic difference between the two kinds of rationalism, the Confucian and the Puritan:

> Confucian rationalism meant rational adjustment to the world; Puritan rationalism meant rational mastery of the world. Both the Puritan and the Confucian were "sober men." But the rational sobriety of the Puritan was founded in a mighty enthusiasm which the Confucian lacked completely; it was the same enthusiasm which inspired the monk of the Occident. The rejection of the world by occidental asceticism was insolubly linked to its opposite, namely, its eagerness to dominate the world. In the name of supra-mundane God the imperatives of asceticism were issued to the monk and, in variant and softened form, to the world. Nothing conflicted more with the Confucian ideal of gentility than the idea of a "vocation." The "princely" man was an aesthetic value; he was not a tool of a god. But the true Christian, the other-worldly and inner-worldly asceticist, wished to be nothing more than a tool of his God; in this he sought his dignity. Since this is what he wished to be he was a useful instrument for rationally transforming and mastering the world. [16]

As a liberal scholar interested in the promotion of progressive social reform, Weber had a profound concern with the origins and likely course of evolution of industrial capitalism. His interpretation of the "ethos" or "spirit" (*Geist*) of modern Western capitalism continues to exert its influence on the modern mind. Of course, Weber had not lived long enough to witness the kind of unprecedented ecological crisis that now threatens the very survival of the created order, a crisis, many believe, has resulted from unrestricted "rational mastery of the world." People everywhere have now become increasingly convinced that the dominant concept of mastery of the world, especially in its long history and practice in the West, must be counter-balanced by a well considered strategy of adjustment, an idea that was negatively perceived by Weber as a clear sign of weakness in the religio-ethical traditions of the East.

Philip Hefner sees an impasse in the human attitude towards nature which is deeply rooted in Western culture in particular. It is caught between exploitation and sentimentality:

> (1) On the exploitative side, we see secular understandings that by and large inculcate within us the sense that being "natural" or "only nature" is too little for creatures of our capabilities and attainments. The secular spirit prizes human beings for what they can do with nature, how they can manipulate and "develop" it. We could document this at many points in our past, but in our present century, the two great social philosophies of the twentieth century — democratic capitalism and communist socialism — both value persons on the basis of what they produce and what they consume, in materialist terms. Production is conceived in terms of what can be done with the natural resources at hand, and consumption is synonymous with how much of the human products can be taken out of nature and put into human possession so as to enable the possessor to live a life as unlike the world that is untouched by human hands as possible. Both of these great philosophies have left the natural world in a state of disrepair, violation, and little understood, except as resource for human creativity and manipulation.[17]

> (2) On another front, we find cultural information that can be characterized as extreme sentimentality. This sentimentality ranges from sheer anthropomorphisms to uncritical ascription of sacrality to natural forms and processes, as well as to assertions of nature as a realm of divine love. ... It is common for religious groups to affirm the natural order as a realm of God's love, quite uncritically. ... In this context, it is common to excoriate irresponsible human behaviour with respect to nature as a sin against God that requires confession and forgiveness. At its worst, this sort of theology trails off into a form of "Be kind to nature" attitude. [18]

Hefner consequently tries to forge new understandings that include the following concepts in an attempt to break the *impasse*:

> (1) our kinship with all of nature; (2) the inherent capabilities of the natural order; (3) the future of nature; (4) the shape of human

involvement in nature; (5) the poignancy of the relationship between humans and the rest of nature. A complex of cultural information that provides less than this will not be adequate to the issue of where humans fit in with nature and what behaviour is appropriate to them. When one gives careful attention to these five elements, it is clear that what we are dealing with is nothing less than a full theology of nature. In what follows, I will sketch some of the resources that classical Christian theology offers for an adequate theology of nature.[19]

Hefner's voice is certainly not a lonely one. In the last couple of decades there has been an encouraging concern in the Christian churches regarding the "care for the earth" and voices on the theology of nature have been many. The World Council of Churches, for example, has repeatedly called for respect for the "integrity of creation." However, as Santmire has critically pointed out, "That is a promising development, but this new terminology will remain a '*flatus vocis*' if it is not firmly rooted in some appropriate theological conceptuality."[20] It seems to him that the inherited Protestant theological tradition, especially in the form of Karl Barth's "the anthropological" thought, is "ill-equipped" to do the job.[21] "What is required," Santmire proposes, is "a triangular mode of thought that corresponds to the trinitarian structure of the divine life."[22] He elaborates: "The line between God and nature must be drawn just as visibly as the lines between God and humanity, and between humanity and nature."[23] This "triangular mode of thought" would correspond to the ideal of a "tripartite" relation between God, humanity and nature which was suggested earlier in this paper.

Challenges arriving from the ecological crisis have been rather high on the agenda of the Lutheran World Federation since the early 1980s. In the early 1980s the LWF-sponsored Institute for Ecumenical Research in Strasbourg signalized a major study on "Creation-An Ecumenical Challenge?." Three international consultations were organized: Strasbourg, 1983; Klingenthal, Alsace, 1984; Burlingame, California, 1985. At the Eighty Assembly of the Lutheran World Federation meeting in 1990, in Curitiba, Brazil, delegates representing more than 100 Lutheran churches throughout the world adopted a message as guidance for the work of the Federation until the next Assembly to be held in 1997, in Hong Kong, China.[24] Here are some excerpts of the message under the heading "A Liberated Creation":

> We hear cries from creation as a chorus of anguish. The future of the earth is threatened. There is an increasing awareness everywhere of growing ecological crisis. In all regions of the world we observe the destruction of the environment.
>
> The ozone layer is threatened, and without its protection all life is endangered. The "greenhouse effect" is changing the climate of the earth and these changes could be more devastating than nuclear war. The rain forests are being destroyed in the Amazon area and in Asia and Africa. There are alarming estimates about the rate of the extinction of the species. The effects of acid rain in industrialized countries and the indiscriminate use of pesticides are appalling.
>
> Some look to genetic engineering to meet basic needs for sufficient food, others are convinced that genetic manipulation is an insult to the sacredness of life.
>
> Social catastrophes are arising from the disturbance of the ecological environment. Urbanization and problems of overpopulation lead to transmigrations, which cause further ecological and social problems. In highly industrialized countries an excessive and wasteful use of the natural resources of our earth jeopardizes the long-term supply of basic needs for everyone-the consumption of fossil fuels by millions of cars is an example.
>
> The interrelatedness of the total ecosystem calls for answers to these cries that cannot come simply from technology. There is need for a new set of values and for a re-discovery of the spiritual dimension of human life on earth....
>
> There are an inseparable relationship and interdependence between humanity and creation as a whole, for survival as well as for salvation. We believe "that the creation itself will be liberated from its bondage to decay and brought into the glorious freedom of the children of God" (Romans 8:21).[25]

An LWF sponsored international workshop on "A Concern for Creation" was held at Bossey, Switzerland in May, 1994.[26] Other Christian bodies have also voiced serious ecological-concerns in recent years:

The environmental issue has been one of the priorities of the Christian Conference of Asia (CCA). In the past, a consultation was held on *Environment and Development* in Chiang Mai, Thailand, in July, 1992, a workshop on *Environment and Development: Church's Response to Environment in Asia*, in Jakarta, Indonesia, in July 1994, and a national level workshop on *Environmental Concerns*, in Lahore, Pakistan, in March, 1996. [27]

If the "cultural mandate" given to humanity to have dominion over the non-human creation has, whether through misunderstanding or misinterpretation or by sheer negligence or irresponsible human behaviour, led to the present crisis, certain aspects of biblical teaching may have also been given too much prominence to the neglect of other equally important insights. One immediately calls to mind the Book of Revelation which, over the centuries has become "the apocalypse" of the Christian Church. No committed Christian perhaps should challenge the profound truth that this piece of New Testament writing conveys, and the glorious eschatological hope that it holds out, not just for the Christians, but also for the whole of humanity. However, some of its graphic and figurative language, signs and symbols, and mysteries, when taken too literally will leave little or virtually no room for a logical mind to take things of this world, including the physical creation and its future too seriously. If the Book of Revelation was indeed written by the apostle John during the reign of the Roman Emperor Domitian (81-96 CE) when the cult of Emperor worship was rampant and the persecution of Christians rather widespread in different provinces of the Empire, then it would only be natural and understandable that this *Sitz im Leben* should be reflected truthfully in John's apocalypse in which the present world order is completely doomed and that faithful disciples of Jesus Christ could only look forward to the dawn of a completely new world order: "a new heaven and a new earth" (Revelation 21:1a), "for the first heaven and the first earth had passed away, and the sea was no more" (Revelation 21: 16). There will also be "the holy city, a new Jerusalem, coming down out of heaven from God..." (Revelation 21:2). However, Isaiah 65:17-19, which is probably the Old Testament background of Revelation 21:1-2, is exegetically open to interpretation in two very different directions:[28]

1. Taking the "new heavens and new earth" to mean a redemption and renewal of the old created order after sin and death have been completely destroyed. This interpretation is rather consistent with the dominant apocalyptic hope of the Old Testament which is essentially "this worldly" and holistic.

2. Taking the "new heavens and new earth" literally which presupposes the prior disappearance of the old. This "other worldly" interpretation is not uncommon in Jewish apocalyptic writings and in the Talmud. It is not at all clear in which direction John's vision in Revelation 21:1, 2 is to be understood. Whatever the case may be, it seems that throughout the long history of the Church, it is the "other worldly" apocalyptic vision that remains dominant, especially among those who are more conservative theologically. And this latter position clearly has had a profound influence on the ways that Christians look at the created order and its present crisis. Without in any way trying to belittle the profound eschatological insights and the glorious hope that the Book of Revelation brings, this paper, however, tries to show, especially from Romans 8:18-25, that eschatological hope can also be expressed in terms of an unbroken continuity between this world and the next and that the redemption of human beings can be understood in the context of solidarity with the earth.

St. Paul's letter to the Romans is commonly acknowledged as the most complete theological treatise among his existing writings. It was written around 57 CE, some twenty-five years after his "conversion" from staunch Pharisaism to Christ (see Acts 9). The letter begins with a very bold statement concerning the gospel: "it is the power of God for salvation to every one who has faith" (Romans 1:16). Immediately following this open declaration is St. Paul's gloomy portrayal of universal human sinfulness that is under God's judgment. This is because humanity, in their wickedness, "suppress the truth," including truth about the "invisible nature" of the Creator-God which can be "clearly perceived in the things that have been made" (Romans 1:18-20). For St. Paul, humanity's refusal to acknowledge God as the Creator-God is a deliberate and culpable act:

For what can be about God is plain to them, because God has

shown it to them. Ever since the creation of the world his invisible nature, namely, his eternal power and deity, has been clearly perceived in the things that have been made. So they are without excuse; for although they knew God they did not honor him as God or give thanks to him ... (Romans 1:19-21a).

St. Paul evidently is not trying to formally advocate any "natural theology" or "natural revelation" here. His real intention-and this is of utmost importance for the Pauline theology-is to state clearly that God's wonderful creation is an apt vehicle, however incomplete and inadequate, for divine revelation. Whether empirically this is often the case or not in the human experience is quite another matter. The rather long section that follows St. Paul's indictment against sinful humanity (Romans 3:21-5:21) is his well known exposition on "justification by faith" through grace. The next three chapters of this Roman letter are concerned with the Christian life that is now in Christ or in the Spirit. Yet paradoxically, salvation in and through Christ remains constantly in strong tension. It is "already" and "not yet" at the same time. As such, even those who are "already" in Christ still have to endure "suffering" in their spiritual pilgrimage. Even God's children, "heirs of God and fellow heirs with Christ," are still expected to "suffer with" Christ in order that they may also be "glorified with him" (Romans 8: 17).

Romans 8:18-25 is St. Paul's elaboration on the theme of suffering. The most revealing thing about this section is that St. Paul is *not* talking about human suffering in isolation, but in *solidarity* with the whole of creation in the hope that they may obtain liberty or redemption together:

I consider that the sufferings of this present time are not worth comparing with the glory that is to be revealed to us. For the creation waits with eager longing for the revealing of the sons of God; for the creation was subjected to futility, not of its own will but by the will of him who subjected it in hope; because the creation itself will be set free from its bondage to decay and obtain the glorious liberty of the children of God. We know that the whole creation has been groaning in travail together until now; and not only the creation, but we ourselves, who have the first fruits of the Spirit, groan inwardly as we wait for adoption as sons, the redemption of our bodies. For in this hope we were saved.

> Now hope that is seen is not hope. For who hopes for what he
> sees? But if we hope for what we do not see, we wait for it with
> patience (Romans 8:18-25).

St. Paul begins the passage by comparing "the suffering of this present
time" with "the glory that is to be revealed" (Romans 8:18). In his
opinion, the former is "not worth comparing" or "bears no comparison"
with the latter, because the two are not "of like value."[29] The word "I
consider," (Greek: *logizomai*) in 8:18 is not used casually in this context,
but denotes, as in 3:28 and 6:1, "a firm conviction reached by rational
thought on the basis of the gospel."[30] In other words, it is a conclusion
that the writer has finally reached after serious reflection and thought.
It indicates the serious nature of the subject matter. Romans 8:18 is
therefore "not just introductory and transitional ... but the theme."[31]
The fact that St. Paul is able to speak with such conviction about the
Christian is because the Spirit of God and of Christ has already been
given to them (Romans 8:1-17). Hence the Spirit becomes "an earnest
pledge of what is to come,"[32] i.e., redemption and liberation. This and
this alone, is the basis of the Christian hope. But before all this can
happen, sufferings must first be endured.

The phrase "of this present time" (Greek: *tou nun kairou*) clearly
suggests that sufferings are already an existential reality for the believers.
St. Paul is thus deliberately approaching the theme of hope "from the
standpoint of struggle."[33] Some see this as "a typically Pauline paradox
(cf. 2 Corinthians 4:10-13)" wherein "the sequence of suffering and
glorification with Christ (Romans 8:17c) is set in the mode of
contemporaneity."[34]

The word "creation" (Greek: he *ktisis*) in Romans 8:19 and the
rest of the passage has been interpreted differently throughout the
centuries.[35] Cranfield thinks that "the only interpretation of *ktisis* in
these verses which is really probable seems to be that which understands
the reference to be to the sum-total of subhuman nature both animate
and inanimate."[36] Fitzmyer takes the word ktisis to mean "material
subhuman creation."[37] Kasemann holds that the main emphasis should
be on "non-human creation."[38]

That St. Paul should regard the rest of creation to be sharing with
humanity in both sufferings and hope may be a surprise to people of

other religious traditions, but certainly not to the Jews. The solidarity that St. Paul so profoundly perceives between humanity and the rest of creation is firmly grounded both in the ancient tradition of the Old Testament as well as in Judaism. As has already been discussed earlier in this paper, the special creation of human beings, their divine calling to rule over the earth as well as their "fall" are all set against a cosmic context in intimate relation to other creatures. Even part and parcel of man's being is believed to have been formed "of dust from the ground" (Genesis 2:7). Although St. Paul is here referring to the solidarity between "the sons of God," or "the children of God" and the rest of creation, the former are, in a qualified sense, representative of humanity. "It may be suggested that St. Paul may have omitted to mention unbelievers here as a separate class contrasted with believers," says Cranfield, "because he did not accept that human unbelief presents God with an eternal fact but saw believers as the first fruits of mankind."[39] Hence the analogy of "first fruits" here connotes hope and optimism. For in the natural order of harvest when first fruits have appeared, more crops are only to be expected.

The Greek word for "eager longing" (*apokaradokia*) — "the creation waits with eager longing" — occurs only twice in the New Testament. The other appearance is in another Pauline letter Philippians 1:20 where it is associated with "hope" (Greek: *elpis*) and signifies "confident expectation."[40] Romans 8:20 explains, by the particle "for" (Greek: *gar*), why the creation waits so eagerly for the ultimate redemption of "the children of God?": "for the creation was subjected to futility, not of its own will but by the will of him who subjected it in hope." With reference to the subjection of the creation to futility here, St. Paul evidently has in mind the "curse" that God had pronounced upon the ground because of Adam's sinful act of revolt (Genesis 3:17) and possibly other Old Testament references to the suffering of creation on account of sinful human behaviour, especially those that are found in the prophetic writings. Similar ideas are also present in the Jewish Apocrypha (meaning "hidden things") such as 2 Esdras 7:11, 12:

> Such is the lot of Israel. It was for Israel that I made the world, and when Adam transgressed my decrees the creation came under judgment. The entrances to this world were made narrow, painful,

and arduous, few and evil, full of perils and grinding hardship."
(*The New English Bible, with Apocrypha*)

The word "futility" (Greek: mataiotes) denotes "the ineffectiveness of that which does not attain its goal," i.e., "the sub-human creation has been subjected to the frustration of not being able properly to fulfill the purpose of its existence ... ."[41] The word also means "emptiness ... purposelessness ... the state of ineffectiveness of something that does not attain its goal or purpose; concretely it means ... chaos, decay, and corruption... ."[42] On the "corruption" of the creation, Fitzmyer comments: "Paul speaks of 'corruption,' even though he did not have in mind what modern industry and technology have done and are doing to the universe and Earth's ozone layer. Yet his words somehow ring true even in this century with its ecological concerns."[43]

The phrase "not of its own will" is obviously deliberate and emphatic. It is meant to remind humanity of their sinful behaviour, and God's response to it by bringing the "curse" on creation. As such, it could justly be said that it was the will of God that subjected the creation to futility. St. Paul seems to be more concerned here with reality and simple logic rather than the question of fairness or reasonableness, that is, whether it was fair for the creation to suffer for human sinfulness. The reality here is clearly the ongoing suffering of the creation. And the logic is: as man, the crown of God's creation and the ruler of the earth, sins, the rest of the creation, almost of necessity of by sheer "fate" simply has to bear the tragic consequences of its ruler's act. Unfortunately this is often true also in the purely human realm, since no human person actually lives in isolation. Yet the good news is, the subjection of the creation to futility is not absolutely irreversible. For the Creator-God who first subjected it to futility has done so "in hope." And the same logic and the principle of solidarity work: just as sinful human behaviour has brought "curse" to the creation, "the creation itself will be set free from its bondage to decay and obtain the glorious liberty of the children of God" (Romans 8:21).

"The glorious liberty of the children of God" is essentially the liberty from the tyranny of sin and death. But "the liberty proper to the creation is indeed the possession of its own proper glory — that is, the freedom fully and perfectly to fulfill its creator's purpose for it, that freedom which it does not have, so long as man, its lord (Genesis 1:26, 28; Psalm 8:6), is in disgrace."[44] It is important to note that creation could not free itself from the bondage of decay to which it has been subjected. It can only hope to share in such liberty in solidarity with redeemed humanity. In this sense, redemption, or liberty, for the creation may be regarded as "an attendant aftermath of the glorification of the sons of God."[45] In perceiving the redemption of humanity in solidarity with the rest of creation, and the latter being "an attendant aftermath" of the former, St. Paul is largely in line with the old prophetic vision (e.g. of Isaiah and Micah).

In the new messianic age of peace and righteousness when peoples everywhere shall be fully reconciled to God, there will also be the restoration of the rest of the creation to its former peace and harmony:

> The wolf shall dwell with the lamb,
> and the leopard shall lie down with the kid,
> and the calf and the lion and the fatling together,
> and a little child shall lead them.
> The cow and the bear shall feed;
> their young shall lie down together;
> and the lion shall eat straw like the ox.
> The sucking child shall play over the hoe of the asp,
> and the weaned child shall put his hand on the adder's den.
> They shall not hurt or destroy
> in all my holy mountain;
> for the earth shall be full of the knowledge of the Lord
> as the waters cover the sea.
> (Isaiah 11:6-9).

> He shall judge between many peoples,
> and shall decide for strong nations afar off;
> and they shall beat their swords into plowshares,
> and their spears into pruning hooks,
> nation shall not lift up sword against nation,
> neither shall they learn war any more;
> but they shall sit every man under his vine and under his fig tree,
> and none shall make them afraid;
> for the mouth of the Lord of hosts has spoken.
> (Micah 4:3-4).

"Vine and fig tree" are here symbolic of God's blessings on the land of his redeemed people.

But all this is still a matter of hope, and until it is finally realized, suffering for both creation and humanity remain the harsh realities of life. Being keenly aware of this, St. Paul continues (in Romans 8:22): "We know that the whole creation has been groaning in travail together until now; and not only the creation, but we ourselves... ."

The "cursing" of the ground in Genesis 3:17 is clearly reflected in the present "groaning" of the creation. With profound prophetic insight and poetic imagery, Jeremiah writes:

> Disaster follows hard on disaster,
> the whole land is laid waste.
>
> ...
>
> I looked on the earth, and lo, it was waste and void;
> and to the heavens, and they had no light.
> I looked on the mountains, and lo, they were quaking,
> and all the hills moved to and fro.
> I looked, and lo, there was no man,
> and all the birds of the air had fled.
> I looked, and lo, the fruitful land was a desert,
> and all its cities were laid in ruins
> before the Lord, before his fierce anger.
> For thus says the Lord, "The whole land shall be a desolation; yet
> I will not make a full end.
> For this the earth shall mourn,
> and the heavens above be black,
> for I have spoken, I have purposed;
> I have not relented nor will I turn back."
> (Jeremiah 4:20, 23-28).

It should not take much imagination of a sensitive soul in the modern world to feel the particular effects of these powerful words of the prophet Jeremiah. Yet, in the divine providence and mercy, there is still hope even in the midst of judgment and disasters: "Yet I will not make a full end" (Jeremiah 4:27b). Similarly, in Romans 8:22, the present groaning of the creation is "in travail" or, as the New English Bible puts it: "the whole created universe groans in all its parts as if in the pangs of childbirth." The use of the two Greek words *systenazein* (to groan together) and *synodinein* (to suffer great pain together) and its personification are most appropriate and effective in the present context in describing the common and universal suffering of the whole of the creation. However, just as in the case of childbirth, the pangs are necessary and are never in vain in the end. The metaphor of "childbirth" in relation to the coming of the messianic age has also a long Biblical tradition:

> Like a woman with child,
> who writhes and cries out in her pangs,
> when she is near her time,
> so were we because of thee, O Lord,
>
> …
>
> Thy dead shall live, their bodies shall rise.
> O dwellers in the dust, awake and sing for joy!
> For thy dew is a dew of light,
> and on the land of the shades thou wilt let it fall
> (Isaiah 26:17, 19).

> Before she was in labor
> she gave birth,
> before her pain came upon her
> she was delivered of a son.
> Who has heard such a thing?
> Who has seen such things?
> Shall a land be born in one day?
> Shall a nation be brought forth in one moment?
> For as soon as Zion was in labor
> she brought forth her sons
> (Isaiah 66: 7-8).

> For I heard a cry as of a woman in travail,
> anguish as of one bringing forth her first child,
> the cry of the daughter of Zion gasping for breath,
> stretching out her hands,
> 'Woe is me! I am fainting before murderers."
> (Jeremiah 4:31)

In Greek philosophy there is also a beautiful metaphor regarding birth pangs: "when — after the winter's cold — the groaning earth gives birth in travail to what has been formed within her." [46]

Not only has the creation been groaning, even God's children who already have "the first fruits of Spirit" have to "groan inwardly" as they wait for their redemption, says St. Paul in Romans 8:23. The metaphor "first fruits" is here used to denote the initial installment or a pledge of what is to come. And since the Spirit is the pledge, what is to come, namely, the full liberation or redemption, is absolutely certain, because the children of God are already "in" the Spirit (Romans 8:9) who raised Jesus from the dead. (Romans 8:11). In 8:23b, St. Paul explicitly refers to the redemption of the "bodies" as the goal for which God's children are waiting. And this redemption could only be effected by the life-giving Spirit on the basis of Jesus' sacrificial work: " ... the Spirit of him who raised Jesus from the dead will give life to your mortal bodies also through his spirit which dwells in you" (Romans 8:11). The "mortal bodies" in 8:11 and the "bodies" in 8:23 seem to be the same as what St. Paul has earlier described as the "body of death"; death caused by sin. St. Paul is here not talking about getting rid of our physical body altogether however burdensome it may be. Nor does he subscribe to the Greek idea of a "disembodied" soul, or the immortality of the soul without the body. As Fitzmyer has rightly pointed out,

> Paul does not mean that Christians long for the liberation of their bodies from corporeality, but refers to the liberation from "this doomed body" or "this body of *death*" (7:24), in which they presently live. That body of death has to give way to the "spiritual body" of risen life: "when the perishable puts on the imperishable, and mortal puts on immortality" (1 Corinthians 15:54). [47]

This point is of utmost importance. For if the apostle is expecting "this doomed body" to be redeemed, or liberated rather than to simply disappear, it is only logical that he also wishes the same for the creation which will share in the same redemption or liberation in solidarity with God's children. Ultimately, St. Paul concludes, it is "for this hope we were saved" (Romans 8:24a). St. Peter also expresses the same conviction when he writes to his fellow believers in a different context: "By his great mercy we have been born anew to a living hope through the resurrection of Jesus Christ from the dead, and to an inheritance which is imperishable, undefiled ..." (1 Peter 1:3,4).

Hope that does not see implies steadfast waiting and watching. "Now hope that is seen is not hope. For who hopes for what he sees? But if we hope for what we do not see, we wait for it with patience," concludes the apostle (Romans 8:24b, 25). Kasemann sums up this idea of hope in a remarkably challenging way:

> He thus creates room for love and service not just in the community but also to tormented creation. If disciples are no longer on the road they have no more to say and give either to themselves or the world. They can thus be regarded only as the champions of one ideology among others. Those who groan with creation, and this not merely in fervent prayer ... , are truly potential and called instruments of the Spirit. [48]

It is most appropriate for Kasemann to end his concluding comment on this section (Romans 8:18-25) with an accented note on the Spirit, since St. Paul's vision for the redemption of the creation in solidarity with the children of God is set in the immediate context of the whole chapter of Romans 8:1-39 concerning life in the Spirit. Moreover, if not for the creative power of the Spirit there would not have been any life "in the beginning" (Genesis 1:1-3). As Job humbly acknowledges, "The Spirit of God has made me, and the breath of the Almighty gives me life" (Job 33:4). To Nicodemus who is seeking for the meaning of regeneration, Jesus answers, "Truly, truly, I say to you, unless one is born of water and the Spirit, he cannot enter the kingdom of God" (John 3:5). Some commentators take "water" here to be referring to the Christian sacrament of water baptism. This "sacramental" view evidently has the support of St. Paul in Titus 3:5 where the apostle reminds fellow-believers that "he [God] saved us, not because of deeds done by us in righteousness, but in virtue of his own mercy by the washing of regeneration and renewal in the Holy Spirit." The phrase "washing of regeneration" seems to be a clear reference to the sacrament of baptism.

The biblical view of the sacraments, the Holy Baptism and Holy Communion in particular, is a very holistic one. It admits no dichotomic view between "matter" and "spirit." In the unfathomable mystery of divine operation, the Spirit takes on ordinary created matter to achieve wonderful purposes for God. Even Adam himself is said to have been formed "of dust from the ground" (i.e. created matter). But once given the vital "breath of life," he became "a living being" (Genesis 2:7). The Son of God, the eternal logos, through whom "all things were made" (John 1:1-3) also "became flesh and dwelt among us" (John 1:14). What is spiritual does not cancel out the material, but rather enables it to achieve God's intended purpose often in ways far too profoundly mysterious for the human mind to ever comprehend. If God could use the physical body (Greek: *soma*) or flesh (Greek: *sarx*) and blood (Greek: *haima*) of Christ as worthy instruments for the atonement of human sin, he obviously could also use the created matters such as water (in Holy Baptism) as well as bread and wine (in Holy Communion) sacramentally. In fact it is not without good reason that the Latin word for sacrament, *sacramentum* should have derived from the Greek term *mysterion* ("mystery"). In the sacramental view of nature, ordinary created elements such as water, bread and wine which have originated from the crop and fruit of the earth, can become "means of grace" for humanity, when these are mediated in and through the mysterious operation of God's Spirit and his creative word. In this sacramental sense, there is truly a "real presence" of Christ in the created elements, just as Christ was present in the world in his incarnation. A biblically based sacramental theology is essential for the human understanding of the "sanctity" or "sacredness" of the creation. And the understanding of it certainly provides the much needed spiritual undergirding for serious ecological concerns and commitment. Otherwise, ecological concerns could only express itself in purely mundane terms and thus void of the dimension of what has been described by Rudolf Otto as *mysterium tremendum et fascinans*.

"A crisis of degradation is [indeed] enveloping the earth. Never before have human beings wielded so much power over creation," warns Calvin B. DeWitt, editor of the book *The Environment and the Christian* (Grand Rapids, 1991) and Professor at the Institute For Environmental Studies, University of Wisconsin. And what threatens the survival of humanity and the earth are not imaginative, but concrete: global toxification, atmospheric contamination, cultural subversion, land exploitation, species extinction, soil destruction, waste mismanagement, modern science and technology, the myth of unlimited economic growth, over-consumption and population growth. The task to effectively deal with them is dauntingly hard and insurmountable. And human beings "formed of dust from the ground" are in desperate need of something no less than that of a "heavenly mission" for inspiration and perseverance to take on the task. It is the conviction of this paper that a biblical hope for the redemption of the creation is a solid basis for ecological concerns and commitment.

Notes

1. Robert Davidson, "Genesis 1-11," *The Cambridge Bible Commentary on the NEB* (Cambridge, 1973), p. 23 ff.

2. *Genesis* (Revised Edition, Philadelphia: The Westminister Press, 1972), p. 57.

3. Ibid.

4. Ibid.

5. Ibid., p. 58.

6. Ibid.

7. "Lecture on Genesis, Chapters 1-5," *Luther's Works*, vol. 1, ed. Jaroslav Pelikan (Saint Louis: Concordia Publishing House, 1958), pp. 61-2.

8. von Rad, p. 58.

9. Ibid.

10. "Lecture on Genesis, Chapters 1-5," *Luther's Works*, vol. 1, p. 66.

11. Robert Davidson, p. 25.

12. Luther on *Genesis*, p. 204.

13. H. Paul Santmire, "Healing the Protestant Mind: Beyond the Theology of Human Dominion" in *After Nature's Revolt*, ed. Dieter T. Hessel (Minneapolis: Fortress Press, 1992), p. 57.

14. Ibid., pp. 62-63.

15. See *The Protestant Ethic and The Spirit of Capitalism* (New York: Charles Scribner's Sons, 1976).

16. *The Religion of China: Confucianism and Taoism*, ed. and trans. Hans H. Gerth (3rd printing; The Free Press of Glencoe, 1962), p. 248.

17. "Beyond Exploitation and Sentimentality: Challenges to a Theology of Nature," from Viggo Mostensen ed., *Concern for Creation: Voices on the Theology of Creation*, (Uppsala: Tro and Tanko, 1995), p. 124.

18. Ibid., p. 126.

19. Ibid., p. 127.

290 Interpretations of "Hope"

20. See *Concern for Creation*, op. cit., p. 72.

21. Ibid.

22. Ibid.

23. Ibid.

24. *Concern for Creation*, op. cit., pp. 39-40.

25. Op. cit., pp. 25-27.

26. Ibid., p. 11.

27. *CCA News*, July/August 1996, pp. 17-18.

28. See G. R. Beasley-Murray, *The Book of Revelation* (London: Oliphants, 1972), pp. 305-310.

29. C.E.B. Cranfield, *Romans*, vol. 1 (Edinburgh: T & T Clark, 1975), p. 408.

30. Ibid.

31. Ernest Käsemann, *Commentary on Romans*, ed. and trans. Geoffrey W. Bromiley (Grand Rapids: Eerdmans, 1980), p. 232.

32. Ibid., p. 231.

33. Ibid.

34. Ibid.

35. See Cranfield, op. cit., pp. 411-2, and footnote on p. 412, also Käsemann, op. cit., pp. 232-3.

36. Cranfield, op. cit., pp. 411-2.

37. Romans, *The Anchor Bible* (New York: Doubleday, 1993), p. 505.

38. Op. cit., p. 233.

39. Op. cit., p. 412.

40. Cranfield, ibid. p. 410.

41. Ibid., p. 413.

42. Fitzmyer, p. 507.

43. Ibid.

44. Cranfield, op. cit., p. 416.

45. Fitzmyer, op. cit., p. 509.

46. Heraclitus Stoicus c. 39, p. 58, 9, quoted in p. 801 of A *Greek-English Lexicon of the New Testament and Other Early Christian Literature*, ed. and trans. W. F. Arndt and F. W. Gingrich (12th impression, The University of Chicago Press, 1971).

47. Op. cit., p. 510.

48. Käsemann, op. cit., p. 239.